IT TAKES A
WOMAN

Dear Mr & 1/85
Carter,
I hope you enjoy
this season of my
life . Regards

Nana Hemtings
18/1/2019

IT TAKES A
WOMAN

A LIFE SHAPED BY HERITAGE, LEADERSHIP
AND THE WOMEN WHO DEFINED HOPE

NANA KONADU AGYEMAN-RAWLINGS

Former First Lady of the Republic of Ghana

Hillcroft Bay Press

Library of Congress Cataloguing-in-Publication Data

It takes a woman: A life shaped by heritage, leadership and the women who defined hope, by Agyeman-Rawlings, Nana Konadu

Editor: E. Obeng-Amoako Edmonds

ISBN:
978-1-7323519-0-5 Hardback
978-1-7323519-1-2 Paperback
978-1-7323519-2-9 E-Book

Includes references and index
1. Agyeman-Rawlings, Nana Konadu   2. Leadership and culture   3. Ghana - Politics and government   4. Memoir   I. Title

In order to maintain anonymity, in some instances the author has changed the names of some individuals, some identifying characteristics and details such as physical properties, occupations and places of residence.

Cover Photograph by Glitz Magazine

First Edition

Praise for *It Takes a Woman*

"In this heartfelt and engaging memoir, Nana Konadu Agyeman-Rawlings traces both her formative years and those of her country. Her perspective, with its personal insights and much-needed focus on the vital role played by women makes this book insightful reading for anyone wanting to know more about Ghana's early history."

– Kofi Annan, Former Secretary-General, United Nations

"Beneath the public person as a former First Lady is a warm, caring and kind human being. This narrative is a compelling heroine's journey, against the background of an awakening Africa, undergoing dynamic political and social change in the 21st century."

– Shawki Haffar, M.D.

"Epitome of what an African leader should be. You give us light at the end of the tunnel. Queen mothers in Ghana salute you."

– Nana Agyakoma Difie II,
Paramount Queen Mother of Asante Mampong Traditional area.

"Our opportunity to gain insight into the life of a girl through her formative years and later to the woman the world came to know and respect. Her leadership has inspired countless women in her home country and across the globe. Count those of us on this side of the Atlantic as among the many and let all take the lessons of her leadership and make our world a better place."

–– Sheila Jackson Lee, United States Congress, House of Representatives

"Nana led Ghanaian women to free themselves, not in rivalry to men but in the context of their own capacity and personalities. Even those who may not share her political ideology still respect her drive for excellence, a strength of character and her great love of education, art and culture."

– Professor Kwabena Frimpong-Boateng, Ministry of Environment, Science,
Technology & Innovation

"A woman of substance, dynamic and affable. She stood at the forefront of empowerment of the womenfolk, giving them hope, as well as creating job opportunities for the women."

– Nana Adwoa Otubea II, Queen Mother, Nkonya Traditional Area

"A powerful voice which demands to be heard. She stands in her own right as an activist and advocate for women's rights and development. A gripping account of a life, well and fully lived."

– Rt. Hon. Lord Boateng, PC DL, House of Lords, Westminster, London-UK

"She is a product of a historic and turbulent period in Ghana's history that she helped shape, and which in turn impacted her life immensely. In this book, readers will know the woman behind the household name, what she is made of and what she stood for, - one woman can indeed make a difference."

– David Ampofo, Broadcaster and Public Affairs strategist

"She loves Ghana and has a passion to work to protect Ghana and especially its women and children… a beautiful account, gracefully written."

– Ohemaa Nana Yaa Asaa Safoa II, Akwamufie Hemaa

"She redefined the role of a First Lady as reflected in the programmes of the 31st December Women's Movement, which she founded and nurtured to be a vehicle for women empowerment. It is refreshing to observe the path she blazed."

– Nana Otuo Siriboe II, Omanhene of Asante Juaben, Chairman of the Council of State

"A remarkable read, filled with memories of a young woman finding her voice. Very reminiscent of our years together in Achimota School (1961-1966) where a confident and fun-loving Nana Konadu seemed ready, even then, to meet the challenges of life head-on."

– Marjorie Quist Abdin

Dedicated to the memory of
my father J. O. T. Agyeman, my mother Felicia Agyeman;
my extended Ashanti families – Agyeman, Akosa, Bonsu, Osei, and Prempeh;
and my extended Akyem families – Owusu, and Sarpong.

Also dedicated to the women whose stories nurture our legacy.

Mɛnkatakyie etwa sa kɔ to kro no,
Na mmaa awo ama kro no ase adore.
– Akan Proverb

The mighty man will fight for a land,
Yet the woman births its strength and future.

FOREWORD

Nana Konadu Agyeman-Rawlings stepped into Ghana's political, social and economic life in June 1979, almost forty years ago. For two decades, she and her husband, Ghana's former President, His Excellency, Flt. Lt. Jerry John Rawlings remained the most formidable political couple in Ghana. Nana Konadu has always been the pillar behind Mr. Rawlings. Indeed, in the Ghanaian context, the term "First Lady" virtually became synonymous with Nana Konadu Agyeman-Rawlings.

She is a very proud Ghanaian with a solid and impeccable Asante pedigree. She was named after the 11th Asantehemaa, Nana Konadu Yiadom II, - the Ashanti Queen Mother whose reign as Asantehemaa commenced in 1917 when her brother, the 13th Asantehene, Otumfuo Agyeman Prempeh I was ensconced in the Seychelles Island as a British Exile. Indeed, it was Asantehemaa Nana Konadu Yiadom II who in 1931 nominated my father, Otumfuo Sir Osei Agyeman Prempeh II, to be the 14thAsantehene.

Her father, Uncle John Osei Tutu Agyeman, J.O.T. as he was affectionately called, was a grandson of the Golden Stool. J.O.T's father, Oheneba Owusu Sekyere Agyeman was the son of the 11th Asantehene, Otumfuo Mensah Bonsu (1874-1883). Nana Konadu's mother, Auntie Felicia, Madam Yaa Safowaa (Auntie Felicia's older sister), and my mother-in-law Madam Ama Banahene were very close friends in their youthful days. They lived together in the "Ashtown" vicinity near Manhyia Palace, Kumasi. As a daughter of Asante, Nana Konadu has taken on the duty of sharing the guidance of her footsteps with her generation and the ones that will come after her.

The title *It Takes a Woman* could not have been better chosen. Her courage, independent personality, intellect, and forthrightness come across easily throughout the book.

Nana Konadu reminds me of the famous Asante heroine, Nana Yaa Asantewaa, the legendary Queen Mother of Ejisu, who was the first woman to defeat the British in their many fights against the Asantes. In March 1900, the Governor of the Gold Coast, Sir Frederick Hodgson led a British contingent to Asante to demand the Golden Stool, the highly revered, sacred, physical symbol and emblem of Asante Power. While some of the Asante Paramount Chiefs were pussyfooting, it took a woman, Nana Yaa Asantewaa to galvanise the Chiefs and people of Asante to stand up, fight and defeat the British in their most sacrilegious adventure.

Nana Konadu has always fought against the marginalization of women and children. Columnist Africanus Owusu Ansah once wrote: "She is credited with the formation of the 31st December Women's Movement, which taught women how to generate income and save money for community projects. The Movement gave opportunities for women to be part of the decision making process. Women were propelled to adopt policies on health and education. They were keen on adult literacy, discouraged early marriages, and were formidable in the affairs of children to the extent of pushing Ghana to adopt the UN Convention on the Rights of the child."

My encouragement to her is to let the support of the people who look up to her, continue to give her the strength to fight for the work to which she is committed.

Oheneba Akwasi Abayie (Lovelace Prempeh)
Akomforehene to Otumfuo Osei Tutu II

ACKNOWLEDGEMENTS

Writing this book began long before I had the chance to put my first thoughts onto a paper. As such, I have been immensely fortunate to have had so many great people through the years who inspired everything I am today, and for all of whom, I am profoundly grateful.

My deepest gratitude goes to my mother, Madam Felicia Agyeman, whose encouragement and contribution to unearthing much of my family's history set me on this journey. My father's most important wish was to see his daughter embrace a life that made a difference for her community and her people, and I am forever grateful for his guidance and for the honour of allowing my children also to keep the name Agyeman.

My grand Aunt Afua Konadu gave me the best historical grounding any child growing up could ever have, and I thank her for the example of integrity, duty, and honour.

To my curious husband Jerry John Rawlings who was dying to read the contents of my book before publication. Also to my children Zanetor, Yaa Asantewaa, Amina, and Kimathi for their boundless curiosity about our family's heritage and background. Each of you brings incredible joy to me, and I thank you for pushing me to work even faster on this book. Aunty Alice Adwoa Agyeman remains a rock of our family, and her reassuring words carried me.

To Erika Amoako Agyei for having the confidence in my story, that it ought to be told. Kissy Agyeman-Togobo deserves my huge ovation for the countless hours reviewing the early drafts in line with the Oxford version of the English language. My immense gratitude also to Mildred Annan who spent many weeks and months typing my handwritten notes over and again with an incredible commitment and gentle smile, and never a single complaint.

I also thank E. Obeng-Amoako Edmonds, whose patience, advice, encouragement and precious time poured into the manuscript made the words come alive.

There are many more people for whom my words will not aptly express my full gratitude, but for whom I am eternally grateful for their influence and support.

The pages of my life are filled with many men and women, from the villages and cities across the world who inspired me, admonished me, and most importantly, taught me. For all the lessons I carried along, perhaps none had been more salient than knowing that every unsuspecting moment and encounter has a way of shaping a person's life.

CONTENTS

INTRODUCTION

Nothing could have prepared a young woman for the tumultuous years to come in the late 1970's Ghana, an era when every moment seemed uniquely important to the strides the country was taking away from the shadows of its pre-independence years. There were spells of uncertainty in a country that was quickly changing, and a people hungry for economic stability and social development. In the dizzying pace in search of progress, women had an incredibly significant role in society. They were the mothers and daughters standing alongside the men who stood at the forefront, while having to fight through the restrained expectations that culture placed on them.

At a very young age, Nana Konadu Agyeman-Rawlings, whose name *Konadu* means "fight 'til the end," learned a striking truth that was to shape the rest of her life. The Asantehene (King of Ashanti) was the preeminent figure of the Ashanti and wielded tremendous influence over the destiny of the empire and his people, yet, as tradition would have it, it took a woman—the queen mother—to nurture his ascent to power.

Named after the valiant Ashanti Queen Mother, Nana Konadu Yiadom II, who ruled the Ashanti kingdom in the absence of the exiled Asantehene Nana Agyeman Prempeh I in 1896, Agyeman-Rawlings' journey has been one with stunning subplots in a country where every man, woman, and child could find hope of a future. The lives of the women, and indeed, the men, who mentored her along the way became reminders of the urgency of service to the nation, despite the long and undefined road ahead.

It Takes a Woman retraces the early life of Agyeman-Rawlings who rose to prominence and served as the First Lady of the Republic of

Ghana (1982-2000). She redefined the privilege of serving a nation and sought every platform to champion the causes of underserved citizenry and women. While her husband, former President Jerry John Rawlings embarked on a relentless pursuit of transforming Ghana into a model of African democracy, Agyeman-Rawlings founded the 31st December Women's Movement, an organisation which played a pivotal role in the empowerment of women, and in addressing issues of systemic gender inequality, not only in Ghana but across the African region.

The narrative captures the family history of a spirited little girl, and as she walks us through the refreshingly detailed scenes from her childhood, we are transported to a hopeful and quintessential Ghana, where a sense of national pride resounded powerfully at the time of independence. But as she recalls Ghana's struggles post-independence, we are also confronted face to face with her juxtaposed emotions of elation and frustration, hurt and joy, certainty and dread. She was not to know that her personal life being upended early one morning in 1979 would also become a turning point in the nation's history and thrust her into the glare of international publicity.

Born in an era when women were overtly marginalised, Nana Konadu Agyeman-Rawlings' strong relationship with her father, mother and family elders formed the core of much of her formative years. Fortified by her unique family history, she was raised never to accept the notion that "*there were some things she could not do, simply because she was a woman.*"

Agyeman-Rawlings' values, outlook and indeed, life itself, have been sculpted by the nurturing hands of strong female leaders in her life, from her grandmothers, her mother, to sisters and mentors. Her father stands tall as the patriarchal inspiration throughout her life whose voice echoed that of the women who encouraged her to fulfil her potential. Her journey of political activism and women's empowerment is etched into a broader narrative of Ghana's political history and destiny.

It Takes a Woman, written with unflinching candour, is an absorbing portrait of a life devoted to public service and shaped by heritage. Above all, it is an account of resilience. The voices of the women who stood tall will forever inspire Agyeman-Rawlings to stand for many more whose voices may not be loud enough to stand on their own.

CHAPTER ONE

DRIFTING INTO SUNSET
Accra, Ghana

It was June 4, 1979. Just before dawn that morning I was home in bed, soundly asleep when suddenly, I was awakened by the roaring sound of jet planes and helicopters. They seemed to be hovering directly overhead. Under the spell of overpowering fatigue, I quickly dismissed the oddity of the early morning commotion and drifted back into deep slumber.

I needed the rest.

The sudden flurry of activity following the recent arrest of my husband, Flight Lieutenant Jerry John Rawlings—a fighter pilot with the Ghana Air Force—had left me feeling physically and mentally spent. With my husband on trial for his life, it felt as though I was already in the midst of a brewing crisis. My only relief was sleep, which for a short time, seemed to allay some of my anxieties. I could not have known that the crisis was just about to escalate.

Around 5:30 that morning, I heard a faint knock on the front door of our two-bedroom flat. "Huh?" I mumbled sleepily, stirring but not waking up. It felt like a dream. The knock grew louder and more forceful – it felt like the door was being pounded. Startled and confused, I forced myself to my feet and grabbed my morning coat but my pace didn't match the persistent hammering, as I wondered irritably who could be knocking at this time of the morning. My sleepy eyes strained to make out objects in the dark, but the shadows seemed impenetrable. As I inched closer to the door, groping about with one hand, the other clutching a table, then a chair, I could hear the utterance of a muffled voice, "Nana, open up!"

I opened the door. I saw the face of a frantic woman who was visibly shaken. It was my mother. My eyes grew wide, and I felt my heart sink. My first thought was, *have they killed him?*

Panting, my mother pushed herself through the door. She spoke quietly and cautioned, "There's something going on. I think it is Jerry. We have to get you and the baby out of here." The baby was our one-year-old daughter, Zanetor, who was our only child at the time.

Knowing Jerry was in prison and due back in court later that same morning, I looked at my mother in disbelief and said, "Maa, you're imagining things."

Impatiently, she snapped back, "*Ohhh no.* You've got to listen…"

Just then, Elizabeth, a lady we both knew and who worked as a journalist at the time, came to my door. She was equally frantic, and blurted, "Jerry has run out of jail."

I stiffened. All I could think was, *I don't believe it!* Just four days ago, he had promised me that he wouldn't do anything outrageous. Then I began to reflect on our last conversation while he was in detention. We were given only a few minutes of privacy during the trial. This was the first time I was allowed contact with him in the two weeks since his arrest.

"Nana," he whispered within the confines of a small room, "these people are not really watching me that well. I could run off if I want."

His eyes were wide and full of hope, searching my face for a reaction.

"No!" I said firmly. I was concerned about his safety and unwilling to encourage any thoughts of escape. "Don't do such a thing. That is probably what they want you to do so they can kill you," I stressed, holding his gaze. "*Don't give them a chance.*" Reading the distress in my face, he relaxed his posture and feigned a smile. "Ahhhh, don't worry

Nana," he said reassuringly. "I was just joking," he added, pausing, as if to say, "You have my word."

That was what I thought. Looking back on that early morning, thoughts ran through my mind over and again that perhaps I should have taken Jerry's first words more seriously. Beyond the realm of anything I could imagine, plans for his escape must have already been in the works.

I replayed the conversation over and over in my mind, each time feeling a bit more restless and terrified. I started to pack a small suitcase with some necessary provisions for Zanetor and some personal belongings for myself—a dress, a toothbrush, and whatever else I could quickly grab. By around 6 a.m. we were in a car with my mother, fleeing to her home for shelter.

My neighbour, Miriam, who lived upstairs in the same building in Accra, drove us that morning to Maa's house. I vividly recall how each time the car slowed down or came to a halt, I held my breath, wondering whether we were being followed. To avoid suspicion, I forced myself to look composed and clung tightly to the baby who sat alertly on my lap. She seemed eager to break free from my protective hold. I had to look calm. I didn't want to attract the attention of someone who might drive up alongside us and look in our direction while waiting at an intersection, but this only added another layer of anxiety. I was a young mother and a wife, unsure of what the next moments held.

The route from our block of flats on Independence Avenue to Maa's house in Nyaniba Estates was very familiar to me. I had driven it many times. But on this warm and rainy Monday morning, the way seemed strange, full of a sense of foreboding, stemming from feeling like a fugitive. In fact, a fugitive I had become. Within ten minutes of leaving my flat, I learned that three men from Military Intelligence (MI) had descended upon our premises looking for me, apparently to take me into custody until Jerry surrendered. But Jerry didn't surrender. Nor do

I believe he would have—even in the face of my captivity. The situation in Ghana had become so desperate that, given a chance, I knew my husband would relentlessly pursue what he was convinced was a worthy sacrifice of his own life—at almost any cost—to save what was left of Ghana.

Many across the country felt the pain of a home we were proud to call our own, but one that was gradually falling apart, and unsure of what the next minute would bring. By the late 1970s, Ghana had been stripped bare. The country had become like an automobile whose working parts had been stolen by thieves, with only its metal frame left behind.

In a span of a decade, the country had been under the changing hands of corrupt civilian and military regimes. Poverty, neglect, and stagnation had pervaded both the infrastructure and the people of Ghana. Fathers and mothers struggled to provide for their families, and it felt as though the society had been plunged into unrestrained chaos.

In Accra, the filth of open gutters lined the edges of the streets and carried rainwater mixed with garbage and sewage across the city. It was as if this was a symbol of our once promising future now washing away with every moment. It felt as though there was no attention being paid to the country's basic infrastructure since the overthrow of the first president, Dr. Kwame Nkrumah in 1966. Roads had fallen apart, hospital supplies had become a scarcity, and industrial and farm machinery had been tucked away for there were no spare parts to repair them.

With little hope for the future, Ghanaians wondered how much longer it would be before we drifted further into the abyss. Journalist David Lamb echoed the sentiments of the time: "Can this destitute, demoralised place be the once thriving 'Black Star of Africa,' which in 1957 became the first black African nation to win its independence?" The questions and uncertainty filled every heart, and it felt as though it was only a matter of time before all the hope on which we stood would evaporate. Every new day seemed to come with a shattering blow, more piercing than the one before.

At the time of regaining independence, Ghana was one of the world's largest producer of gold, cocoa, and manganese. But after this turning point, Ghana was brought to its knees by several of its own leaders. Men and women pillaged for no other reason than personal gain. That had sadly become the open secret; they did not even care to hide their greed. Now under the leadership of a regime known as the Supreme Military Council (SMC), the country had slipped into the grip of the worst political and economic crisis of its history.

When we reached my mother's home, I immediately sat in the sturdy living room chair. The atmosphere in the house was tense. Curious neighbours and worried friends and family had already gathered inside. I sat aloof. I felt both dazed and bewildered. Slowly, I turned inward for quiet contemplation, and I became absorbed in deep thoughts of doubt and terrifying suspicion. *"If he has broken out of jail,"* I thought, *"then he better leave Ghana—for good."* It was a rather agonising reality, but with every flutter of the heart, I thought to myself that *"If they catch him this time, they will not spare his life."* The stakes were high. With Jerry on the move again, the humiliation felt by the SMC would only harden the government's determination to silence him once and for all.

Underpinning my feelings of grief was paranoia. It was a fear so overwhelming and reminiscent of the sheer sense of engulfment I used to feel as a child when I was left alone in the dark. The sensation was an indescribable presence of something so massive and horrifying that the darkness seemed alive. Long ago as a child, I remember how my fear would be so intense that Maa always made sure I spent the night in the same bed with one of my sisters so that I could drift off to sleep.

Now with the passing of each hour, I could feel a reality that was far from anything I'd imagined my life would become. Vivid images of my husband's brutal killing kept flashing into my mind. It was tormenting, but there was nothing I could do about it. The thought of gunmen emerging from out of the bushes, encircling Jerry, and unleashing fire on my husband was beyond terrifying.

For hours, I sat quietly in sober meditation. A flurry of emotions kept running through my mind, and I struggled to remain hopeful. I was completely withdrawn as I prepared myself for news of the worst—news of Jerry's death. It would be devastating for me, and I could not imagine having to pull my unravelled world back together. In futile attempts to console me, the people in the house would chime in with kind words intended to lighten my distress.

"Don't worry. He will be fine. Just try and relax." I tried to relax. I could not breathe.

Another politely added, "Really Nana, if you worry, you only make it worse."

"Nana, maybe you should try and eat something…"

The only thing I could take in was a cup of coffee, and the only movements I could make were frequent visits to the bathroom. Even then, as I walked, my thoughts were completely dissociated from the movement of my body. In the bathroom mirror, I saw the reflection of a face so filled with anguish, tension, and uncertainty that I did not recognise it as my own. All that was familiar to me was my deepening despair. No matter how hard I tried to contain it, my grief, like a river overflowing its banks, surged forth in all directions.

I returned to the living room and collapsed back into Maa's sturdy chair. At that moment, a sympathetic voice whispered a simple piece of advice that stirred me more than any other: "Nana, think of the baby." Of course, I had a little baby to think of.

Each time I glanced over at my daughter, who clung innocently to my mother, my thoughts were once again held hostage to involuntary scenes of torment. Turning one year old only three days earlier, Zanetor was the only extension I had of Jerry—the one precious gift that both of us proudly shared. How could I ever explain to her that her father had been a hero, but was sadly killed the day he escaped from a government prison? Although she was so little, she was living this nightmare with me. As I sat there, overcome with dread, I wondered how I would ever look into her eyes and explain the outcome of this fateful day.

The psychological strain from anxiety was becoming unbearable. Finally, I reached into my handbag and pulled out a small vial of stress relief tablets. I took two. Within fifteen minutes, I felt a wave of calm come over me, followed by a dull, numbing sensation. As I sat there, wandering in and out of consciousness, I began to feel as relaxed and as comfortable as I could, under the circumstances. Even the darting and vivid images in my mind's eye had been stilled.

Then, without warning, that fragile state of calm was fractured by the abrasive crackling of the afternoon radio which broke through with: *"This is Flight Lieutenant Rawlings,"* my husband shouted with breathless anxiety. His voice jolted me out of my momentary reverie and my fears were rekindled. I sat up tense and alert, my heart racing and my stomach felt queasy.

"The ranks have just got me out of my prison cell. In other words, the ranks have just taken over the destiny of this country," his voice, rising, at times almost screaming, was punctuated by the staccato sound of gunshots in the background. *"Fellow officers, if we are to avoid any bloodshed, I plead with you not to attempt to stand in their way because they are full of malice, hatred—hatred we have forced into them through all these years of suppression. They are ready to get it out—the venom we have created. So, for heaven's sake do not stand in their way. They are not fools. If you have any reason to fear them, you may run. If you have no reason to feel guilty, do not move... We can't restrain them."*

He then requested that all units send representatives to the new Revolutionary Council that would replace the SMC which was, as he stated, *"No more."* Jerry then gave what had to be a crucial reassurance to the civilian population: *"The Ghana Armed Forces will be handing power over to the civilians in due time. Elections will take place."*

As he continued, my husband was careful to reflect the feelings of frustration of the long-oppressed rank and file soldiers: *"But before the elections go on, justice, which has been denied to the Ghanaian worker will have to take place, I promise you... Some of us have suffered for far too long."*

The marginalised Ghanaian population knew that the only way to change the status quo was through free and fairly managed elections. But how this was to be guaranteed was far from certain at the time. It had been ten years, two coups d'état and two consecutive military regimes since the country had held democratic elections. Even though fear still gripped me, I felt the weight of the moment. I knew that Jerry's promise of elections during this broadcast would hold great significance for Ghanaians. I hoped so.

I imagined millions of listeners across Ghana hearing Jerry's passionate plea for calm in the midst of a highly-charged and explosive situation. But what many perceived as a brilliantly planned and dramatic escape from the custody of an abusive government, I saw differently. I viewed the morning's events as a possible plot to kill my husband. During the broadcast, I detected in Jerry's voice a tremor which alarmed me. In my mind, it was clear that he was under some duress. As he read the announcement, I was paralysed by an image of him with a gun behind him or pointing at his head.

At this stage, what no one knew was that Jerry himself was uncertain about his own position in this emerging revolution that had been led by the ordinary ranks of the Ghana Armed Forces. He certainly was not the "leader of the uprising." His rescue from prison had been the focal point that prompted the revolt and thrust him into a leadership position. For the first time in the history of our country, ordinary-ranked soldiers had taken the reins and were boldly expressing their dissatisfaction with the rot and corruption within the military hierarchy and throughout society at large.

What had now developed was a spontaneous revolution of the lower rank and file against the established authority of the Ghana Armed Forces. To some extent, Jerry himself was part of that 'authority' structure—merely by his ranking as an officer.

But just over an hour after his broadcast to the nation, everything changed. Government forces regained control of Broadcasting House where my husband had made his announcement on the nation's only radio station, Ghana Broadcasting Corporation. They announced that the coup had been foiled and called on all ranks to return to their barracks. The Army Commander, Major-General Odartey-Wellington, then added: "I also urge Flight Lieutenant J.J. Rawlings and any following he has with him to meet me at (the police) headquarters."

That balmy afternoon of June 4 1979, while my husband's shrill voice through the radio sent shivers down my spine, I could not help but wonder who else was listening. I was afraid of what could happen to our young family, but I understood the weight he must have felt on his shoulders. I clutched onto a sliver of hope that anyone who heard him, understood him, and perhaps would see through the lens from which he viewed our beloved country.

Ghana, not long ago, had been the beacon of hope for other African countries to look to, and find their own inspiration. If the country's optimism for a bright future unravelled at its seams, we would all soon become threadbare-nothing would bind us together. In such a world, the tapestry of our rich culture and language would not matter, nor would any of the languages that gave us our identity. Home would have lost its allure – the former refuge of promise now ruined by patronage and worst of all - we would have no one to blame but ourselves.

One thing was sure; we were a people who could draw strength from our varied experiences from the different regions in the country. We could only hope that the turmoil that was slowly surrounding the moment added to the colourful future we dreamt of, one that was to somehow emerge in the horizon. Our distinctive cultures gave all of us a chance to see Ghana from our unique vantage points, and even in the desperate moments, we could only hope that our challenges would not deflate all of the promises our motherland held in its bosom.

The weight of the time was awful. Even if for a moment, I began to dream of a time when my life was unassuming and carefree. Everything

I had known all my life seemed to flash through my mind, one scene after another. There was this eerie feeling that I could not take another step without everyone peeking over my shoulder. Who I was, and the place from where I had come, was almost unimportant. Ghana was made up of a people whose diversity was our strength to cherish, and the fear was that soon the burden of the moment could rip apart what held us all together.

This had turned out to be the longest day of my life. It felt as though nothing I had lived through could have prepared me for this. I remembered how the confidence in my father's smile and the reassuring embrace of my mother's arms had once been enough comfort for any distress I experienced as a child. But now, as a mother and a wife, society expected - and family depended on, my stoicism, even on a day so agonising as this. It was a dawning realisation that my life had changed forever.

CHAPTER TWO

A DIFFERENT KIND OF GLARE
A World through My Eyes

I come from a long line of strong, independent and ambitious women. Yet I was born in an era when women were marginalised politically, socially, culturally and economically. Even as a little girl, I was attuned to the inequalities in our society.

Unlike my generation, I quickly found out how a professional woman of my mother's generation did not even have the luxury of dreaming of balancing the demands of family and career. The British colonial government waded into family affairs also by making the choice for the young woman: under British law, married women were forbidden from entering into the workforce. They were no longer allowed to work or contribute to the economy and broader society. The women were forced to stay at home and look after their husbands and children.

My mother, Felicia Agyeman, was no exception. After only one year of professional work as a school teacher, she was forced to abandon the career she loved the moment she married my father. This colonial government's obligation gradually discouraged many female professionals of my mother's era from marrying in their youthful years, and in some cases, not marrying at all. My mother had to live through the disadvantage but remained determined to make the best of her journey.

I learned that around the time my mother was eight-and-a-half months pregnant with me, she was ascending a flight of stairs when she suddenly slipped, lost her balance and suffered an excruciating fall. The impact from the fall immediately threatened her pregnancy and left her barely able to walk. Fortunately for her – albeit unjustly, given the endemic over-reliance on networks to get things done - my father's professional ties within the white expatriate community were fortuitous at this time. My mother was provided with easy access to the modern facilities of Cape Coast Hospital, where she was rushed to for urgent care. I was born in the pre-dawn hours of the following morning, on November 17, 1948, under the care of a resident European doctor.

When I was born, Ghana was still the Gold Coast, a British colony known for its plantations and for being the world's largest producer of cocoa. The resident governor in Accra was an Englishman named Sir Gerald Hallen Creasy, who represented the British monarchy in the colony, and our Head of State was Queen Elizabeth II of England, Scotland, and Wales. The population of the Gold Coast had reached a little over four million and much of the landscape in the nation's two largest cities, Accra and Kumasi, was dominated by whitewashed colonial-style housing surrounded by neatly manicured lawns in spacious, residential neighbourhoods. These were the planned communities primarily reserved for the families of European civil servants.

At the time of my birth, my father, John Osei-Tutu (J.O.T.) Agyeman was stationed in the coastal town of Cape Coast as a senior manager working for the United Africa Company (UAC), a well-known British trading firm that was a branch of the multi-national corporation Unilever. I was born third of my parents' seven children. My sister, Yaa Achia was the first, followed by my older brother, Owusu Sekyere (also called Daddy O.S.), who was born two years before me.

I am told I was a precocious child. My mother says that by the time I was eleven months old I was speaking several words clearly. Moreover, by the young age of three or maybe four, my fondness and efforts at duplicating 'lady-like' behaviours became the subject of great laughter in our home—to the extent that my family amusingly nicknamed me

Lady. As far as I can remember, my earliest childhood joy was dressing up in fancy dress, placing a flower in my hair and sneaking into Maa's closet to put my little feet into her high heels. Repeatedly and with great conviction, I began asserting, "As for me, *I am a lady.*"

No one took greater advantage of this than my older brother Owusu. Closest to me in age, Owusu was my first childhood playmate. I followed him everywhere. However, when he or any of the other children would start fighting in my midst, I would step back and haughtily declare, "I do not fight, and I do not quarrel because *I am a lady.*"

I suspect this provoked my brother's enthusiasm for pushing me around and continuously harassing me. Tired of my complaints, my mother would advise, "Lady, when he beats you, don't just stand there, *beat him back!* And when he knocks you with something, take that something and *knock him back!*" Rather than listen, Maa told me that I would gesture boldly and defiantly with my little body, and declare that I could not do that because I was a lady. Well, one day this strong conviction nearly cost me my life.

We had recently moved from Cape Coast to Tarkwa, a booming little mining town in the Western Region of Ghana. Maa had gone to town one afternoon to buy foodstuffs from the local market, leaving Owusu, Yaa Achia, and I home alone with the maidservant.

When she returned home that morning, Maa said she asked Owusu, "Where is the Lady?"

Owusu casually replied, "Lady? Well, she drank something so now she's asleep."

"Asleep? What did she drink?" Maa demanded.

"I filled a glass, gave it to her and told her that ladies only drink from glasses, so she drank it," Owusu replied.

Maa said she quickly found out that what Owusu gave me was kerosene!

"*Oh, God Almighty!*" Maa screamed. "Owusu, I've told you that you will kill your sister—*you will kill her!*"

Maa said she found my little body tucked away in the corner of a room in a deep sleep. After struggling to wake me, she quickly beat a fresh egg and gave it to me to drink. She then put her finger down my throat to induce vomiting. It worked, but soon afterward, Maa said, I quickly drifted back into a deep sleep, which made her panic once again.

The local hospital was about 12 miles away in the small town of Abosso, but there was no transportation, so she waited for my father to return home from work with the car and they took me in together. I was put on admission, and Maa said a European doctor told both her and my father that once I had vomited, I would continue to sleep until the effect of the kerosene wore off.

After two days of wearily waiting by my bedside, Maa said she began losing hope. Nearing the end of the second day, however, I finally awoke, breaking through the spell of kerosene, which I thought was the drink of choice for ladies – it was served in a glass, after all.

With UAC outlets all over the colony, I grew up on the move, from one small town to another. My father was transferred to various regions of the country's interior, except his native Asante—a deliberate move on the part of the company to prevent ethnic sentiments and family ties from interfering with local trading activity.

From Cape Coast, we moved to Abosso, and from Abosso to Tarkwa, where my younger sister, Afriyie, was born. From Tarkwa, we moved to Dunkwa, then to Axim, then to Hunni Valley. So just before I turned five in 1953, we moved to Nkaw Nkaw, a small town in Ghana's Eastern Region. Although my father's work required that we move often, his position with the UAC exposed our family to a level of comfort and stability which I knew we were blessed to have. Among the standard perks that came with his postings were a car, driver, live-in domestic help and estate housing in well-furnished, British-built bungalows.

In the gated communities of UAC compounds, each bungalow usually came equipped with amenities such as a refrigerator, ceiling fans, and a wood-burning stove and oven. The furniture was supplied by UAC management and made locally of mahogany and cedar wood. We sometimes ate breakfast on the airy verandas which wrapped around two sides of the bungalow and were netted in with fine wire mesh to keep out flying insects. This was effective, and my parents enjoyed having a cross-breeze that blew in through the house from one open window and out through the other.

Before either my husband or I was born, our fathers happened to be acquaintances and colleagues of one another within the UAC. My husband's biological father, James Ramsay John, was a Scottish-born pharmacist who had migrated to the Gold Coast in 1935 with his English wife to work for the UAC. He was managing Kingsway Chemist in Accra when he met Jerry's mother, Victoria Agbotui, a beautiful Ewe woman from *Dzelokupe*, near Keta, in Ghana's Volta Region. She was a caterer at the State House in Accra who eventually cooked for each Head of State from the time Ghana regained its independence.

My mother, although petite in stature, had a very strong constitution. After she had me, she bore five more children, all girls, including one who died as an infant, leaving seven children total. Each of us was named by our paternal grandfather, Owusu Sekyere Agyeman, a well-educated Asante businessman who, in his day, made a vast fortune and a name for himself as a pioneering cocoa broker. While many mission-educated children of my grandfather's generation named their children after British imperial heroes and heroines like Victoria, Elizabeth, Wellington or Adelaide, my grandfather, a direct descendant of the Asante royal family, drew inspiration from the Asante stool.

As a result, my sisters and I were all named after Asante queen mothers, thus given the honorific title "Nana" to precede each of our names. We were Nana Yaa Achia, Nana Konadu, Nana Afriyie, Nana Serwah, Nana Sefa and my youngest sister, Nana Yaa. Originally, the title "Nana" was reserved solely for members of the royal family or those naming a child after a revered elder. However, nowadays, it is used more liberally. My only brother, Owusu Sekyere, was named after my grandfather himself. There was a certain pride and humility that came along with knowing the influence and legacy of the person whose name we carried. I had always been proud to bear the name of an Asante queen mother, and I could not help but appreciate that by adopting this tradition, my grandfather had ingrained in me a sense of loyalty to both king and country that would last throughout my life.

As our family grew, conversely, the UAC bungalows suddenly seemed to shrink. They were built to accommodate the typical European colonialist who either had a nuclear family or lived alone. Living in the country's interior, and in mostly expatriate (European and American) communities, I was somewhat insulated during early childhood from the harsh realities affecting the average African.

However, I would often have conversations with my father, which led to an early awareness of the world around me. My father was not only well-informed but also one of the most studious people I've ever known. He possessed worldly intelligence and could speak widely on a variety of topics. His love for politics profoundly influenced my interest in world affairs. A trait which I loved so much about him was his willingness to share his knowledge with me and the patience he exercised in explaining the complexities of geopolitics and Ghana's political history, starting with the year I was born.

"*Misewaa*," he would say, wide-eyed and enthusiastic, "the year of your birth coincided with a time of critical importance in this country." My father called me *Misewaa*, the Asante word for aunt, since I was named after his paternal aunt, Afua Konadu. I called him "D" (Dee). It must have been short for *darling* or a term of endearment, but it was a nickname my mother had given him soon after they were married. Somehow, every one of his children also called him *Dee*, never even pausing for a moment to wonder why we did not call our father "Daddy" like other children we knew.

"By the time you were born," his lesson would continue, "a large part of Asia was in the midst of gaining its independence from the British Empire. This stirred dreams of freedom in many other colonies. In 1947, the year before your birth, both India and Pakistan had achieved their independence. What encouraged most Africans in the Gold Coast was India's fight for freedom. It showed the world how the masses could defy their colonial masters."

By 1948, it was clear that the winds of change had begun to blow. World War II had been over for three years, and African ex-servicemen were returning to the colony after fighting for the British in overseas expeditions. Using coercion to increase their numbers, the British had recruited thousands of Gold Coast Africans to serve on the front lines with promises of future prosperity, including higher wages, job opportunities, improved housing conditions and other enticements, but only upon their return from the battlefields.

Sadly, however, after serving with distinction in places like Ethiopia and Burma, the vast majority of the ex-servicemen, totalling over 50,000, returned home to worse conditions than before they left, now confronted with high unemployment, inflation, housing shortages and other political and economic woes of the post-war period. Worst of all, my father told me, was that their appeals for help from the colonial authorities who recruited them fell on deaf ears. This left African veterans feeling embittered, angry and betrayed.

What colonial authorities failed to realise, however, was that the years of service in the war had not only sharpened their skills, but it had also broadened the horizons of African servicemen—making it difficult for them to return and readjust to the same humble and substandard positions set aside for Africans by the British.

My father would say that even in the battlefields, while fighting alongside Indian soldiers, African servicemen began to reason, *"Here I am fighting against somebody I don't even know, and the person using me to fight is the very person who is oppressing me."*

So after returning home to lives deeply entrenched in poverty, inadequate health care, and unemployment, African veterans began to view colonisation in the Gold Coast as one of the worst forms of oppression, similar to the oppression they had just fought against on the front lines of World War II. Like a volcano in eruption, these sentiments sparked a movement of open resistance against the British imperial system.

In the early afternoon of February 28, 1948, my father recounted how thousands of unarmed ex-servicemen took to the streets in an organised demonstration. They marched through the streets of Accra to Christianborg Castle,—then the official seat of government,—to carry a petition to the British governor seeking answers to their grievances. The immense crowd was orderly and peaceful and included six and seven-year-old children excitedly hopping alongside the band of World War II veterans.

But, without warning, the march turned deadly. A British policeman callously opened fire on the crowd, instantly killing three of the marchers, including their leader, Sergeant Adjetey. The shootings sparked a violent rampage of looting and burning of white-owned shops and offices in what became known as the Gold Coast Riots of 1948. During these riots, angry mobs looted and set ablaze a number of European and Asian-owned companies in Accra, including the Accra-based offices and shops of the UAC, my father's employer. Mercifully, none of the violence reached our family in Cape Coast, but in Accra, pandemonium swelled.

The gates of Usher Fort, the central prison, were forced open and many inmates escaped. My father remembered how the country was placed under a state of emergency and the military had to be brought in to help the small number of police regain control. Between February 28, 1948, when the riots began, and March 16, when they were finally brought under control, several more deaths occurred and over 200 people were left wounded.

In later years, I remember my father telling me just how flabbergasted the British were at the explosive outburst of national expression. The riots were the first event to shake the complacency of the white expatriate society, threatening both white prestige and imperial power.

For my young parents, living in the colonial era must have been a constant struggle between the traditional ways of the past and the imported Western values they encountered daily. In the case of my mother's fall, for instance, during her late stage of pregnancy, modern medicine was clearly the fastest and most convenient way of treating the urgent nature of her condition. But soon after I was born, my parent's faith in Western medicine would be tested against the traditional use of African herbal remedies to treat ailments in our family.

Only weeks after my elder brother Owusu was born, he contracted infantile paralysis, also known as polio. This crippling condition horrified my parents and they often worried about his future. They sought help from several Western medical doctors, but all to no avail. I am told that just days before I was born, Owusu, aged two, was completely incapable of walking or even crawling on his own. However, the day before my mother brought me home from the hospital, my father came bursting in the hospital room with good news. "*Owusu is walking!*" he said beaming from ear to ear.

Apparently, Owusu's miraculous turnaround was the work of an old, female herbalist who was the mother of my father's long-time friend and classmate, Nene Mate Kole, the paramount chief of Manya-Krobo, an area in Ghana's Eastern Region. In their school days, the chief and my father had both attended Achimota College, an elite British-established college in Accra that was heralded as the most prestigious school in the colony, and throughout most of West Africa.

The chief had been visiting my father when he saw the debilitating condition of my brother. Startled, he immediately told my father, "I am sending someone back to Odumase (a Krobo village) to consult my mother about your son. Whatever my mother sends, make sure you use it on him, and he will get up."

So, while my mother was still away with me at the hospital's maternity ward, Chief Nene Mate Kole sent a messenger to his village. The messenger returned with some herbal roots, some clay, and some strict instructions: Owusu was to be bathed early in the morning with a mixture composed of the roots, clay and a pint of water. Then, come evening, he was to be given a normal bath.

The routine was strictly adhered to for the next five days, after which time I am told my brother made an astonishing turnaround. Rising slowly to his feet one day, Owusu began motioning to walk. Many Western doctors who had been aware of my brother's condition were stunned by the turnaround and told my parents they were very fortunate. Yet, to this day, as custom demands, we do not know the exact concoction made by the herbalist who healed Owusu's condition. The good news, however, is that my brother continued to develop normally throughout adulthood and no sign of his early childhood affliction ever reappeared.

Much like my brother, I was also burdened from a very young age with health issues. Before I was one, I would frequently come down with periodic attacks of wheezing, laboured breathing and coughing spells. At times, this became so alarming that I would often endure sleepless nights and make frequent hospital visits.

During the initial attack, I was diagnosed at the hospital as having bronchial pneumonia; however, my maternal grandmother, Margaret Appiah, who I never got to know well, was of a different opinion. She immediately dismissed the diagnosis made by white doctors after having suffered the same symptoms herself from infancy. My grandmother recognised my illness as the breathing disorder known as asthma.

So, she quickly advised my mother that the condition could be managed with the use of certain local herbs. But for some reason, both my parents refused her advice and dismissed her diagnosis. Despite the success of my older brother's health, thanks to local herbs, my parents opted this time around to follow the recommendations of modern doctors. With my father's access to Western medicines and the best trained medical professionals in the Gold Coast, both he and my mother continued visiting the hospital each time the attacks occurred, but no permanent remedy was ever found.

My mother recalls, "Wherever there was a neem tree in bloom, bearing fruits and flowers, an attack was sure to come on." By the time I was two years old, my young parents realised that my grandmother was right. My breathing condition was not going away, but instead needed to be managed as the symptoms occurred. Throughout my life, this was something I was going to have to live with and manage, the daily discomforts of asthma.

While British law forbade my mother from continuing in the workforce, it embraced my father's early knack for understanding the world of trade. While still in secondary school at Achimota College, his British instructors recognised his keen aptitude for commerce, economics, and business, and used those attributes to carve out a path for his future in the Gold Coast.

"Had it been my choice," my father would say, "I would have studied medicine, not business. My dream was to become a medical doctor."

"But Dee, why didn't you?" I once asked him. "You always tell me that so long as I keep to my books, I can become whatever I want to be when I grow up. So why didn't you follow your own dream and study medicine instead of business?" I demanded with childlike innocence.

"Misewaa, you are right. That is what I tell you, and that is the truth," he replied earnestly. "With education, you can become anything you want," he continued. "Education will open doors where none seem to exist and will make people listen to you, talk to you and help you; people who otherwise would not bother. And most importantly, education will lift those artificial boundaries and limitations that others try to impose upon you," he said with passion and intensity. Despite the prevalence of female oppression in our society, my father always stressed education and independence of thought to my five sisters and I.

"Misewaa, education is the key that will open up a new world and life for you and your children, a world far different from that of either your mother's or mine. In my time, things were quite different. No matter how smart or well educated we were, the British controlled our destiny. Everything we, the Africans, did was for the benefit of building their empire and serving their interests. Not ours. In those days, our voices were silenced, our choices were limited and in their eyes, we existed only to serve their needs. So, I became a businessman because that is what I was told to do."

Even as a primary school pupil, my father's words hit me like a bolt of lightning. A long silence stretched between us, during which I reflected upon his words. I looked at my father, he looked at me, and at that moment, I vowed to never allow any foreigner, or any self-serving individual for that matter, decide my fate.

During the colonial era, the career choices of African students were directed and determined at the discretion of the British and according to the needs of the state. This was British law. What my father had aspired to do was to become a medical doctor like his best friend and classmate, Dr. Charles Easmon, who was sent abroad to do medicine because he was good at biology. He returned to the Gold Coast as one of the first African surgeons in the country. But since Dee's instructors had decided that his strengths were in commerce and not biology, his personal career ambitions were forced to give way to the predetermined path chosen for him by the British. Moreover, he was an Asante and people from Asante were often pegged as being good traders.

"John, you will pursue business," his British instructor told him. So, after completing his primary and secondary education at Achimota College, my father left the Gold Coast for London to continue his education at the London School of Economics, where he obtained a master's degree in commerce. Upon graduating, he returned to the Gold

Coast to start professional work—first with Elder Dempster Lines, a major international shipping company that was based in Liverpool but operated a large number of cargo ships that ran between West Africa, Great Britain, and the United States. From Elder Dempster Lines, he eventually moved on to work for the UAC.

The UAC was a large and diversified business enterprise of major significance in British West Africa. It functioned as an autonomous company within Unilever. Originally formed in 1919, the UAC was a merger between two British trading companies. So, it was no surprise when only Europeans held executive and managerial positions while Africans were generally limited to junior and subordinate positions.

But by the time I was born, Dee would have broken this pattern when he became one of the first Africans to rise to senior management level. Taking nothing for granted, he always recognised how fortunate he was. "Misewaa," he would say in a reflective tone, "I was one of the lucky ones. Because my father could afford to put me through school, I was able to use my 'brains instead of my back,' to earn a very decent living to put my children through school and support my entire family. For that, Misewaa, I am always grateful."

Dee certainly did receive an outstanding education—a rarity for most Africans of his time. As a consequence, many prominent European officials would willingly vouch for his business and managerial skills at a time when most Africans were denied any such recognition.

It was not until much later in life that I truly understood what my father meant by being able to use his brains instead of his back. The economy of the Gold Coast was based upon the export of raw materials, most notably, cocoa—the colony's main export earner—followed by gold and timber, to the developed world of Europe and North America. By 1950, the Gold Coast was exporting more than half of the world's cocoa supply, making it one of the wealthiest and most economically-advanced colonies in all of Africa. The problem, however, was that the British made themselves the sole beneficiaries of our nation's wealth,

human labour, and abundant natural resources, especially after the
Second World War.

Since Europe was confronted by financial crises both during and
after World War II, the Colonial Office in London was determined to
transfer as much wealth as possible in natural resources from the Gold
Coast directly to Europe. Such was the pattern of the colonial economic
system, which was designed to preserve African colonies as sources of
raw materials to strengthen a crippling post-WWII British economy.

Regardless of the world market price, the British made it a practice
to pay African cocoa farmers a low fixed rate for the latter's produce.
For instance, if the world cocoa market reached a level of £450 British
pounds a ton, the African cocoa farmer received no more than £150
British pounds a ton. This created a net surplus of £300 a ton that went
straight into the coffers of the British government.

Beyond the lucrative cocoa market, the prices of all other raw materials exported from the Gold Coast were determined in far-off financial
centres such as London. In the same way, this was the case for the prices
of all manufactured consumer goods (e.g. tractors, trucks, machinery,
fertiliser, clothing, books, household utensils, etc.) from the developed
world, which we, in the underdeveloped economy of the Gold Coast,
were expected to import. In other words, the developed Western world
dictated the terms of trade with the Gold Coast and all other African
colonies.

The injustice inherent in the colonial economy was clear. In times of
crisis in the developed world, cocoa and gold prices were reduced while
those of manufactured goods remained constant or were increased. This
meant that the Gold Coast would have to export more of her cocoa and
her timber just to import the same amount of manufactured consumer
goods. Under this system, any economic weakness in the developed
world could be off-loaded onto the backs of African labour.

Certainly, this was not in the same direct manner as during the
slave trade, but nonetheless an unequally-yoked relationship. Adding to

this, the nation's gold, diamonds, and other rich mineral resources were entirely owned by foreign companies who paid only a token compensation in rents and royalties to the ancestral owners of the land based on terms many Africans in those early days did not fully understand but were forced to accept. This was an economic system that Dr. Kwame Nkrumah would later coin as 'neo-colonialism'.

My father, J.O.T., was a quiet intellectual who intuitively understood the inner workings and unfair trade practices of foreign merchants operating in the Gold Coast. Because the British government controlled the markets for the country's export commodities, Africans could not explore other, and possibly more favourable, markets for their own products. Moreover, foreigners owned all the commercial banks in the country, so African-owned business enterprises were often discriminated against, making it impossible for them to establish credit.

In spite of my father's high position within the UAC, he, too, was subject to the deeply ingrained system of discrimination. As one of the few Africans who served at the senior levels of the company, his salary was far below that which was paid to his white counterparts. Yet his advanced training and performance overseas in the same centres of learning as his European and American colleagues were proof enough to him that, given the opportunity, the African is in no way inferior to the white scholar. Upon this realisation, my father also advocated the mindset that Africans could, and must, manage their own affairs and resources for the benefit of African people.

My ancestral home finds its roots in the central parts of Ghana. The tributaries of several rivers criss-cross the landscape, giving life to beautiful cascading waterfalls, deep green rolling hills, and dense tropical rainforests. Verdant and lush during the rainy season, this portion of Ghana had become the centre of the ancient kingdom of Asante (Ashanti), where both my parents descended from a long line of royal ancestry.

My father's uncle had been the king of Asante, Nana Agyeman Prempeh I, who was exiled in 1897 by the British before the colonial government finally imposed its power on the Asante kingdom in 1902. But even in defeat, the Asante royal family was held in high esteem, and it continued to be a focal point of the history and culture of this region and the African continent itself.

I remembered how surrounding the former Asante Empire was rich fertile land which was home to large cocoa plantations and the most important gold mines in the country. Farther inland, on the main road that extended through the country all the way down to the southern coast, the terrain became more dramatic. The road wound up and down rolling hills, and when the leaves were out, you could barely see the housing nestled in the greens of the hillsides.

As a child, I always found it terrifying travelling these roads, even from the comfort of my father's car, from one small town to the other. The moment we hit the rolling hills and steep valleys of the narrow, dusty, interior roads, I would fall sick from the undulating motion of the car. My stomach would be in knots, and I would fight to suppress the urge to externalise the internal contents of my stomach. Unfortunately for my sister, Afriyie, three years my junior, she would lose the battle on the backseat of the car all too often. So, as a young child, even the thought of sitting in the back of my father's car for any length of time became a reason for alarm. But the irony was that my parents would proudly declare that my siblings and I would be *treated* to these road trips "for good behaviour."

It was not until I overcame this trepidation that I could actually appreciate the splendour of my motherland's natural beauty. The luscious landscape seemed to awaken as the touch of rain released a sweet aroma which particularly appealed to me. And so too did the uniform fertile fields of pineapples and bananas that surround local towns and villages as you descend into the lowlands of the southern coast.

Along the southern shoreline was a beautiful string of white, sandy beaches where people would go to picnic under rows of coconut trees and swim in a sometimes-treacherous ocean. Accra, being the capital, was the most prominent part of the southern coastline.

Like most Ghanaians, some families had left our hometowns and settled there, where it felt like the centre of the universe. As the political and commercial heartbeat of Ghana, even during my childhood, Accra was crowded, busy and noisy; pulsating under the vibrant, colourful motion of a city alive with promise. And though close to the equator, waters from the Gulf of Guinea sprinkled the city's shoreline with welcome reprieve, so even when it was sweltering hot during the day, the night air was tempered by cooling ocean breeze.

The people of Ghana mirror our landscape in diversity, yet there is always a sense of cohesion like a world full of people without an urge to fight for their glimpse of the shining sun. Roughly 80 ethnic groups speak a similar number of indigenous languages. The largest of these is the *Twi*-speaking Asante, the ethnic group to which I belong.

The Asante people are part of the larger *Akan* ethnic and linguistic group who hail from southern and central Ghana and make up nearly half of the country's population. Besides the Asante, the Akan people are made up of many other ethnic groups, including the Fante, the Akyem, the Akuapem, the Brong Ahafo, and the Kwahu, each of whom speak dialects of *Twi* that are mutually understood and collectively known as the *Akan* language.

But for me in 1979, it felt as if those differences had faded into the background. Sharing a common language was the great unifier: it was uncanny to come across two Ghanaians from the same ethnic group conversing in English, despite the colonial legacy. But it was when fellow Ghanaians of different ethnic hues came together that English found a comfortable place as a bridge to bring countrymen (and women) together, which was the case with my husband and I. *Ewe* is Jerry's mother tongue, being from the Volta Region of Ghana, while mine was *Twi*.

Despite the city in which I had been raised, the different cultures in Ghana did not rip us apart. Our mothers and fathers seemed to always embrace the people who travelled from both near and far to be their neighbours with open arms, just as I could imagine other people did to us. There was nothing that lurked in the backdrop of our ordinary lives that would make us feel the need to guard against one another, simply because they looked different from us. Of course, even as children, we were not oblivious to the fact that our cultures were different. Yet none of it seemed to matter.

Accra had become a melting pot with diverse populations calling it their home. The predominant local Ga language in some of the areas was not difficult to grasp. In a rather fascinating manner, people who spoke Ga did their best to learn Twi also, as if to reassure themselves that everyone could make a home in the largest city in the country. Then, there were the children from other countries whose families now lived in Ghana. Their presence also brought along awareness—if it didn't exist already—that indeed there was much more to the world around us than our little space in which we spent our days.

Even in the schools we attended and churches to which we belonged, the hodgepodge of cultures having descended into Ghana made the English language common to all of us. The British had made their home in what had been the Gold Coast, and their influences were to remain, long after our independence. We knew little of the challenges of racism and prejudice that other countries could not seem to shake off, and somehow in our world, there were none of those distractions in our ordinary day.

Differences existed, but there was no reason to emphasize them, at least from my vantage point. The stereotypes that existed in our communities somehow didn't paint a demeaning picture of the person who stood next to us. I remember vividly how occasionally the people we saw working in the neighbourhoods seemed to have all come from regions outside Accra. They had a certain enviable skill for the work they did, and even though we would occasionally hear condescending remarks, we still respected them for who they were and what they did. They were no different from our neighbours, and they were not strangers.

Our journeys seemed to have been measured in motions, not by our traditions. We didn't know what it felt like to let our hometowns tell us who ought to be our friends and whom to dislike. Where people had come from was almost inconsequential, and I could only hope that such beautiful innocence would not be upended someday in the future by our stereotypes and prejudices.

It could all change, just as quickly.

CHAPTER THREE

TAPESTRY

Strands and Threads for a Childhood Memory

My early years in school mark the clearest beginnings of my childhood memories. In 1953, our family moved to Nkaw Nkaw, a small town in Ghana's Eastern Region. My mother was pregnant with my sister, Nana Serwah, while still caring for my baby sister, Afriyie. With a fifth child on the way, Maa decided it was too much for her to handle Afriyie and I, while still trying to manage all the duties of the home. So even though I was underage and very small in size, she made a decision to put me in school early with my two older siblings, Yaa Achia and Owusu, and three of my cousins who were living with us at the time.

In those days, every child entering the school system was expected to be big enough to reach his or her right-hand overhead to touch the left ear. At that age, I was too small to pass the test, but just before my fifth birthday, I was allowed to sit in class one anyway. The headmaster of Nkaw Nkaw Methodist School agreed to accept me, but could not officially enrol me as a pupil due to my age and size. I sat in the same classroom with my older brother and cousins, but I was not yet big enough to play with the other children during free time. For my own safety, I was told I would have to remain by the 'foot of the teacher' if I wanted to remain in school.

Despite the limitation, entering school opened up a whole new world for me. I was immersed in a vast place of other children and adults whose lives often differed from mine. I remember loving the atmosphere and feeling liberated as I left the house each day in my white and blue uniform. I was incredibly proud to follow the big children from my home to the local schoolhouse. In their presence, I never felt alone, homesick or intimidated at school. I can never remember being shy or aloof. Even if I kept to myself at times, I was generally outgoing, active and as some of my childhood friends would later say, quite bossy.

From the earliest days in the classroom, I knew I was in my element. School became a place of freedom. I was a bright pupil, eager and willing. Throughout elementary school, learning was a joy. Each new English grammar, nature study, history, arithmetic, or geography assignment was carried out with gusto.

In Nkaw Nkaw, just like any other small town we lived in, the UAC bungalows were clustered together but evenly spaced apart, on a large tract of land in the rural area. Off in the distance, surrounding the bungalow compound were the homes of the local townspeople. Many of the local dwellings were without electricity or piped water.

Back in those days, interior roads of the Gold Coast were free of traffic, so by 4:00 pm each day, Maa would send all the children in the house out for daily walks. She used to say, "C'mon, all of you, out! Go for a walk to strengthen your bodies and enjoy the natural beauty of the outdoors." But I suspect she sent us out, in large part, for her own peace of mind.

On these walks, we were often accompanied by Maa's domestic help or by older children from the neighbourhood. When we lived in Tarkwa, for instance, a young Kofi Annan, who would later become Secretary General of the United Nations, would accompany my brother and I for walks. Our parents were not only neighbours on the UAC compound but close friends as well. And since Kofi was older than us, Maa would have him supervise my brother and I on our walks.

As we strolled past village homes, we took in the sights and sounds that accompanied everyday life. Meals, for instance, are an endless and all-consuming chore in the village. A woman sits low on a stool next to a mortar as another woman stands to pound boiled yam and plantain to be moulded into shiny, round balls of *fufu*, to be eaten with an evening meal of hot soup. *Thud, thud, thud* echoes the deep, pounding sound of the pestle, as it rhythmically strikes the bottom of the mortar in a small, open-air kitchen.

As a young girl, I was fascinated by the sight of a woman throwing the heavy pestle into the air and dropping it down with a thump that jarred her body. Between each strike of the pestle, she appeared to wipe the glisten of sweat from her forehead on the sleeve of her cloth without missing a beat. All the while, children ran playfully around their mothers or were strapped to the backs of women who laboured tirelessly under the warm rays of the afternoon sun.

In those days, our walks took us along dense, green forests filled with giant trees that usually surrounded UAC compounds. It was always cool and dark in the forests, even when the weather was hot, sticky and sunny outside, and it was so dense that a person could walk in it for miles among the flowering shrubs, fragrant fruit trees, and exotic birds and butterflies. But I don't know anyone who would want to, because the thick forest surrounding the bungalows was full of crawling creatures and forest animals like monkeys, bush babies, wildcats and big forest squirrels with large bushy tails. Also common were wall geckos, spiders, lizards, mice, beetles, cockroaches and worst of all, snakes.

I was petrified of these creatures. As we strolled along tracks of unpaved narrow roads, the sighting of an African beauty snake would send me sprinting, elbows pumping, at speed, straight back to the bungalow compound where we started. Such drills may have served as sufficient training for the athletic ability I later acquired as a competitive track runner.

The outdoors was a big part of how my parents enjoyed spending their leisure time. I suppose their love of nature accounts for much of my own personal love and interest in preserving the environment today.

My mother was an avid gardener. Wherever we lived, Maa had large pots of colourful flowers and exotic plants on the veranda and around the house. Year round, Maa's garden was filled with flowers—purple trumpet-shaped blossoms of hibiscus, bright red and yellow bulbs of heliconia, vines of pink, purple and orange bougainvillea, and clusters of orange woolly-textured celosia. All of these were among tropical palms and green ferns. As we got older, my siblings and I took turns tending to them.

Although my father's hobby was photography, he spent hours in the forest on hunting trips. In Nkaw Nkaw, he enjoyed spending time and hunting with our neighbour, Mr. Archicocks, a white European man who loved to eat traditional groundnut (peanut) soup with their catch. It is entirely possible their friendship might have been easier to manage in the countryside than in Accra because in those days it was still considered inappropriate to invite Africans into white homes.

My father was a firm believer in preserving the ecology. He would always warn us by saying, "Unless you plan to eat what you kill, you should never harm the living creatures around you." He never wanted to see butterflies, lizards or wall-geckos killed unnecessarily. I remember him using brute force on a couple of occasions to reinforce his message. When he caught one of us with a dead lizard or wall-gecko, he would serve it on a dinner plate. As punishment, he would make whichever one of us he caught sit in front of the plate for hours and say, "You killed it, so you must have wanted to eat it." I always believed this was unusually cruel punishment for children, but by the time we got up from the dinner table, we had a newfound appreciation for the living creatures around us.

One of my strongest childhood memories was waking up to the heavy sound of raindrops pelting onto the corrugated iron roof of our bungalow. I would lie quietly in bed and listen until my concentration was broken by the warm smell of breakfast being prepared by Maa on Saturday mornings.

Even though Maa had house help, she would always be at the centre of preparing a family meal. I suppose she also spent much of her time instructing the maidservants, but to us children, it was Maa who made the meals. Meals in our home were one of those serious moments because it was mandatory that we all sit together. Dee would always start each meal by blessing the food with a prayer.

Maa was an excellent cook and she believed in an elaborate presentation. Breakfast was always very big—fried potatoes, bacon, eggs, sausages, bread and kippers—I found the fish horribly salty and appalling as a child but, today, I quite enjoy them. We would wash our morning meal down with a warm cup of *Ovaltine* doused with lots of milk. My father's work with the UAC ensured that food was never in short supply in our home. This good fortune prompted my parents to keep taking in the children of struggling relatives, particularly those from my father's huge extended family. My parents never hesitated to share their abundance with others—and my mother always saw to it that every little mouth around her table was well-fed.

I don't remember much about lunch at our home, but dinner was my favourite meal of the day because I loved rice. This earned me the nickname 'Cru lady'. *Cru* was a term we used to refer to somebody from Liberia as it was known that Liberians ate a lot of rice. I preferred a hearty meal of rice and corned beef stew as opposed to any of our other staple starches, such as *fufu*, which I never really enjoyed because I found the texture too sticky.

Dinners were never complete without two things–a sweet and delicious dessert and a speech from Maa and Dee. If my parents felt bad behaviour from any of us needed correcting, we would hear about it over dinner, usually at the tail end over a sweet dessert of either banana fritters, custard and cake, fried plantain or pancake. Dee would use great tact and diplomacy to address individual behaviour problems as he sat next to Maa at the head of the table. And just by the tone he would start with, a person knew what was coming their way—either a good scolding or praise for something well-done.

My parents were an interesting match. Perhaps due to her training as an educator, my mother was a strict disciplinarian in our home. Conversely, my father was a peacemaker, explainer, and comforter. Nevertheless, they both felt a tremendous duty towards their children and it was part of that duty to bring the family together regularly for special activities in our home. This is one reason I looked forward to Friday evenings because that was when my parents held family spelling bees.

Maa and Dee would be the judges as all of us seriously took on the challenge of spelling words of increasing difficulty correctly. The togetherness we experienced during this time brought so much joy, excitement, and laughter. The opportunity to step forward and spell a word correctly gave us each a chance to shine individually in front of our parents. The best part of Friday spelling competitions, however, was the reward from our parents afterward for demonstrating good spelling, usually a treat of hazelnut chocolates. On the other hand, the worst part of the evening was being knuckled on the head for losing by the chocolate-grabbing winners.

More than anyone, my mother kept us grounded. Her tight reign as family matriarch humbled us—sometimes beyond comprehension. When I think of humbling experiences, the earliest and most vivid recollection that comes to mind happened soon after I entered school in Nkaw Nkaw. Each afternoon when my siblings, three cousins and I reached home from school, it was normal protocol for Maa to meet us at the front door and give us each a quick look over. On one particular afternoon, I heard my mother suddenly wince as something caught her attention in the hair of one of my cousins. Looking repulsed, she quickly turned to the head of another cousin, then another, then my sister, then my brother, before angrily declaring, "All of you have brought head lice home from school!"

Initially, this meant little to me until Maa loudly snapped, "None of you are to move out of my sight!" She then feverishly started moving things around as she told us, "I'm not going to treat the lice. Rather than take chances, I am going to shave each one of your heads." And that's exactly what she did. As we all stood there horrified and in disbelief, Maa steadfastly sat each one of us down, one after the other, and shaved each one of our heads down to the scalp.

As if being bald was not humiliation enough, the next day as we left for school Maa made all of us wear these ridiculous-looking white bonnets to cover our scalps. Needless to say, our new look drew huge amounts of laughter, teasing, and harassment from the other students. As we entered school, children surrounded and taunted us. They flicked off our bonnets with their fingers, burst into hearty laughter and pointed at us until we burst into tears. It got so bad that the headmaster, Mr. Ofosu-Appiah, a giant of a man with a thick build, had to call the entire student body into an assembly. With the whole school gathered, the six of us—mortified and in distress—were called, front and centre, to stand by his side. The feelings only worsened when he asked each one of us to remove our bonnets. It was like standing stark naked in front of the whole school.

Looking stone-faced and extremely agitated, Mr. Ofosu-Appiah bellowed out to his audience, "These children are better off! They had lice in their hair and their mother did the right thing by shaving their heads. They were smart enough not to come and infest any of you. Many of you here have lice in your hair, sucking your blood and making you sick. And you do not see the need to deal with it. You are worse off! If I hear of any of you throwing off their hats again, I will be very angry and I will sack you from school!"

And with those words, our torment ended, but our humiliation did not. The next day we all begged my mother not to send us back to school, but she felt no pity for us and simply reaffirmed, "You will go to school and next time you will know better than to put your head next to somebody with lice and bring it home."

Above everything else, Maa was principled, sometimes to the point where it made her appear cold or unfeeling. She was a strong and decisive woman who raised her children and ran her household according to her own strict beliefs and did not allow much leeway in either area. Maa was continuously instructing us about proper etiquette or how to enunciate a word or how to cook or clean a particular area of the house.

Our home was always immaculate, and the slightest hint of disorder thoroughly distressed Maa. She was driven by order and punctuality. Meals were served on time. School work had to be done on time. And when each of us was of age, we had to complete all daily chores, such as laundry, sweeping and cooking to her taste and on schedule. She expected all of us to be as methodical as she was.

Even though Maa was not able to work outside the home, she still used her teaching skills inside the home. One way she did this was by giving each of us regular tutorials on mathematics, English, and elocution. Her insistence on tutoring us at home ensured a solid educational foundation, not only for each of us as her children but also for all the children of relatives she raised and cared for like they were her own. There was no doubt that Maa was strict, but she also had a very compassionate side. The one thing I always admired about my mother was her unwavering instinct to nurture those far beyond her closest family.

She had her own way of engaging us at bedtime. By early evening she would round us all up. First, we would sing a song of worship. Then she would make each of us quote a passage from the Bible before listening to us collectively recite the Lord's Prayer. After this, bedtime was between 7 and 7:30 pm.

Married life must have been difficult for my mother. My father was an unapologetic workaholic and was rarely home. For the most part, it was Maa who single-handedly maintained discipline and order in our home as she tended to my five sisters, one brother, several of my cousins and I. So, when the occasion called for it, I loved watching her from the corner of her room as she got ready with girlish excitement for a special evening out with my father.

In Nkaw Nkaw, Maa and Dee would attend formal evening dances like the UAC ball. I took great pleasure in studying Maa's every move as she slid her petite frame into a colourful, form-fitting dress that hugged her curves. To accentuate her small waistline, she would wear a large matching belt and meticulously craft her thick, natural hair into an elegant 'pompadour' hairstyle, which was swept upwards from the face and all around and worn high over the forehead. Then she would powder her face and colour her lips with the most complimentary shades of make-up. To complete her make-over, she would slip her feet into a sleek pair of fancy high heels. I would gaze at Maa's finished look with marvel. Her transformation from a modest housewife to a glitzy and stunning woman was truly amazing. She would leave the house holding Dee's arm with the giddiness of a school girl, walking with a spirited skip in her step and a carefree smile that we rarely got to see.

One of my favourite places to explore, when neither of my parents was home, was Maa's dressing table. It stood in the corner of their bedroom against the far wall. Made of dark mahogany, it had a tall, oval central mirror, with two smaller, movable side mirrors. There were three drawers, each holding a fascinating array of cosmetics—lipsticks, powders, rouge—and accessories—hairpins, combs, and hairnets. Filling the room was the soft fragrance of Maa's talcum powder. Standing there I could experiment with tiny dabs of lipstick or powder, or dot my cheeks with rouge, knowing full well I'd have to be ready to wash the make-up off quickly if my mother returned home unexpectedly. Because it was exclusively hers, this was an area I never dared to explore when my mother was in the house, but it seemed to capture a much happier and more youthful side of her.

Another ritual after my parents would leave would consist of me going to Maa's wardrobe, putting on her high-heeled shoes and parading around her room with animated lady-like movements. I would boldly declare to my cousin, Afua, "*Myyyy goodness*, when I grow up I am going to dress just like Maa. I'll colour my lips, puff up my hair, wear high heels and put on a beautiful tight dress. Then I'll go dancing just like Maa and Dee."

CHAPTER FOUR

POLITICS, SERVICE AND DEE

Dr. Nkrumah Calls on Dee

Even though British law rendered Maa and other married women virtually powerless in the Gold Coast, addressing the issue of gender inequality was nowhere close to being a priority in our nation's agenda. A far more pressing issue at the time was the widespread subjugation of the African population under the control of European colonial masters. This was a deep-rooted problem that, at some level, affected every African in the colony.

Under the yoke of colonialism, modern conveniences were provided primarily for the use and comfort of the transplanted European. While African labour was being used to build schools, construct roads and erect 'European' hospitals that served the interests of the British, there was practically no involvement from the African population in the political processes of the country. What's more, black workers were forced to toil night and day just to eke out a living so that whites in the colony could enjoy one of the highest standards of living in the developing world.

It was no wonder British occupants often described the Gold Coast as a 'modern colony' and a 'peace-loving country with extremely sensible people'. The unwillingness of the British to give up any power to the African in the Gold Coast triggered growing unrest and deep anti-British sentiments among the African population. By the 1950s, nationalist movements were rising in popularity and spreading across the country.

But even as African resistance grew, the white expatriate community continued to doubt the readiness of the Gold Coast to rule itself. I remember my father telling me, "Misewaa, even when African political parties organised marches that passed right by the European Club in Accra, members would raise their voices and go on discussing polo and trade as if the gathering outside was in hopelessly bad taste." He explained British leaders felt little, if any, pressure, to implement any kind of change that would place real power in the hands of the African. As a result, executive power remained firmly in the hands of the British governor, who was neither answerable nor required to take notice of any political activity or advice from the African.

As a young girl during these times, I remember overhearing my parents and their friends as they sat deep into the night engaged in spirited political debates. In the workplace, my father would stay clear of politics, but at home, he would gather together with friends and family and debate passionately about the future of an independent Gold Coast. They would sit on the veranda and sip on Johnnie Walker Black Label scotch or drink Lipton English tea as they discussed and debated the political viewpoints of emerging leaders such as Kwame Nkrumah and Kofi Busia—both of whom were personal friends of my parents and former schoolmates of my father at Achimota. Now both men were leading political figures, but with fiercely opposing viewpoints about the vision of the country's future development.

"*You wait!*" Dee would say with vigour. "It's only a matter of time! Our people are tired, and the British are scared." Even as a child I could tell by the inflection in my father's voice and the intensity of arguments presented that something big was about to happen in the Gold Coast. Kwame Nkrumah was a man of extraordinary energy, idealism, and patriotism. He had spent a decade in the United States and Europe travelling and studying during the thirties and forties.

While in the US, he struck a friendship with my Uncle Harry Osei

Asibey Agyeman, my father's younger brother, a student at Columbia University in New York. The two met while standing on the corner of 125th street in Harlem, hawking fish in the dead of winter. Overhearing my uncle speak *Twi*, Nkrumah approached him and asked his name. Upon answering, Nkrumah peppered my uncle with questions, "Did you say Agyeman? Which of the Agyemans? Any relation to J.O.T. Agyeman?"

"Yes, J.O.T. is my older brother," my uncle replied bursting with pride. With that answer, the two of them became fast friends. Years later, Nkrumah called on my uncle to offer him a job. Still, in New York, my uncle accepted the offer, left the US and would become Nkrumah's personal secretary since he was the only person in his office who could use the typewriter.

When Nkrumah returned to the Gold Coast in 1948, the colonial history of Ghana took a decisive turn. Unlike his predecessors—a small group of elitist African lawyers who had been at the forefront of the nationalist movement—Kwame Nkrumah had risen from humble beginnings. When he travelled overseas, he supported himself on his meagre income, which he had to work hard to earn. So, the people of the Gold Coast found it easy to relate to him as one of their own class. Campaigning on the slogan "Self-Government Now," Kwame Nkrumah's leadership was a sharp departure from the leaders of the past and he quickly became a national hero.

His ascent into government began in 1951 when his party, the Convention People's Party (CPP), won an overwhelming majority in parliamentary elections. Remarkably, when Nkrumah was first elected into office, he was serving a prison sentence for leading a general strike in the name of complete self-government. This became known as the campaign for "Positive Action."

It caused such uproar in the Gold Coast that he and his strategists were arrested and put in prison for a year. But nothing could stop the changes that were coming. In fact, the imprisonment of Nkrumah and his political strategists, like K.A. Gbedemah, Kojo Botsio, and many others made them heroes in the eyes of the masses who viewed them as selfless men and women suffering cruel persecution for the sake of the people at the hands of the imperialists. This alone enraged the people of the Gold Coast who became more determined in the political struggle and stood behind Nkrumah in full force. Neither imprisonment nor repression could slow down the party's march to victory.

Within a relatively short time of founding the CPP, the party's message had dwarfed all other nationalist movements and soon became the only threat to British colonial rule in the country. The party's leadership was made up of a group of mostly young men known as the "Verandah Boys," who, initially, identified more closely with the ordinary working person.

In contrast to earlier political movements whose activities were generally confined to the middle and upper classes of society, the CPP cast a wide net to embrace all classes of people, drawing its strength instead from the youth and the low-income workers and farmers throughout the country. The party also won the support of influential market women who served as important channels of communication at the local levels of small-scale trade. Nkrumah and his followers were convinced that prior movements were too conservative in their approach and lacked the revolutionary spirit needed towards the goal of total independence, which is what the masses were clamouring for.

The colonial governor, Sir Charles Noble Arden-Clarke, released Nkrumah from prison and invited him to become the leader of government business—a de facto prime minister. Nkrumah was to be responsible for internal government and policy, while the British governor remained chairman of the executive council and British officials remained in control of the ministries of defence, external affairs, finance, and justice. Nkrumah accepted. Although it was an enormous step forward, the structure of government in 1951 fell far short of the CPP's call for full self-government now. Nonetheless, with his eye firmly fixed on the future, Nkrumah began his first term alongside the British governor with friendly cooperation.

The following year in 1952, Nkrumah officially assumed the office of prime minister. By this time, the country was several steps closer to gaining full independence. As prime minister, Nkrumah was able to embark on an ambitious programme for social and economic development. As he began this agenda, he reached out to my father and invited him to take on a position in his administration as the commissioner for trade and industry in the ministry of commerce.

Dee's extensive business and managerial experience within the UAC was the primary reason Nkrumah's administration recruited him to run the government's business sector. Consequently, in 1955, my father officially resigned from the UAC and accepted his new post. I was seven years old when my father entered formally the world of government. This was the time when our family moved from Nkaw Nkaw to settle finally in Accra.

Compared to the many small towns we had lived in, Accra was a bustling city with a large and crowded central business district. High Street, the city's main commercial street was lined with business, judicial and administrative buildings. This is where Dee would go to work each morning at the Ministries building in the city centre. The city was also home to the country's first university, the University of Ghana, which had been established by the colonial government in 1948.

By the mid-1950's, Accra was filled with many lively neighbourhoods. The British government had planned and financed a series of exclusive residential developments primarily to house the growing influx of European civil servants, businesspeople, and their families, but like our family, some Ghanaian civil servants were also housed there. Ridge and Cantonments were two such areas and, although we changed houses three different times, we always lived in or near the residential area of Ridge.

Our family finally settled in a home that sat on Egypt Road, House No. 3, just a few meters from the George Padmore Library and across from the Ridge Church. Our neighbourhood consisted of neat rows of whitewashed, colonial-style housing constructed of thick concrete walls and slate red roofing. Many of our neighbours were families with young children—and many were foreign or African civil servants. Reverend and Mrs. Farr, an American couple, had three young girls—Jane, Sarah, and Sue. And Mr. and Mrs. Armstrong, another American couple, also had three children. The Fisherber family were from Cyprus, the Maclarens from Canada, and the Angelakos family had also moved to Ghana from Greece. Mr. Knight was British and had been married to a Ghanaian lady. Among the Ghanaian families, our neighbours included the Techie-Menson family, the Sackey family, Mr. and Mrs. Gardner, Mr. and Mrs. A.L. Adu, and Mr. and Mrs. Ribero-Ayeh.

Later on, two other families moved in: Mr. and Mrs. Quist-Therson with their three little girls and Mr. and Mrs. Enoch K. and Theodosia Okoh, who had two sons and a daughter—Ernest, Stanley, and Amma. So, from one house to the next, I always had playmates nearby, and many of our parents became close friends as well as neighbours.

The first school I went to in Accra was a public school called the Osu Progress School, a government establishment that sat just behind the Osu Cemetery. "Progress schools" were initiatives that Nkrumah had started as experimental schools to decipher which form of education was best suited for our country. The curriculum was aimed at preparing pupils for the common entrance exams, so they served more as preparatory schools.

When I entered the progress school, my siblings, cousins and I quickly realized that we awkwardly stood out once again—this time for being the only pupils in the school to wear socks and shoes. In the 1950s, it was rare to see children coming to school with shoes, let alone socks—with the exception of children of white colonialists. To our surprise, we appeared so out of place to the other pupils that they started calling us "white children." They teased and laughed at us simply for wearing "Achimota sandals" to school— these were shoes imported by Achimota College from Clarks of U.K. and required to be worn by all Achimota students.

In primary schools, however, mostly international pupils and only a handful of African pupils wore them. In spite of the teasing, my parents required that each one of us leave home each day complete with a clean pair of socks and shoes. We knew our mother would not bend on this, so we had to find our own way out of this misery. And sure enough, we conjured up a plan to make our strangeness less glaring.

On the way to work each morning, my father would drive us to school and drop us off directly in front of the school's main entrance. After about a month of this routine, we requested that he drop us about 200 meters away from the school. Naturally, he asked us, "Now why don't you want me to drop you in front of the school?"

We told him, "Everybody else walks to school and we want to walk too—to exercise our legs." He felt this was a brilliant idea and soon after, we changed our morning routine. My two siblings, three cousins and I all began alighting from Dee's car at a nearby junction surrounded by overgrown bushes. Upon bidding Dee farewell, we would walk slowly until his car disappeared into the distance.

As soon as it was out of sight, we would stop, quickly unbuckle and remove our Achimota sandals. We would then slip off our clean white socks and throw them all into the bushes. At the end of the day, we would retrieve our hosiery and footwear from the same bushes before returning home! Now, just like everybody else, we were able to walk to school barefoot and with peace of mind.

But once our appearance became more acceptable, it was then our lunches which became a point of interest to several of our schoolmates. While each of us brought food from home that Maa had prepared, the other pupils were buying their lunches from street vendors that were set up under large shade trees. Maa would pack us varieties of cold sandwiches or *jollof* rice topped with fried eggs, while our schoolmates were eating hot *waakye* (rice cooked with black-eyed beans) or fried plantain with *aboboi* (boiled beans) or groundnuts with roasted plantain wrapped in the previous day's *Daily Graphic* newspaper. Typical of children, we found their food more exciting and appealing than ours.

To our delight, the reverse was mutual—pupils relished the opportunity to partake in what we brought from home. Soon, they were lining up daily to negotiate lunch exchanges with us, and we happily complied. For years, throughout different schools in Accra, we continued these exchanges without Maa ever knowing. Had she found out, she would have been outraged and most likely would have responded with a good knock on each of our heads with her knuckles. Because in her opinion, it was a taboo to buy food prepared by outsiders—particularly the delicacies I enjoyed eating, which often came warmly wrapped in banana leaves and packaged in a newspaper.

Once my father joined the civil service, his work schedule became even more demanding. Despite this, I always found him easily approachable. Even as a young child, he answered my questions earnestly and was willing to converse with me as if every word I uttered was the most important he had heard all day.

Around the age of eleven, I recall waking up one morning around 2 am startled by awful thoughts and images of my own demise. This had been a recurring dream for about two weeks. But this time, I found the images too disturbing to go back to sleep. So, I arose from bed and went to knock on my parents' door. My father asked, "Who is it?"

"Dee, it's me, Nana Konadu," I replied in a loud whisper.

"What's the problem?" my father grumbled in a voice still heavy with sleep.

"I need to talk to you."

"Misewaa, is it a matter of life and death?"

"Yes, it definitely is!"

Because I was asthmatic and often had bouts with the illness in the middle of the night, Dee immediately thought I was sick. He opened the door as he tied the belt of his morning coat. Searching my face for an illness that obviously was not there, my father scolded me, "Misewaa, do you know the time? It's 2 o'clock in the morning." Ushering me away from the bedroom door, he whispered, "Come on. Let's go to my study."

My father had an office at home that we called his study. If my visits to his study caught him without work from the office, I usually found him reading a book or in deep thought, but if I were to knock he would always put down his book and give me his full attention. I spent many of my most intimate moments with my father conversing in his study.

And this particular morning was no different. We sat down, and he gave me his undivided attention. I started telling him about my fears of death and aging. He seemed surprised but continued to listen. What I could not tell him, however, was what triggered these fears.

You see, a few weeks prior, some friends and I sneaked over to a house where a funeral was being held. Curious about death, I moved in close to where the lifeless body of an old woman lay. I stared into her wrinkled face which appeared still and cold and without expression. My hands trembled, and I shuddered at the thought of her body being forever enclosed in the darkness of a coffin. For nights after that, my mind remained unsettled. When I shut my eyes in search of sleep, only the vivid images of that day played back in my mind—the corpse, the wrinkled face, the sullen look.

Looking back, the woman was most likely in her 80s. But in my youthful mind, I thought she must have been about 40! So that day, I told my father, "Dee, if I am not dead by the time I am 40, I want you to kill me."

"Is that right?" he said without flinching. "And why is that?"

"Because I don't want to be wrinkled or walk with a walking stick or have my teeth fall out."

My father was quiet for a moment. Then he gazed at me questioningly, as if awaiting further instruction. "Is that all?"

"No!" I said. "I also don't want to be put in a box. With my asthma, I won't be able to breathe and I'll suffocate."

"Oh, I see," he entertained, holding a straight face. "So, when you are dead, you don't want to be put in a box because you won't be able to breathe."

"Yes," I affirmed. "And I would prefer to be burnt so that worms will not eat my eyes."

"You mean cremated."

"Yes," I said.

When my father resolved that I had finished, he calmly said, "Okay, Misewaa. I've heard you. And I'll do as you say. Now let's go and have some sleep."

And with that reassurance, a feeling of relief came over me—never realising at the time that my father himself was well into his forties.

My father's greatest virtue was his patience, even for the extremes of a child's imagination. Publicly, he became widely regarded as a scholarly and pragmatic business leader who resorted to logic over emotion in solving problems in the workplace. Privately, at home, he was able to do the same. Perhaps this explains the strong sense of calmness which seemed to surround him constantly. His presence was never overpowering, but neither did he go unnoticed. He was pro-active, assertive and out-going.

His appearance and grooming were impeccable. He would leave for work in the mornings clean-shaven and dressed in neatly pressed trousers, a crisp white shirt, and well-polished black leather shoes. He was trim, soft-spoken, and a self-possessed man of medium-height and dark skin. He had a gentle countenance and an inviting smile that always reminded me of his genuinely open nature. In Nkrumah's government, Dee emerged as a distinguished and reputed thinker and business leader. I was always proud of my father, the first male influence in my life.

As my father's influence and visibility with Nkrumah grew, so too did the run-ins he encountered with an angry opposition. Just before we moved to Accra, a group calling itself the National Liberation Movement (NLM) was formed. While the CPP had pursued a policy of political centralisation, the NLM was mostly made up of Asante nationalists who wanted a federal form of government, including securing Asante autonomy. At one point, they even argued for the secession of the Asante region. The party was to be led by Dr. J.B. Danquah and eventually prime minister (1969) Dr. Kofi Busia, who were both staunch opponents of Nkrumah.

The new party worked in cooperation with another regionalist group, the Northern People's Party. The fact that there was a tribal aspect to the NLM probably made it a more ominous challenge for Nkrumah. The NLM in Ashanti area—the former seat of West Africa's last great empire and the location of most of Ghana's mineral and agricultural wealth—was fiercely provincial. Under the British, the Ashanti chiefs had retained most of their kingly privileges and authority. But Nkrumah's agitation for independence and centralised rule threatened to undo this arrangement.

In 1956, there was another election, and the CPP won 79 of the 104 seats. The NLM and its allies won the remaining seats making them the primary parliamentary opposition. Soon after these results, the NLM began conducting its campaigns with violence, staging dramatic bombing raids in the streets of Kumasi and threatening to use force to overthrow the government. In the midst of Nkrumah's rising popularity, people alleged that their aim was to make the country ungovernable under the CPP so that the Colonial Office would have little choice but to intervene and delay progress towards the granting of independence.

Between 1955 and 1958, they carried out numerous assaults, often burning the houses of Nkrumah supporters in Kumasi and targeting anyone whom they suspected was a member of the CPP. In 1955, Nkrumah survived the first of several assassination attempts on his life. It was a bomb attack in Accra. Fortunately, no one was seriously injured, but for nearly two years, the threat of violence was so significant that the prime minister of the Gold Coast could not even visit the Ashanti Region.

It was not long after my father had started working with Dr. Nkrumah's government that he, too, was targeted. One morning while working in Accra, my father received urgent news from his cousin, James Mensah-Bonsu, who told him that his house in Kumasi had been ransacked by NLM supporters and turned into a community trash dump. Alarmed by the news, my father immediately made plans to travel to Kumasi with his cousin James.

When he arrived at the house, the first thing that hit my father was the overpowering stench from large piles of garbage, faeces and rotting material. Waste matter spilled from within the home and covered the surrounding outer premises. The place swarmed with flies and the heat of day heightened the putrid odours. My father stood bewildered, gazing at the filth around him. The magnitude of damage was hard for him to grasp. In a dazed stupor, he surveyed his once valuable property, not realizing he was being watched.

Before he and his cousin knew it, someone shouted, *"Nkrumah's chickens have come to the place!"* Suddenly a group of NLM boys charged at them in a wild rampage, beating both of them senseless with handheld whips while venting their hatred for Nkrumah and the CPP. While my father tried surrendering to his attackers, showing no resistance, my Uncle James, enraged, forcefully fought back. They beat my father until he was almost unrecognisable. His face was bloody and battered, both eyes blood-filled and swollen half shut from blows.

The lashings Uncle James received were even worse, as his attackers took their whips to his back, beating him mercilessly until streams of blood poured from gaping wounds. After the ordeal was over, both men lay subdued. They then managed to get sympathisers in the area to help them return safely to Accra. Once back at home, both my father and his cousin were bedridden and hospitalised. My father spent the next six weeks recuperating.

At the time, I was too young to understand everything that had happened, but it was incidents like these that concerned me most about travelling to the Asante region. Despite the brute politics and physical attacks of the NLM, support for Nkrumah's CPP government continued to grow.

CHAPTER FIVE

"Mate Masie"
Tracing Yesteryears: Paternal Family Roots, 1859 – 1948

In Asante culture, there has always been the belief that a girl child inherits her blood from her mother and her spirit from her father. The roots of my character found their home in the values of a lineage of doers, leaders and independent thinkers with strong wills and deep convictions. Perhaps, in keeping with this heritage, I had never been able to accept the notion that there were some things I could not do or some things I could not change simply because I was a woman. Contrary to the colonial environment I grew up in, I was raised to understand the important and legitimate roles women had always played in upholding our family legacy.

After Ghana's independence, I remember how all school children were taught that Queen Mother Yaa Asantewaa had been an iconic Asante war heroine who boldly defied male traditional rulers in an attempt to preserve the Asante empire. Students learned and appreciated the truth that by using her position as queen mother, Yaa Asantewaa declared war on the British and led the Asante army into battle in the final Ashanti-British war of 1900-1901.

But beyond this piece of history, I was always taught a much more intimate version of her heroism—one that included the painful years she spent in exile alongside my father's uncle, *Asantehene* (King of Asante) Prempeh I. In our home, Yaa Asantewaa was much more than just a historical figure. She was a revered and intertwined piece of our family history. Fortunately, in my family, the memoirs of past generations were preserved and passed on to my generation through a ritual of storytelling.

Oral history was a deep-rooted tradition in our family, and before bedtime, our family elders would use that medium to entertain us as children, much like television and video games were to capture the imagination of future generations. In traditional Ghanaian culture, it is believed that the past should serve as a guide for living in the future. So, by reflecting on the hardships and experiences of our ancestors, our elders would recite these stories and teach us proverbs, all in an effort to remind us to live more consciously.

I learned much of my paternal family history by listening to two of our family elders: my father's aunt, Afua Konadu, and my father's father (my grandfather), Owusu Sekyere Agyeman. Each of them spoke eloquently about the heroics and hardships endured by our Asante ancestry. As children, we sat fixated and mesmerised as we hung on to their every word. As a little girl, I could not fathom the magnitude of the impression the stories made on me. They turned out to serve as a moral and cultural compass which would guide me for the rest of my life. The intricate web of kinship that traced the tangled limbs of our ancestral tree became a guiding light to my own humble pursuit of a future.

Both sides of my family tree are deeply rooted in the history of Asante, the former centre of an empire that once controlled much of present-day Ghana. Through wars and conquests, the Asante set up a powerful kingdom at the end of the 17th century, and a strong and sophisticated government that extended from the central forest region of the south all the way up to the savannahs of present-day northern Ghana.

The single most sacred object for the Asante people is a historic Golden Stool, a royal and divine throne. According to Asante history, the Golden Stool descended from the heavens and landed in the lap of the first king of Asante, Nana Osei Tutu, in the late 1600s. It was conjured from the sky by the king's priest, Okomfo Anokye, one of the two chief founders of the Asante confederacy.

According to legend, the Golden Stool houses the *sunsum* (soul) and spirit of the Asante people: living, dead and those yet to be born. It is a symbol of Asante unity and independence and, therefore, the king's priest declared that the strength and unity of the Asante people depended upon the safety of the Golden Stool. Without it, he warned, the unity of the Asante would disintegrate, and the empire would crumble.

The Asante grew wealthy in two areas—the gold trade and more ominously, the slave trade.

Long before colonialism, in a darker historical era, Ghana was one of the main locations from which many of our people were forcibly taken, sold into slavery, and transported as human cargo across the Atlantic Ocean to the plantations of America and the Caribbean. Between the 15th and 19th centuries, European traders seeking riches built 32 forts and slave castles—probably the most in any sub-Saharan African country—along Ghana's southern coastline to use as trading posts for human beings. This southern coastal region became the centre of all European activity in West Africa.

But as much as early Europeans were to blame for the horrors and atrocities of the trans-Atlantic slave trade, the sad, and often neglected, the truth remains that our own forefathers within the Asante Empire were some of the biggest perpetrators of the notorious slave trade. The Asantes, the Ewes, Gonjas, and Akwamus were all major human traders.

The Asante Empire simply recognised early that the human slave trade was the fastest and easiest way of gaining wealth. As a result, the empire used its military prowess to secure slaves through slave raids and wars in which fellow Africans from other clans were abducted from the interior and transported down south to the coastal forts and into the hands of European merchants. Waiting expectantly, European traders brought export goods considered valuable to Africans, such as rum, cloth, guns and other commodities to trade in exchange for human beings. Centuries later, the dark days of the infamous trans-Atlantic slave trade would create a footprint of pain and a distorted history.

The most vivid storyteller during my childhood was Afua Konadu, who we called our family historian. Both she and I were named after the Asante Queen Mother, Nana Konadu Yiadom II, bearing the name Konadu (*Ko-na-du*) meaning '*fight 'til the end*' in the Asante *Twi* language. During story time in my childhood home, she would always remind me of the importance and the strength of character attributed to my name. What left an indelible imprint on my mind about her was that she never tried to omit the deplorable truths from our history, like the story about the slave trade. Instead, she kept things as factual as possible while using these stories as a basis for teaching us life lessons.

I remember her fondly. Afua Konadu visited us frequently, and as children, we were often left in her care. I was especially intrigued by her. She was a tall, dark-skinned woman of slim stature and high pronounced cheekbones. She had a stern manner and did not spare the broomstick when disciplining my siblings and I. But she also had a loving nature. When she gathered all of us around her for bedtime stories, she captivated us—entertaining and teaching us at the same time. I was barely five years old when I first started learning the history of my family, and I can remember the joy and excitement this brought me as a little girl. Sitting amongst my siblings, I recall all of us listening, wide-eyed and completely engrossed, to the unfolding history of our family tree.

No matter how many times I heard it, there's one story that marvelled me more than any other. It is the account of how my father's young uncle, while still in his teens, became one of the most memorable kings of the Asante nation. His reign was perhaps the most dramatic and tragic of any in Asante history. It not only affected our family for generations to come but also stirred the political spirit of our nation during the early twentieth century.

Historically, the Asante have always been a proud people whose opposition to the British in West Africa is one of the most significant examples of African resistance to European occupation. As my grandaunt Afua Konadu told us, the Asante grew fierce in military might by conquering neighbouring kingdoms to expand their own.

Through their conquests of groups like the Denkyiras, and collaborative relationships with neighbouring ethnic groups such as the Gonjas, and Ewes, the Asante not only sold victims into the slave trade, but they also absorbed valuable aspects of their culture and made them their own. This includes the hand-woven, ceremonial kente cloth which was originated by the Ewe and the gold weights which came from the Denkyiras, and the *Atumpan* (large talking drums) from the Gonjas.

Their rapid expansion, however, threatened British commercial interests in the region. By the 19th century, the British had won control of the coastal trade from other European nations and their interests could no longer tolerate any further Asante expansion. The British army knew the only way to obtain supremacy on the Gold Coast was to fracture and humiliate the longstanding Asante Empire, but as my grandaunt Konadu proudly emphasised, "to their surprise a victory in this way would not come easy." From 1811 to 1874, the Asante and the British clashed in fierce battles seven times. The exchanges of defeat and victory between the two warring factions continued throughout most of the 19th century.

In the midst of this turmoil, my father's family remained at the centre of leadership in the ruling royal family of Asante. In 1859, my father's great-grandmother, Nana Afua Kobi Serwaa Ampem I, began her reign as the *Asantehemaa*, Queen Mother of Asante, until 1884, making her the most powerful woman in the Asante monarchy. As queen mother, she occupied the most prestigious position a woman could hold. She took part in court intrigues and influenced political events that gave successions to two of her sons to ascend the Golden Stool.

In Asante custom, the role of the queen mother is crucial for many reasons. She is the custodian of custom and tradition, but more importantly, she holds the power of kingmaker. In large part, her role is to submit the names of individuals she would like considered as the heir apparent to the Golden Stool. These names are presented to the council of kingmakers and advisors for deliberation, yet the queen mother's influence and final word remain of utmost importance. *So even though the king is an important man, it takes a woman to champion his cause and bring him to power.*

Such was the case during the reign of my father's great-grandmother Nana Afua Kobi I, who was instrumental in orchestrating the successive rise of her two sons to the status of Asantehene. Starting in 1867, the queen mother's eldest son, Nana Kofi Kaakari, ascended the throne as the 10th Asantehene until 1874, when he was succeeded by his younger brother (and my paternal great-grandfather), Nana Mensa Bonsu, as the 11th Asantehene. During her sons' reigns (between1867-1883), Nana Afua Kobi I was the power behind the throne. From the first day, she influenced and nurtured her sons in preparation to ascend the Golden Stool.

When her reign ended as queen mother, she was succeeded by her daughter, the king's younger sister, Nana Yaa Akyaa, who was my father's paternal grandaunt. Like her mother, Nana Yaa Akyaa selected her eldest son, Nana Kwaku Dua II, to succeed my great grandfather, Nana Mensa Bonsu, as the 12th Asantehene. But only 40 days into his reign, Nana Kwaku Dua II suddenly died from a horrible bout of chicken pox.

The tragic loss left a power vacuum in the Asante Empire, sparking years of conflict over who should be the next successor to the Golden Stool. But even after the sudden death of her eldest son, Nana Yaa Akyaa remained a strong and formidable woman who now insisted that her younger son be the ruler of Asante. Despite great resistance within the empire, the queen mother eventually got her way, and in 1888, her 18-year-old son, Nana Agyeman Prempeh I, made a historic ascension to the Golden Stool as the youngest king ever to hold the venerable title of Asantehene.

So, while still in his teens, all power was given to Nana Agyeman Prempeh I, who, in formal terms, was my father's first cousin *once removed* ("once removed" because they are separated by one generation). In traditional terms, however, we refer to the young king as my father's uncle, and my granduncle. He became chief justice and commander in chief of the Asante army. And just three years into his reign, Prempeh I, as he was known, was seen as a unifier of the Asante nation and, therefore, a threat to British colonial expansion.

To keep closer tabs on him, the British politely offered 'protection', which my granduncle firmly and gallantly refused. Unlike his predecessors, he resorted to diplomacy, writing letters and dispatching a delegation to England to meet with Queen Victoria. But the British government refused to see the Asante delegation and instead issued an ultimatum. After the refusal of multiple offers from the British Empire to make Asante a British protectorate, British troops once again marched to Kumasi and prepared to fight, except this time the Asantehene, Prempeh I, offered no resistance. Not a shot was fired as the king, and his elders peacefully met with the governor and accepted British rule.

My granduncle later attributed his acquiescence to the painful memories of the civil war and his desire for promoting peace. The British, however, would settle for nothing less than the total humiliation of the Asante Empire.

So in 1896, they rounded up and arrested members of the Asante Royal family, starting with Nana Agyeman Prempeh I, along with his mother Nana Yaa Akyaa, his father, brother, two heirs to the throne, and his war chiefs and took them all into British captivity. As if that was not enough, the British then sent the royal family into exile. They were first sent to Cape Coast Castle and then to Elmina Castle, but the British still feared that the Asante would stop at nothing to rescue their king. This was especially true upon hearing of an Asante army that had been formed by the main agitators of the king's return.

So, on January 1, 1897, Prempeh I and his party were deported to Sierra Leone. By the time the army started advancing in pursuit of him, the British had again uprooted the royal family—this time from Sierra Leone to the far-away Seychelles Island off the coast of East Africa. Prempeh I left behind his wives, children and several of his siblings.

Knowing the value of the sacred Golden Stool, the British Governor Sir Frederick Hodgson demanded that the defeated Asantes hand over to him the Golden Stool upon his arrival in Kumasi in March 1900. This was the symbol and soul of the Asante Kingdom, and its people were infuriated by this and other gestures by the British to humiliate and subdue the Asante. One notable woman embarked on a last-ditch effort to preserve Asante sovereignty. She was Nana Yaa Asantewaa. She was the queen mother of Edwiso, a state in the Asante union; and she began a resistance movement against the British.

Described as a tiny woman in her mid to late 50's, she first tried to rally the support of many male Asante leaders, such as the chiefs and senior war officials, but they all refused to lend her support. While the male leaders stood idle, it took a woman to raise an army to take up arms to prevent the British from capturing the legendary Asante Golden Stool. Without the assistance of these leaders, Yaa Asantewaa was able to mobilise Asante troops. She rallied resistance to the British in a speech:

> "Now I have seen that some of you fear to go forward to fight for our king. If it were in the brave days, the days of Osei Tutu, Okomfo Anokye, and Opoku Ware, chiefs would not sit down to see their king taken away without firing a shot. No Oburoni (white man) could have dared to speak to a chief of the Asante in the way the governor spoke to you chiefs this morning. Is it true that the bravery of the Asante is no more? I cannot believe it. It cannot be! I must say this, if you, the men of Asante, will not go forward, then we will. We, the women, will. I shall call upon my fellow women. We will fight the white men. We will fight till the last of us falls on the

battlefields".

And so began the Yaa Asantewaa War of Independence, which began on March 28, 1900. Assuming the role of commander-in-chief, Yaa Asantewaa raised an army of some 20,000 Asante warriors to confront the British and their allies. Under her supervision, an Asante army surrounded a British-established fort in Kumasi that housed the British governor and several hundred of his entourage inside the Kumasi Fort, where many died as a result.

For six months, the Asante army cut the British off from relief supplies and reinforcements by blocking all routes leading to Kumasi, preventing the British from capturing the Asante capital. It took thousands of British troops and artillery to break the siege. Despite her bravery, Nana Yaa Asantewaa was eventually betrayed by an Asante man from her hometown which led to her capture. After taking her into custody, the British sent Yaa Asantewaa into exile where she joined my granduncle, Prempeh I, in Seychelles islands. Over the ensuing years, the British used the Seychelles as a place to banish political prisoners of status from colonies all over the world.

By the turn of the 19th century, the British had deprived the Asante of much of their authority and wealth—plundering the Asante treasury of gold—but never were they able to capture the sacred Golden Stool, as it was hidden deep in the forests for the duration of the war. In 1902, Kumasi (and the kingdom of Asante) was annexed into the British crown colony of the Gold Coast, making it a formal part of the British Empire. A year after the Asante annexation, the British annexed the northern territories, shaping modern Ghana with the addition of a new group of disgruntled ethnic groups.

Even in defeat, the Asante remained a proud people and continued to honour their monarchy, even from a distance. They gave little or no deference to colonial authorities and still largely governed themselves. But imagine what it must have been like for people of my grandfather's generation to wake up one day in the same place our family had been living autonomously for generations to find themselves suddenly answering to a white colonial master who spoke no word of their indigenous language.

As children, these scenarios challenged our thinking. With intriguing accounts of our family history, my father's aunt, Afua Konadu, kept the tradition of storytelling alive. Even though she could not read or write, she was a master of oral tradition, and she recited the epics of battles and court cases of times past with great detail, passion, and animation. My grandaunt's uncanny ability to turn mere words into unforgettable pictures fused night after night into a series of riveting narratives. Through her, my siblings and I learned the history, economics, and customary law of the Asante.

Aside from entertainment, there was a lesson embedded in every story. We were taught about right and wrong, good and evil. No matter what the storyline, the message that came along with it continuously reinforced the values of truth, honesty, integrity, humility, and determination. Whenever she ended a particular tale, saying that it was past our bedtime, we would implore her to tell us more—a request she always heartily granted until my mother stepped in or we children quietly dozed off.

Since we had the same name, she had a soft spot for me and often reminded me of our connection to the queen mother we were named after and the importance of proper conduct. She would tell me, "Konadu, carry yourself with dignity and lead your siblings by example." She had a strong impact on me, and in fact, my early interest in history was encouraged by her.

Prempeh I's mother, Nana Yaa Akyaa, had thirteen children. The last-born child was a girl named Nana Konadu Yiadom who succeeded her mother's reign as queen mother in 1917. She emerged as a strong, fearless and capable leader who was driven to continue the work of her exiled brother and the legacy of the Asante kingdom. So, in addition to being queen mother, Nana Konadu Yiadom, served as regent over Asante, taking over many of the royal duties of her brother. She successfully presided over court cases, made executive decisions and maintained peace and order in her brother's absence.

Fearing British revenge, she even went to the extent of strategically uprooting and spreading members of the royal family throughout Asante. This was a tactical move to preserve the family line and the larger *Oyoko* clan, which is the ruling family in Asante and the occupants of the Golden Stool.

Meanwhile, the Asante people continued to agitate for the return of the Asantehene. Despite the imposition of a white government, the role of the king remained an esteemed and venerable one, commanding the loyalty and respect of the people. One of the main proponents of the return of the exiled king was my paternal grandfather, Owusu-Sekyere Agyeman, who was the king's first cousin. I remember my grandfather well. He had been a prosperous businessman and cocoa broker. As a child, he towered over me and appeared very tall. He was dark in complexion and naturally dignified. A well-educated and shrewd businessman, my grandfather was a man of many talents.

As a young girl, I remember him in his later years filling our childhood home with joy, laughter and the melodious sounds of organ music. Singing with his deep voice, my grandfather would play the organ we had in our home and teach us songs from the Presbyterian Church. I was always amazed by his mastery and coordination with this instrument. He would play the keyboard with his hands while playing the pedal board with his feet and guide us as we all sang along. I found the complexity of this instrument fascinating, and I always aspired to one day learn it myself, although it never came to pass.

Much like his younger sister, my grandaunt Afua Konadu, my grandfather was an avid storyteller. In his later years, he spent a great deal of time in our childhood home telling my siblings and I of his early days as an entrepreneur in Kumasi and the troubled journey that followed.

My grandfather's career began in the early 1900's in the burgeoning Gold Coast, which was now one of six British colonies that made up what was then known as British West Africa. The other colonies included Nigeria, Gambia, Sierra Leone, Trans-Volta Togoland, and Cameroons. Now that the Gold Coast was under an occupying force, European missionary schools began sprouting up all over the colony and missionaries began intervening in all local affairs. In large part, the missionaries were brought in to soften the African people and disorganise them spiritually before the political colonialists stepped in. To that end, missionaries were also serious politicians in their own right, but of a different angle and nature.

My grandfather was educated at a German mission school east of Asante at Akyem Begoro. He was fluent, outspoken and articulate in both English and his native Asante Twi. He was also a dashing young man with drive and ambition. In Asante, Owusu Sekyere Agyeman became the pioneer of exporting cocoa as an individual cocoa broker.

Cocoa trees had first been introduced to the Gold Coast in 1878 and became the first cash crop brought to African farmers of the interior. My grandfather was one of those farmers. Soon after, cocoa became the mainstay of the nation's economy. By the early 1900's, it was the number one foreign exchange earner in the Gold Coast, creating a cocoa export boom in the colony.

Around the year 1910, my grandfather, then an up and coming businessman, married a young woman named Yaa Akyaa, an only child who also descended from the Asante royal family and was named after the mother of Prempeh I. As a lesson, we were told the story of Yaa Akyaa's parents to help us understand the importance of customary law as it relates to marriage.

Long ago, marriage within the royal family was preferred to marriage with an "outsider." But there are some exceptions that were considered taboo. In Asante, we say that a child gets their blood from their mother. That is to say, lineage in Asante custom is traced through the mother's bloodline, and thus all family members are related by matrilineal descent from a particular female ancestor—in our case, Afia Kobi of the royal Oyoko Clan. Since a child's ancestry is traced through the mother's side, then marriage between members of the same clan (i.e. the same matrilineal bloodline) is customarily forbidden. Unfortunately, in the case of Yaa Akyaa's parents, the union that produced her broke this sacred custom because both her parents descended from the same matrilineal clan—the royal Oyoko clan.

As it happens, Yaa Akyaa was the daughter of Nana Kwasi Berko, the acting king of Asante in the absence of Prempeh I. Nana Kwasi Berko was a first cousin to the exiled king. He met Yaa Akyaa's mother, Nana Serwaa, as a young and stunningly beautiful virgin girl, when she was first presented before him by her uncle, Nana Owusu, during a customary puberty ceremony.

In those days, when a girl reached puberty it was customary for her to be formally presented to the Asantehene in a ceremony that marked the crossing of a threshold into adulthood. Captivated by her youthful charm, the acting king lured Nana Serwaa to his room, with promises of gifts before inquiring of her family lineage. Blinded by lust and acting on selfish desire, he broke her virginity, and she conceived, giving birth to Yaa Akyaa nine months later.

Upon finding out that both he and Yaa Akyaa's mother both shared Oyoko lineage, the acting king shamefully and regrettably told her family that custom would not allow him to marry the young girl. He then confessed that his action was a crime punishable by death. Fortunately for him, Prempeh I was in exile, so the acting king went unpunished, though he promised to help raise and see to the welfare of his daughter, Yaa Akyaa.

More than likely, the uncle, Nana Owusu, who presented my great-grandmother to the acting king, was chosen because of his established place in local society. A few years before then, he was responsible for leading early European missionaries to Asante to establish Christianity. Because of this, Nana Serwaa's family were among the first Asantes to become Christians and, thus, Nana Serwaa grew up as a devout Presbyterian. So she was devastated, and understandably so, by her encounter with the acting Asantehene. She had been brought up to believe that being touched once by a man precluded her from ever being touched again. As a result, she never got married and her daughter, Yaa Akyaa, remained her only child. My grandfather, Owusu-Sekyere Agyeman, told us this story to open our eyes to the cultural beliefs reflected in customary law.

Years later, when he married Yaa Akyaa, they had three boys together. The first boy was my father, John Osei Tutu Agyeman, born on the fourteenth of January in 1912. After him were Thomas Boakye Agyeman and Henry Osei Assibey Agyeman. My grandfather was one of the first Asantes to give a surname to his children. Prior to this, most Asante children bore only their given names, which usually did not include a family name. But my grandfather made a conscious decision to give all his children the surname, Agyeman.

Influenced by their Christian faith, Owusu Sekyere and Yaa Akyaa, baptised each of their sons with English first names, also known as their Christian name. But when Owusu Sekyere made his first journey outside of continental Africa, his view of this custom would drastically change.

With no sense of inferiority to whites, Owusu Sekyere's charm, outgoing personality, and business savvy endeared him to trading partners both in and out of the Gold Coast. As his business flourished, he became more enterprising; not only buying cocoa from other farmers, but also acquiring ten of his own cocoa farms. By the standards of his time, my grandfather became a wealthy nobleman and eventually set up Agyeman Brothers and Company with a few of his brothers and peers. His business grew large enough to compete with the long-established UAC.

With an ambition to see his business achieve even greater heights, my grandfather made the bold move of taking his cocoa business to the United States around 1919, making him the first Asante to travel to America for trade. Not surprisingly, the British were not happy with this move, and the UAC now saw this young rising entrepreneur as a formidable threat whose ambitions required a more watchful eye.

Just before he set sail to America, Owusu Sekyere and Yaa Akyaa discovered that they were expecting their fourth child. After three boys, it was their heartfelt wish to have a girl. Since Asantes are a matrilineal people, it is often said that "when you give birth to a girl, you give birth to a nation," because children are said to belong to the family of the mother. So, bringing forth girls was always a reason for celebration, and therefore the news of Yaa Akyaa's fourth pregnancy was embraced with joy and anticipation by both she and her husband.

Upon bidding farewell to his pregnant wife, Owusu Sekyere set sail on a long journey to Philadelphia, Pennsylvania on the eastern coast of the United States with high hopes that his return to the Gold Coast would be met with good news of his first daughter. His historic voyage to America was filled with great excitement and anticipation by both him and those he left behind.

Commercially, America proved promising, and my grandfather's journey opened up several avenues for business, most notably his first overseas buyers of Gold Coast cocoa—a monumental breakthrough for an African working as an individual broker. But his entrepreneurial spirit did not stop there.

Outside of the cocoa business, he purchased commodity products, such as plastic combs, powdered soap, and other American-made beauty products to export and sell back home. He wanted to make the most of his time away from home, so he spent several months in America tirelessly looking for business prospects and interacting with Americans of various backgrounds. But above all, his interactions with blacks in America had the greatest impact on him.

Owusu-Sekyere came face to face with the reality of racial oppression in America. He was shocked by a people who physically resembled many of his own, yet displayed all signs of being forcibly stripped of their African heritage and identity. This startling encounter re-awakened his African consciousness and his pride in local customs and values.

Through his travels, my grandfather discovered the value of Africa's rich heritage which had been set aside during the years of contact with European colonialists. Accordingly, he strove for a restoration of his own cultural values and resolved to stop using English names for his children. From this point forward, he would start instilling African pride in his children from birth by bestowing only African names upon them. This practice would stay in my family for generations to come.

While his commercial dealings were very successful, my grandfather missed home and often thought of his pregnant wife and three sons. Nearing the end of his journey, Owusu Sekyere awoke one morning horrified by a dream that aroused intense fear. He said he had dreamt his wife was dead and the haunting imagery of this nightmare caused him to question the safety of his family back home. Anxious to return home, he wrapped up his business dealings in America and set sail for the Gold Coast in 1920.

His safe return to the shores of West Africa was a mark of both personal courage and professional victory, as it defied the limitations imposed upon Africans by their colonial masters. His broadened horizons and newfound business success fortified him. Nothing, however, could prepare this adventurous explorer for the tragedy that would meet him back in Kumasi. As hoped for, the baby his wife was carrying was a girl, but unfortunately, Owusu Sekyere would never see his new daughter or his wife again. Struck by jaundice eight and a half months into the pregnancy, Yaa Akyaa went into premature labour, during which time both she and the baby suddenly died. My father, their eldest child, was a promising eight-year-old boy attending a local Methodist mission school when his mother died suddenly.

It was at times like these when Owusu Sekyere Agyeman was in dire need of the strength and capability of his most trusted confidant and advisor—his sister, and my grandaunt, Afua Konadu. When her brother was angry, she was the only one who could humble him. In times of difficulty or weakness, she would confidently intervene and take leadership both in and out of her brother's home, maintaining a sense of normalcy for the family until her brother was back on his feet. Her courage and grace under pressure always brought relief to him. She was a strong and a morally upright woman with a deep and abiding loyalty to her family. It is no wonder he loved and adored her so much and hoped for her legacy to live on, in naming me after her.

To my own recollection, these qualities in my grandaunt never changed. When we were under her care as children, she exemplified these traits in the home. She set an example that moulded me. In our culture, it is believed that certain attributes can be ascribed to the name a child is given. I remember observing her conduct and style carefully, and I like to think I inherited much of her spirit.

Although, much like other great women I grew up observing, my grandaunt's greatness was often eclipsed by the male dominance prevalent in our society. Whereas my grandfather was able to manifest his many talents through his business ventures, Afua Konadu's role and influence in society were relegated to the narrow confines of the home.

The gap between the influence exerted by men and women in larger society was a generally accepted norm, but one I came to view as contradictory to the values and expectations bestowed upon me by my parents and grandparents. As I matured, I struggled with the disparities I observed between the genders, and for years this growing awareness remained lodged deep in my consciousness.

Over time, Owusu Sekyere's prominence, wealth and influence grew more visible, especially following his journey to the United States—an undertaking that aroused equal amounts of respect and envy from observers both near and far. My grandfather went on to use much of his wealth and influence to campaign for the return of his exiled first cousin, the king of Asante, Nana Agyeman Prempeh I, who was still a political prisoner of the British in far-away Seychelles.

He organised and financed a delegation to England to petition King George V for the return of Prempeh I. Among the group were southern lawyers from Cape Coast and Accra and other prominent Asantes, including a number of his brothers. The expedition was successful, and their petition was among many other appeals made by various Asante organisations. This led to the king's pardon and on Wednesday, November 12, 1924, Nana Agyeman Prempeh I returned to Kumasi, but this time as a private citizen, after almost 30 years in exile.

Dissatisfied by the king's status as a private citizen, my grandfather gathered his delegation once again and sent them on another expedition to England—this time requesting the British monarchy reinstate Prempeh I as Asantehene. These negotiations lasted much longer than the previous one and proved much more difficult and expensive. In stages, however, the British slowly started accepting pleas and in 1926, Prempeh I was enstooled as *Kumasihene* (Chief of Kumasi) as a first stage. Yet to all Asantes, my granduncle was, and still remained, the Asantehene.

Eventually, Owusu Sekyere remarried and before long, proudly fathered his first daughter, Ama Serwaa (who later became instrumental in the union of my mother and father). My grandfather went on to develop strong ties with his American trading partners. His determination to grow his own cocoa business, which incidentally caused the loss of market share to the UAC, put him under the radar of the British. With prior failed attempts to dissolve his business, the UAC would now resort to more direct and dubious means to thwart my grandfather's business growth. In large part, this marked the beginning of the rivalry between the UAC and the indigenous African commercial class.

The goal of the British UAC was to disgrace and discredit Owusu Sekyere to the Americans. They set out to sow seeds of doubt about my grandfather's character by surreptitiously contacting his American business partners. They sent cables overseas and, in a clandestine operation, they invited the Americans to the Gold Coast without my grandfather's knowledge on one particular occasion, as if to ensnare him. They challenged the Americans to re-evaluate their business ties in the Gold Coast after observing the "uncivil" lifestyle, customs and surroundings of their African business partner.

Despite his mission school education and worldly travels, my grandfather was never one to deny his culture. In daily life, he was guided not by the ways of the colonial masters, but by Asante custom. At home, he ate and enjoyed local foods with his hands, even though he could readily afford available corn flakes and English tea. He was polygamous and went on to father several children—I was told as many as sixty-six, but fifty-two of them survived through adulthood—for each of whom he provided education and support.

He was an upright man who was not afraid to assert his traditional prerogative as a royal descendant and as an influential community leader. But the British aimed to shift focus away from my grandfather's business acumen and integrity to the negative and demeaning stereotypes of Africans that existed in those days.

When the American delegation arrived in Adum, a Kumasi suburb, they made their way to my grandfather's home—a modest two storey building (the British restricted the kind of homes Africans could build). In the privacy of his home, Owusu Sekyere, and his wives had just sat down together for a typical Asante breakfast: *ampesi* (boiled yams and plantain) and *kontomire* (spinach stew) topped off with boiled eggs. Midway through this traditional morning meal—which all were eating and sharing by hand—my grandfather's American business compatriots strolled into his home unannounced. Startled by their arrival, Owusu Sekyere's jaw dropped, and his eyes widened as he momentarily froze. Then he and his wives rose from the breakfast table and awkwardly scurried to offer them chairs. "Why didn't you inform me that you were coming to Kumasi?" he asked, trying to regain his composure.

The Americans, equally stunned, replied: "We came to see your environment."

No one knows exactly what conclusion they may have reached that day, or if seeing my grandfather in his own dwellings had any effect on them. But, by making Owusu Sekyere appear unrefined and uncivilized; the UAC was able to undermine the confidence the Americans had in their African business partner. This British ruse proved successful, and my grandfather's business soon took a steady turn for the worse. This seemed to mark the start of his downfall in Asante. By 1931, all small competitors, both foreign and African, had been eliminated by a small group of trading companies dominated by the Unilever subsidiary, UAC.

In 1931, Prempeh I died, and the traditional seat of the Golden Stool was once again vacant. While the heir to the stool is always a man, it takes a woman to nominate him and bring him to power. Among the Asantes, who are matrilineal, it is only the relatives of the king's mother that can contend for the stool. Customarily, it is the nephew – that is, the son of the king's sister – who takes on great significance and is among the first considered.

The Queen Mother, Nana Konadu Yiadom, who was sister to Prempeh I, was fraught with a personal dilemma. It just so happens that long before either she or Prempeh I was born, their mother, the Asantehemaa Nana Yaa Akyaa, had children with a man from a previous marriage. One of those children was a woman whose name was Nana Akua Akakoma. She had a son that was now the eldest of eligible successors for the Golden Stool. But the Queen Mother, Nana Konadu Yiadom, knew that the disrespectful and bully-like behaviour of her sister's son excluded him from consideration by the royal council. Despite his eligibility by traditional standards, the royal council simply lacked confidence in his ability to lead.

So instead, the queen mother wanted to give the stool to one of her own sons, Bonsu. On the other hand, my grandfather, Owusu Sekyere, believed the stool should go to his son-in-law, an Asante royal named

Nana Kwesi Appau, who was the husband of his first daughter, Ama Serwaa. But the queen mother's eligible nephew would settle at nothing in his quest for the Golden Stool and, in the end, would become Prempeh I's successor, later known as Prempeh II.

During the intense deliberations, the royal council and the decision-making body consisted of Nana Konadu Yiadom and various Asante chiefs, known as the kingmakers. In closed chambers, the council gathered to assess the list of all viable candidates, of which Prempeh II was not part. In fact, by general consensus, Prempeh II was considered the least likely candidate to inherit the stool, even though he was the eldest boy on the queen mother's side. But he was a persuasive man—although defiant, bullish and quick-tempered—who knew he stood at a disadvantage in the eyes of decision-makers.

Prempeh II resorted to negotiating, first with his aunt, the Queen Mother Nana Konadu Yiadom, appealing for his customary right as the eldest son of the king's older sister to be considered as the occupant of the Golden Stool. His request to her was simple: that she follows custom and mentions his name among the other eligible candidates on the day of decision, and if he was not hailed by the council of kingmakers, he vowed that he would quietly accept defeat.

Convinced by his proposal, the queen mother consented to his request. Then, as a final recourse, Prempeh II quietly travelled to meet with each senior chief individually to offer favours and money in exchange for their support. Despite previous discussions and an agreement within the royal council, many chiefs were swayed in the final hour by Prempeh II and promised to hail at the mention of his name. As a result, Prempeh II was chosen as the next Kumasihene in 1931. By some accounts, his reign marked the beginning of bribery and corruption in the choosing of an Asante chief. His singular act of lobbying for the stool permeated all levels of chieftaincy in Asante going forward.

In an astonishing turn of events, my grandfather, Owusu Sekyere Agyeman, went public in protest to the decision of Prempeh II as heir to the stool. With the backing of some chiefs, elders and his sister, Afua Konadu, my grandfather took Premeph II to court, challenging his eligibility as occupant of the Golden Stool. Owusu Sekyere alleged that contrary to Asante doctrine which stated that all candidates vying for the stool of Asantehene be completely free of any body modifications, including cuts, markings or scars, Prempeh II had been circumcised. These allegations drew much tension and debate in Asante, and Owusu Sekyere and his supporting chiefs and elders were arrested and kept in custody while the case went into a lengthy litigation. It finally ended with Prempeh II having to expose himself to the plaintiffs as evidence of his defence—an embarrassing and humiliating task, but one that would ultimately work in his favour.

Even so, my grandfather said he was never convinced of what he saw in court that fateful day, as he strongly believed that the "evidence" had been tampered with. Nonetheless, the case was dismissed and my grandfather and his party were set free by the courts.

Prempeh II, however, was unhappy with the proceedings. Seeking distance between him and his accuser, he filed an order of protection by formally requesting the intervention of the colonial governor. He sent his request through the British resident representative in Kumasi known as the chief commissioner of Asante. After Prempeh I was exiled to Seychelles, the British had appointed a resident commissioner to Asante, who was given both civil and criminal jurisdiction over the territories. In his grievance, Prempeh II stated that under the demeaning circumstances for which he was subject, he could no longer live in Asante with Owusu-Sekyere Agyeman. The chief commissioner reported this grievance to the central governor of Gold Coast, adding that he, too, was facing problems with my grandfather and many of his followers.

In response, an order of deportation was handed down by the governor in 1935 ordering the banishment of my grandfather and a few of his supporting chiefs from Asante. At this point, my family history ironically repeats itself. Much like my granduncle, Nana Agyeman Prempeh

I, forty-one years earlier, my grandfather, Owusu Sekyere Agyeman, was condemned to exile. Only this time, my grandfather was banished from his hometown, rather than country; he was forced to live outside of Asante.

In his absence, his sister Afua Konadu, just like the former king's sister, Nana Konadu Yiadom, from a generation before, would be the one to look after my grandfather's properties, businesses, wives, and children. Sadly, instead of sympathy, news of Owusu Sekyere's exile subjected the family he left behind to public ridicule from other Asantes. In front of their home, my grandaunt, Afua Konadu, would boldly confront and turn away choruses of Asante women singing teasing songs in unison—a scene from which she never backed away.

A few years into his reign, in 1935, the British restored recognition of the Asante confederacy and Prempeh II was designated as the first Asantehene under the British government. Although, with Asante now part of the Gold Coast and the kingdom now dissolved, the once powerful role of Asantehene as ruler of the Asante kingdom, had been limited to that of a paramount chief.

In Accra, Owusu Sekyere went on to settle and establish a new home for himself in an area called Osu. It would be twenty-two years later, not long before his death, before my grandfather could legally cross beyond a 40-kilometre radius of Kumasi. This milestone was made possible by a pardon he received in 1957 from Ghana's first Prime Minister, Dr. Kwame Nkrumah.

There was a lot of history's glow that took a young girl's breath away. I still had a lot more to remember. Yet none of the people and the places seemed so distant that I could forget. I could imagine my grandfather's pain and his own children's fear. My family had done all they could for their sons and daughters to understand from where we had come, and their journey that had been fraught with heartache. There was much to uncover, still, and even more to learn. For a child, I had to listen intently, and I had to keep the lessons in every footstep close by, as they were bound to someday serve as treasured reminders for my own life.

I could not forget. I could not ignore the weight of the history. Like the *adinkra* symbol, every emotion I carried in my heart was treasured knowledge woven into the wisdom of two words: "Mate Masie," meaning "What I heard, I kept."

CHAPTER SIX

A River Runs Deep

Maternal Roots: Sarpong Family History

Unlike my paternal grandparents, I never knew or spent time with my mother's parents, due to either death or distance. But through discussions with Maa, I came to see their journey as equally fascinating and enlightening as that of my father's side.

My mother's family has a long history of missionary education. In much the same way as my father's side, formal education in my mother's family was rooted in the early establishments of Christian mission schools. Originally founded as the German Missionary Society in 1815, the Basel Mission, and its successor organisation, the Presbyterian Church, began sending missionaries to the Gold Coast in the 1820s.

By the early 19th century, the Mission ran the colony's first organised school system, from the village primary school to the Teachers' Training College. As far as three generations back, my mother's paternal grandparents, my great-great-grandfather Mr. Sarpong and great-great-grandmother Maame Awiwa Sarpong, were some of the first students to learn to read and write in the Eastern Region of modern Ghana, home of the *Akyem* people. The Basel Mission also baptised each of them.

In subsequent years, my great-great grandparents gave birth to a son, my maternal grandfather, whose name was Charles Sarpong. His adult life and first marriage were marked by a chilling mystery—unsolved in his time—that led to the tragic deaths of each of his ten children.

Despite having only a primary and middle school education, he went on to work at a government health establishment where he was trained as a pharmaceutical dispenser. He had a love for children and a fondness for animals. He was disciplined, hardworking and a strong believer in education, especially for his children.

Hailing from Ghana's Eastern Region, my grandfather spent most of his childhood in the town of Oda. But near the close of the 19th century, he married a young woman from his hometown in Otumi. Eager to start a family, it was not long before the young couple started on the path to parenthood. After giving birth to one healthy baby after another, with little break in between, an unexplainable illness slowly emerged in the Sarpong home. My grandfather, Charles, and his wife started noticing that their young children were easily prone to prolonged infections accompanied by fatigue and in some cases, breathing difficulties or jaundice.

But the most alarming symptoms were the regular bouts of chronic bodily pains that the children suffered—sometimes to the point of crippling their movement. None of the doctors they visited understood this illness or the reason why it was confined to the children of the Sarpong home. Adding to this enigma, several of the children would regularly emerge from these painful spells, and various other symptoms, appearing healthy and active. Yet, for some mysterious reason, the symptoms always recurred—for some children, more frequently than others.

Despite the varying degrees to which each child was affected, the fate of all of the children came to the same miserable end. Randomly, they each became violently ill, usually after the height of a painful attack, and then all life from their little bodies would slowly succumb to the grip of death. This plague continued until it took the last of my grandfather's ten children. In times of such unexplainable tragedy, many people in our culture resort to superstition. Superstition brings comfort by explaining those circumstances we do not understand or which arouse severe feelings of fear.

Fraught with grief and despair and unable to receive any answers from the medical community, my grandfather turned in frustration to blame the person closest to him—his wife and mother of all his children. He labelled her as a "cursed" woman with a bad omen. With no means to make sense of this tragedy, he divorced her and left his hometown in search of a new beginning. His wife remained in Otumi, and for her, the situation remained a stigma.

Although I know nothing else of this woman, my heart aches for her. Especially when I think of the despair, she must have suffered shouldering the weight of such tragedy alone. I wonder what happened to her—if, or how, she was ever able to move on. Unfortunately, because she was a woman in this situation, the societal norm deemed her worthy of blame.

It saddens me that her worth was determined only by a misfortune over which she had no control. In a society where a woman's status was determined by her husband and by her capacity to bear children, the loss of both her husband and children would only lead her to feelings of inferiority and worthlessness. In contrast, by virtue of being a man, my grandfather Charles went on to live a fruitful life. Sadly, neither my grandfather nor his first wife lived long enough to understand the evil omen that took the lives of their precious children.

In a desire to move past this, my grandfather re-married another woman a few years later. When he left Otumi around 1919, he migrated to Kumasi, where he came across a young woman, most likely in her early twenties, whom he wished to marry. Her birth name was Maame Akua Fokuo Appiah, but when she was converted to Methodism, she was given the name Margaret. Margaret was from Mpobi, a village about 20 kilometres from Kumasi, or as my mother would say, "A day's walk." She was the daughter of Maame Ama Dankwaa and Nana Koo Tuffour. Margaret was a petite and delicate woman with no formal education. When my grandfather Charles went to inform Margaret's father of his wish to marry his young daughter, he received a rather peculiar response. Margaret's father forewarned Charles by saying, "This is a woman who is not healthy. She is asthmatic."

Despite this warning, my grandfather went on to marry Margaret Appiah. They had three healthy children together, one of whom was my mother. When my mother and her siblings reached adulthood, however, they each found out that they were carriers of the sickle-cell gene—a trait they learned was inherited from my grandfather, Charles Sarpong. This was the piece of information that helped to explain the tragic deaths of the children of my grandfather's first marriage.

Around the 1950's, a deadly blood disease, sickle cell anaemia, which involves a recessive gene, showed its horrid side to the world. It is a hereditary blood disorder that results when two carriers of the sickle-cell gene have children. Through simple blood tests available after my grandfather's death, my mother and her siblings were able to check medical records and solve the mysterious "plague" that affected the children from my grandfather's first marriage in Otumi. They found that my grandfather's children all died from complications of sickle-cell anaemia, as both he and his first wife were carriers of the recessive sickle-cell gene. Several of my siblings and I have also carried the sick-cell gene, and coincidentally I happened to be the only one of my generation to have inherited asthma from my maternal grandmother, Margaret.

Of my grandparents' three children, my mother was their middle child. She was born in Kumasi on the 27 of October in 1923 and she was christened Felicia Akosua Awewa Sarpong. After my mother's birth, my grandmother, Margaret, spent 40 days in Kumasi before returning to Ghana's Northern Region where the family had made their home.

Two years before my mother's birth in 1921, my grandfather's modest career as a pharmaceutical dispenser took a positive turn in a new direction. The Gold Coast government had decided that there was an urgent need to set up a veterinary services division of government. Because people had no education about animal health care, animals with the slightest ailments were being put to sleep. People were contracting and dying of rabies from the bites of infected dogs, and there was no central place or trained professionals to provide health care for livestock.

So, the government took two initiatives to prevent and control animal diseases. The first was to recruit trained pharmaceutical dispensers, of which my grandfather Charles was one. The second was to bring a trained veterinary doctor from England—the first ever in the Gold Coast—to lead the entire effort. The doctor selected was an English man named Dr. Beale.

Among the dispensers, my grandfather was the only one to accept the offer by the government to move over to the veterinary services division. The other pharmaceutical dispensers, mostly of Ga ethnicity from Accra, preferred the security of their current positions. So, my grandfather and his family were transferred from Kumasi to Tamale, the capital of the northern territory, and the chosen site for this ground-breaking venture.

Tamale in the 1920s was quite different from its thriving neighbours to the south. The serene savannah landscape of the north was dominated by a far more remote and simple existence. Closer to the Sahara desert than most of the other regions of Ghana, the north had a long dry season, as opposed to the moist tropical air of the south. This made for intense heat throughout most of the year. In the distance, the boys herded cattle or sheep and drove their flocks between clusters of villages; a scenery that presents as an almost idyllic setting of a timeless, pastoral life.

In the north, large grazing animals covered much of the grasslands, and due to the concentration of wildlife in this region, the British government chose this location to set up the colony's first veterinary hospital. In the ensuing months, my grandfather Charles trained hands-on under the guidance and direction of Dr. Beale's expertise. This pivotal move in my grandfather's career led to his distinction as being the first black veterinary officer in the Gold Coast.

During this time, the northern law forbade residents from the south from enrolling their children in northern schools. This law was imposed as a means to protect and preserve the "purity" of northern cultures, which were seen as less adulterated and less exposed to European influence than the southern Gold Coast culture. So, neither my mother, Felicia, nor her older sister, Yaa Safoa were allowed to attend school in the north.

When Yaa Safoa—later baptised Christine—reached school age, my grandmother, Margaret, told my grandfather that her asthma was making daily chores, such as fetching water and cleaning house, near impossible. Because of that, she requested my grandfather Sarpong to keep Christine at home instead of going to school to help with the household chores. She kept Christine at home.

Memories of my grandma's asthma attacks during childhood kept her own father, Nana Tuffour, on protective watch over her, even from a distance in her marriage home. Although her father was a polygamist and had several children of his own, he always worried over the health of his young daughter, Margaret, even into marriage.

My grandfather Charles complied with his wife's request to keep Christine home, but he was determined to educate his younger daughter, my mother Felicia. By the time my mother was seven, the opening of a new Methodist boarding school for girls caught my grandfather's attention. The mission school was based in Kumasi. Eager to secure a spot for his young and promising daughter, Charles immediately whisked my mother off to the south. The travel to the school was a long and arduous three days' journey away from their home in Tamale. The school was called *"Mmofra Turo,"* which translates as "Children's Garden" and was taught by all-white staff members, the European Methodist sisters.

Charles proudly arranged and paid all necessary fees for my mother's enrolment and boarding accommodation. Due to the distance and expense for travel back and forth, he instructed his family in Kumasi to keep young Felicia in their care during all holidays, except Christmas, at which time she would return to Tamale. But outside of boarding school, her primary home in Kumasi was that of her mother's brother, her uncle, Osei Kofi Ahenkro, to whom she could turn for basic needs.

I remember Maa talking about how a semester at Mmofra Turo felt like a lifetime away from home because she longed for the love and attention of her own parents and the familiar sights, sounds and smells of home. She missed the nurturing touch of her mother and the bond she shared with her big sister, but most of all, she missed the one person who believed in her most—her father Charles. So, come Christmas each year, young Felicia was always bursting with childlike excitement as she prepared for her long journey home.

Strangely, each year at Christmas time, my grandfather Charles would organise and charter for my mother a local post office van, which would be on its normal 10-day route from Kumasi to Tamale. The driver would be picking up and delivering mail from village to village as he headed north with my mother as his only passenger.

As a child, she did not mind. The excitement was in the journey and the anticipation of being home again. The driver would jokingly call her his wife, buying her sardines and fresh bread along the way. She would nibble on savoury sardine sandwiches and laugh freely as she watched the scenery of her surroundings magically evolve from the lush green and moist, closed-canopy forests of the south to the drier, sparsely vegetated, open grasslands of the north.

Each day as they crossed another village and neared closer to the Northern Region, Felicia envisioned the gentle smile of her father. She also thought of the proud look in his eyes as she demonstrated the few English words she had learned from her white Methodist teachers. In her youthful mind, she was also convinced that speaking her native Asante Twi with a nasally English intonation was equally deserving of praise. This, she thought, was another form of the white man's language.

By the time she reached Tamale, nearly two weeks of her seven-week Christmas holiday were gone. But she did not mind. She was simply overjoyed to be home. As she settled in, the security and comforts of homemade time go by so fast that near the end of her vacation, she would tell her father – tears welling up in her eyes – "I don't want to go back to school. I want to stay here with you."

In an understanding manner, Charles would strive to comfort his daughter by gently explaining to her, "Old Lady, listen to me, I know you will amount to something big in life." He affectionately called her "Old Lady", because he had named her after his mother. Then he would say, "You will be able to educate all your children. People will know you. You will learn how to read and write, and you will learn how to speak perfect English." Before long, it was time for Felicia to set off on another long trek back to Kumasi. But this time, all excitement would turn to sadness.

My mother's older sister, Christine, never had the same educational opportunities. At one point, she was moved to the northern city of Wa, which later became the capital of the Upper West Region of Ghana. There, she stayed with relatives and attended elementary school for a while. But by the time she reached class three, Charles and Margaret discovered that she had been kept home and mistreated at the hands of her host family. Emotionally scarred from a bad experience, she returned to Tamale and vowed to my grandmother, "I will never leave your side again."

Before leaving Tamale, my grandmother, Margaret, gave birth to their third and last child—this time a boy whom they named after my grandfather's long-time mentor of veterinary medicine, Dr. Beale. Their son, Robert Beale Sarpong, became known as "Akwasi Beale". Not long after his birth, Dr. Beale's time in the Gold Coast came to an end, and he returned to England. Before his departure, Dr. Beale said in jest, "Now that I have someone to take my place, I think I must go back to England."

In 1933, the Gold Coast government transferred my grandfather and his family from Tamale to Sekondi-Takoradi, Ghana's Western

Region capital, to expand his veterinary work. He was now training other students of veterinary medicine and leading the efforts of setting up animal care centres in various regions of the country. My mother remained in Kumasi at Mmofra Turo, which developed into an elite girl's preparatory school.

After two years in Sekondi-Takoradi, my grandfather returned to Kumasi on leave for a few months for what was supposed to be a transition period for him and the family before he was stationed to Accra to set up another veterinary centre. But upon his arrival in Kumasi, Charles' health began to deteriorate, and health officials discovered that he had a hernia. Doctors immediately operated on him in Kumasi but, sadly, they could not save his life. He died in Kumasi in December of 1935—a seasoned and well respected veterinary officer who was regarded as a pioneer in his field. My mother was twelve when her father died.

Not only did the death of her father greatly affect my mother emotionally, but along with it came dire and immediate consequences for the future of her education. At the time of my grandfather's death, my mother was still in boarding school. Without the financial support of her father's income, her school fees became unaffordable and her academic future hung in the balance.

At this point, Felicia's maternal uncle, Osei Ahenkro—the same one who watched over her during boarding school—stepped in. Following the custom of matrilineal inheritance, my grandmother's brother, Osei Ahenkro, agreed to take responsibility for my mother and to see to her education to the best of his ability. On the contrary, Charles' relatives from the Akyem area in the Eastern Region came only to collect his belongings and to return to their homes with no further contact with Charles' wife or his children.

Sympathetic to my mother's predicament, the Methodist Sisters met to discuss how they could help support the family and honour the future of one of their first enrolled pupils at the mission school. They proposed to put my mother on a partial scholarship, a benefit that is typically awarded to the children of priests and reverend ministers. My mother's uncle, Osei Ahenkro, became her guardian and he agreed to pay the other half. This enabled her to complete the primary and middle school program at Mmofra Turo, which went up to the British "standard seven."

When the time came for my mother to continue onto secondary school, her uncle's support waned. He did not believe in educating women. Nevertheless, my mother was so eager to continue onto the girl's high school program that she opted to take the common entrance exam with hopes that her results would render her a scholarship.

Her plan proved successful, and young Felicia was accepted into the secondary school program at Wesley Girls High School in Cape Coast in the Central Region on scholarship. In spite of the scholarship, there was still a minimal payment obligation equivalent to about eighteen British pounds a year, which my mother's guardian uncle was unwilling to pay.

Having never gone to school and unable to read or write himself, Uncle Osei Ahenkro did relatively well for himself. He worked as a money lender and owned a fleet of cars that operated between Kumasi and the north. He made it clear to his niece that he saw no value in spending his money on educating a woman whose ultimate fate, he felt, was to end up in the kitchen as somebody's wife. "Find a job that will give you money," he told Felicia, advising her to shift her focus from furthering her education to finding a job, such as a telephonist, that would provide her immediate income.

Remembering the encouraging words of her father, my mother knew better than to give up her dream of an education. She not only begged her uncle to reconsider but also resorted to compromise. My mother shifted her sights to entering a teacher's training program at Wesley College, which was on the same campus as Mmofra Turo, where she was already boarding as a student. This plan proved successful as she was able to obtain a partial scholarship. She presented this new plan as an alternative to her uncle.

"Uncle Osei, this program is not only closer to home," she reasoned, "but also less expensive than the secondary school in Cape Coast. And as soon as I finish, I can get work." Exasperated, her uncle begrudgingly gave in and agreed to support her by paying the other half of the tuition costs.

On the other hand, when it came to my mother's younger brother, Akwasi Beale, Uncle Osei had great expectations for his nephew. Akwasi Beale was very academically intelligent, but he was more inclined towards sports, primarily football. When he completed the same level of education as my mother, Uncle Osei was willing and prepared to send Akwasi Beale to *Mfantsipim*, an elite all-boys secondary school located in Cape Coast at the time.

Unlike my mother, who had to struggle to stay in school, no boy ever had to worry about being denied an education. A boy's education was seen as the family's hope to move up the financial and social ladder. While a girl's education was considered less important both financially since they were unlikely to contribute to the family's income, and culturally, since girls were expected to run a "proper home."

Oddly enough, Uncle Osei had children of his own whom he did not educate because he felt they were not intelligent enough. Thus, all the more reason why he strove to encourage and financially support the education of his nephew, hoping one day to reap the rewards for the family from Akwasi Beale's literacy and math skills. But when Akwasi Beale proclaimed, "I want to pursue football in addition to academics," against his uncle's wishes, Uncle Osei grew angry and quickly withdrew his financial support.

Just as my mother was waiting to enter the teacher's training program, a smallish woman with an elegant smile approached her one morning on the way to school in an area of Kumasi called Ashanti New Town. "Excuse me... young lady... good morning!" she called out smiling broadly.

"Good morning," my mother replied, stopping in her tracks.

"*Wo ho te sɛn?* (How are you?)"

"*Mepa wo kyɛw, me ho ye.* (Please, I am fine.).*"*

"Ahem," she uttered, clearing her throat. "*Awuraba, yɛ frɛ wo sɛn?* (Young lady, what is your name?)"

"*Yɛ frɛ me Felicia Sarpong.* (My name is Felicia Sarpong.)"

"Felicia Sarpong!" the woman repeated. "*Yoo* (Okay).

"Hello, Felicia," the woman greeted, switching awkwardly to English, then paused a moment with a searching expression, as if to study my mother's face. "Pardon my asking," she said, striking a serious posture, "I've seen you passing here before, carrying your books and always so neatly dressed and I've been wondering, what do you do?"

Unsuspecting, my mother, now about 16 years old, politely replied, "I'm a student. And I've just received entrance into the teacher's training program at Wesley College, where I will continue my education."

Nodding her head with enthusiastic approval, the woman smiled widely. "That is wonderful, Felicia. Congratulations. Keep up the good work and God will see you through." With little else to say, the woman bid my mother a warm farewell, "*Yoo,* bye-bye, *Nyame nhyira wo* (God bless you)."

The woman's name was Ama Serwaa, and she was on a mission to find a wife for her older brother, John Osei-Tutu (J.O.T.) Agyeman, the man who would later become my father. She had been observing my mother for a while with keen interest and admiration at how young Felicia carried and composed herself with "respect and humility," she would later say. On the day of their first meeting, she had come to the conclusion that Maa would make a suitable match for her brother, J.O.T.

As yet another intricate link to my lineage, in her mother's family, Ama Serwaa was a granddaughter to the former *Asantehene*, Prempeh I. When Prempeh I ascended the Golden Stool in the late 1880's, he was having trouble conceiving a child, even though he had several wives. So he was taken to a traditional healer, a fetish priest, who advised him to return to his hometown to find a woman there to marry. The king did as he was instructed and the woman he married from his hometown was Ama Serwaa's maternal grandmother, who bore the first child of the young king. From then on, the king began to conceive more children with his other wives.

Upon concluding that my mother would make a suitable match for her brother, Ama Serwaa went home to discuss the situation with her husband, Nana Kwasi. She spoke highly of Felicia on many counts—from her focus as a student at Mmofra Turo to the respect and humility she displayed in public to those around her. She could see Felicia was disciplined and hardworking both in and out of the home, but she was now at an impasse on how to accelerate her mission.

"I would like my brother to marry her, but I don't know how to go about it," she told her husband. "And the girl's uncle is not someone I am comfortable approaching." Her husband then advised her to start off by finding out if the girl in question was even available. Ama Serwaa followed her husband's advice and learned that Felicia was not promised to anyone, so she took it upon herself to act quickly—and perhaps prematurely—by approaching Felicia's guardian uncle.

Nervously, she went to pay Uncle Osei a home visit. Ama Serwaa started the conversation by generously praising my mother and then telling Uncle Osei that she had been closely watching his niece. Uncle Osei showed no emotion. He sat stone-faced as he silently listened. Ama Serwaa then explained to him that the reason for her visit was to ask him for his niece's hand in marriage on behalf of her elder brother.

Appalled by the simplicity of her approach and her total disregard for customary rites regarding marriage proposals, Uncle Osei immediately cut Ama Serwaa short.

"Go back and get an elderly person from your home so that two elderly people can talk on such a matter. You are too young to come and ask me this," he instructed, clearly offended. "I won't talk. Go and get somebody elderly from your family."

Incidentally, this was not the first marriage proposal Uncle Osei had received on my mother's behalf. As was common with girls her age, many men, particularly older men, preyed on young adolescent girls in search of a young wife; usually, a junior wife to play a secondary role to their senior, or first wife, or in some cases, multiple wives. Thus, several suitors had sought Felicia's hand in marriage with little success in impressing her or convincing her uncle.

Ama Serwaa went home and, once again, discussed the situation with her husband, Nana Kwasi Appau, who responded with the calmness of his own elderly wisdom by saying, "Don't worry. I will go."

Nana Kwasi was a strikingly handsome man—tall, dark, stately and softly-spoken. A naturally dignified man, he conducted affairs with humility, respect, and decorum. So, it was no surprise when, on a subsequent visit, Uncle Osei warmly received him as he accompanied Ama Serwaa.

The first discussion between Nana Kwasi, Uncle Osei, and Ama Serwaa went so well that it led to a series of visits. Soon, a trusting and budding friendship emerged between the three, but all went on unannounced to their subject, Felicia, the link that brought them together. My mother would often come home from teacher's training college to find the three of them caught up in a merry discussion, but it never occurred to her that it was her future they were negotiating.

Then one day, Uncle Osei called my mother aside. "Felicia, you know the couple that's been coming here?"

"Yes, uncle. I have been seeing them when I return from school."

"A-haaa. Very good! Well..." he said enthusiastically "it's time I let you know. My friends have come to ask for your hand in marriage... for the woman's brother, who is a worker for the UAC." he added.

Anticipating the usual protest from his niece, Uncle Osei changed his approach this time and authoritatively preached, "Look! This time I am not going to ask you whether or not you like it. *You are going to marry him.* So many men have come, but this one is different. I haven't seen him with my own eyes, but they say he is educated. You say you want someone educated. I heard he went to Achimota College and now he's working for UAC. He's a young man. He's never married and he has no children. Every time a man comes forward, you have something (negative) to say. I'm tired. This man has everything you say you want. So this time, I'm not going to ask you. Whether you like it or not, you are going to marry him!"

At the time, my father was stationed with the UAC in Dunkwa, located in Ghana's Central Region. My mother had started the teacher's training program, so her female cousins, sympathetic to her, assured her that they would look out for her best interest. In their own ways, they each worked on doing their own investigation of J.O.T. Coincidentally, my mother also had some family based in Dunkwa. Every family member who came across J.O.T. immediately took a liking to his calm and humble nature. My mother kept receiving the same message over again: that her suitor, this time around, was simply *owura*, a "gentleman."

It was not long before my mother would meet the gentleman she had been hearing about. One day during her first year at Wesley College, Felicia was told that three gentlemen had come to the college looking for her. Confused as to who the unexpected visitors might be, Felicia straightened herself up and descended from her room to the main lobby.

Awaiting her, she recognised only one of the three guests, a Methodist reverend from her old school, Mmofra Turo. Then one of the other gentlemen began the conversation by introducing himself first, and then each one of his friends. "Hello, my name is Kofi Busia", he said. After mentioning his name, Felicia recognised that he was the brother of one of her friends, Afua Busia. Kofi continued, "And you already know Reverend DeGraft. And finally… this is Mr. John Osei -Tutu Agyeman, also known as J.O.T. All of us are old *Achimotans* (alumni of Achimota)."

At that moment, it clicked for Felicia.

Upon seeing my father, Maa said her first reaction was, "After all, he isn't bad looking." Then jokingly added, "But he was shorter and thinner than I preferred." So, she recalls it was not *love at first sight*. Rather, in the beginning, she resigned to simply attach herself to him, regardless of her feelings, as a way to ward off old, married suitors.

The visits from J.O.T. and his friends continued and Kofi eventually arranged for Felicia to befriend his own girlfriend, Ama Piah, from Achimota, who eventually became Kofi's first wife. After a while, Felicia started returning J.O.T.'s visits to Dunkwa when she visited her family there on holidays.

Between visits, my mother recalls that J.O.T. would write her letters "with the most beautiful handwriting." With time, their friendship grew steadily. Nonetheless, Felicia Sarpong was not one to make rash decisions. So, when her suitor, J.O.T., pushed the topic of marriage, my mother fashioned a reply that would buy her more time.

"First, I have to complete my education. Then I need at least one year afterwards to gain some experience teaching in the classroom," she requested. Not one to argue, my father complied. After a long courtship, the two exchanged vows in 1941 in a church wedding in Winneba in the Central Region of Ghana. My father was twenty-nine, and my mother was eighteen.

Throughout my own life, I came across the trails of courageous men and remarkable women in my family's history. They inspired and taught me. Fortunately, I did not have to wait until later in my adult years to discover my identity in the pages of a history book. I was taught about my people. I was reminded of the burden that will forever sit on our shoulders to tell our sons and daughters the truth about who we are. I carried them with me to university and into public service. My mother's faith challenged my intellect and moral beliefs. Afua Konadu's words emboldened me to take risks, to challenge the status-quo and to question the injustices in our society.

Like a sculptor who sets out to carve what he imagines and to reveal what sits inside a hunk of wood, I was to find how much of all of our lives had not been due to coincidence. The dreadful years of adversity that chipped away fear left behind a modesty and audacity in the men and women. It was as though every stumbling block, disappointment, and triumph along their lives' journey would be precisely what their sons and daughters needed to hold on to as a family's legacy.

Nana Konadu at Achimota School in the Upper Sixth form, as Prefect of Kingsley House

Nana Konadu at 8 years old, with brother Owusu Sekyere, sisters Afriyie and Nana Serwah, together with Gloria Sakyiamah and Awurabena Kitiwaa in her mother's garden, Ridge, Accra. 1956

Nana Konadu in Form 1 at Achimota School

Nana Konadu with Owusu Sekyere, Maame Bafoaa Dadzie, Mr. & Mrs. Agyeman, and Mrs. Armstrong.

Owusu Sekyere, Nana Konadu, Cecilia Antwi, Osei Kweiwia, and Efua Achia at father's building site in Nyaniba Estates, Osu - Accra.

Paternal grandfather Owusu Sekyere Agyeman

Maternal grandmother Mama Akua Fukuo (Margaret Appiah)

Wedding day of my parents at Sufrette House, Winneba which belonged to the Taylor family. Also in photograph (From left to right – front line) are Uncle Gyamfi's wife, Uncle Adu Gyamfi, Auntie Ama Serwaa Agyeman, Papa O.S. Agyeman, J. O. T. Agyeman (Groom), Felicia Agyeman (Bride), Uncle Kofi Ahenkro, Margaret Akua Fokuo (Margaret Appiah), Bob Owusu and HRH Annan of UAC

Mrs. Felicia Agyeman, wife of General Manager presenting a silver tray on behalf of the Management Staff of GNTC to Sir Patrick at the Ambassador Hotel, Accra.

Mr. J.O.T. Agyeman, General Manager of Ghana National Trading Corporation (GNTC) at a reception with colleagues at the Agyeman family residence.

Family after a Sunday service at Ridge Church, Accra.

Back: Nana Konadu, Nana Sefah, Owusu Sekyere, Nana Serwah, Cecilia Antwi (Maa's cousin) and Nana Afriyie
Front: Kwame Otchere, Nana Yaa Ofosuhemaa

Nana Konadu with Kate Narnor as part of the cast in the comic opera with music by Arthur Sullivan and libretto by W. S. Gilbert, Achimota School. 1968

Nana Konadu at Africa Hall, University of Science and Technology.

Nana Konadu at the back of the Agyeman residence, 1970.

Nana Konadu in her final year, with sister Nana Sefa Agyeman in her first year, at the University of Science & Technology

At Mrs. Fischerber's for dinner. Also in the photograph Nana Konadu, Serwah, Sefa, Emil, Anthea Fisherber and Paul Boateng (now Lord Boateng, UK), with Mrs. Fischerber as the table head.

Nana Konadu as first year student at University of Science & Technology, Kumasi.

Nana Konadu with Gloria Awurabena Sakyiamah

Nana Konadu working on a project for Ghana Airways in the Graphic Design department of the University of Science & Technology, Kumasi. 1970

Nana Konadu with sister Yaa Achia in front of the Flower Clock in Geneva, Switzerland. 1968

Nana Konadu with friend Rosemary Baddoo at the University of Science and Technology. 1971

Nana Konadu with colleagues in and the university's graphic design studio. 1971

Mrs. Felicia Agyeman with some children and teachers at her school, Tiny Tots Kindergarten, Ridge, Accra.

Pre-school pupils with Mrs. Felicia Agyeman at Tiny Tots Kindergarten, Accra. Photograph taken in front of the school's building

Jerry, Nana Konadu and Jerry's best friend Anthony Gbeho. 1971

Nana Konadu, daughter of the Managing Director of GNTC presenting a tray to Mrs. Griffiths

Mr. J.O.T. Agyeman (Dee) walking Nana Konadu down the aisle on wedding day at Ridge Church, Accra. 29 January 1977.

The newlyweds receive a Marriage Certificate from Rev. Stevens after the church service. Also in the photograph are Mr. J.O.T. Agyeman, Madam Victoria Agbotui and Mrs. Felicia Agyeman.

Nana Konadu Agyeman-Rawlings signs wedding register after ceremony. 1977

Nana Konadu Agyeman with friend Heidi Hubarn in St. Gallen, Switzerland, while on attachment with Jelmoli company.

A.F.R.C. meets representatives on Political Parties, 1979

A.F.R.C. Chairman addressing senior and junior police oficers at the Police Headquarters,
Accra, 1979

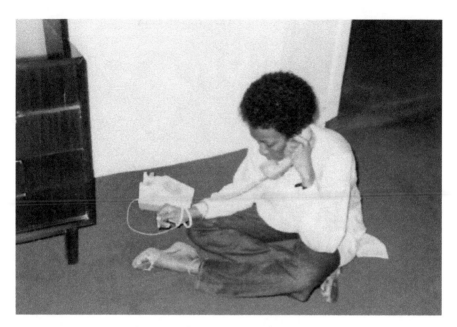

Nana Konadu Agyeman-Rawlings, 1980

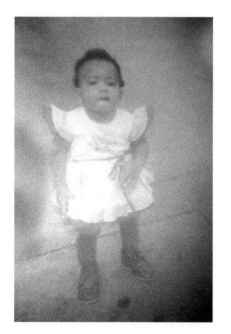

Daughter Zanetor at 1 year old, 1979.

Nana Konadu with daughter Yaa Asantewaa at 6 months year old, 1980.

Paternal Roots : Agyeman Family Tree

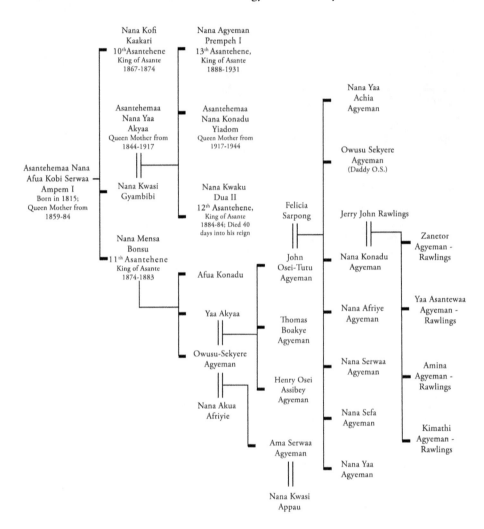

Maternal Roots : Sarpong Family Tree

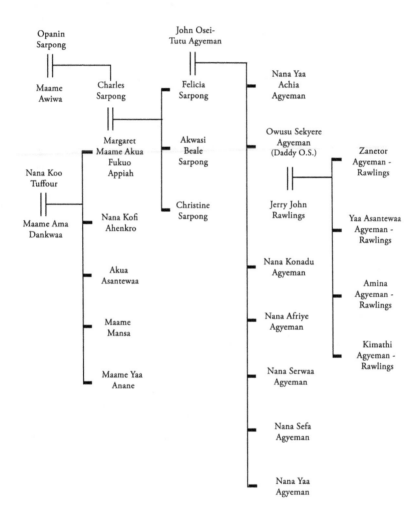

CHAPTER SEVEN

SILHOUETTE
The Bright Dawn of Independence

At the stroke of midnight on March 6, 1957, Nkrumah declared the Gold Coast independent. We became Ghana, named after an ancient West African empire. This was a magnificent day in the country as the rest of the world watched, especially Africans, with a keen sense of what this could mean for the continent. Workers were given the day off, and tens of thousands gathered in Accra to greet the country's first Prime Minister, Dr. Kwame Nkrumah.

The memories have stayed as if they were yesterday. The whole town throbbed with excitement. Church bells sounded across Accra. Crowds filled the city streets with the buzz of celebration and hope as they pushed into the polo grounds outside parliament and cheered as the British flag, the Union Jack (a strong symbol of British colonial rule over the Gold Coast), was lowered in front of half a million spectators. In its place, the red, gold and green coloured flag of the new nation of Ghana was hoisted up, as if elegantly dancing in a light breeze.

Ushering in the birth of a new nation, the new national flag was specially designed by Mrs. Theodosia Salome Okoh. She was a teacher and artist and happened to be our neighbour at the time and a family friend. The flag, as designed by Mrs. Okoh, bore the Pan-African colours— red, gold, and green—in horizontal stripes with a black five-pointed star in the centre of the gold stripe. For us, the red symbolized the blood of those who died in the country's struggle for independence; the gold represented the country's mineral wealth; and the green represented the vegetation and fertility of the nation, while the five-pointed black star symbolised African freedom and the African people.

At the polo grounds, Prime Minister Kwame Nkrumah broke into dance and then spoke of a dream finally realised: *"Today, from now on, there is a new African in the world,"* he declared. *"At long last, the battle has ended. Ghana, our beloved country, is free forever."* Many prominent leaders and activists from around the world were there to bear witness to this event, including Princess Marina the Duchess of Kent, civil rights campaigner, Dr. Martin Luther King and Vice President of the United States, Richard Nixon.

At home, my family and I gathered around a radio and listened intently through the crackling static. *"The independence of Ghana is meaningless unless it is linked up with the total liberation of the African continent,"* Nkrumah said.

I was nine and this was my first memory of a deeply felt sense of national pride. It was exhilarating!

As the first colony in sub-Saharan Africa to break away from its colonial master, Ghana became the symbol of the hopes and aspirations of an entire continent – and further. In a live broadcast while in Ghana, I remember hearing Dr. Martin Luther King on the radio. He told listeners:

"This event, the birth of this new nation, will give impetus to oppressed peoples all over the world. I think it will have worldwide implications and repercussions--not only for Asia and Africa, but also for America... It renews my conviction in the ultimate triumph of justice..."

The day after Ghana's independence had to be one of the most unforgettable of days in every Ghanaian's mind. The country seemed to have been ushered into a new era, one in which we were to hold our destiny in our hands and had every chance to shape our future as we wanted. Dr. Nkrumah and his colleagues had stood at the forefront of this treasured moment, and his hope for Ghana and Africa was seeing its first light of day.

Pan-Africanism filled the air and Ghana was at the edge of an African renaissance. The political ideology that was to pull together and strengthen any pledge of solidarity between people of African descent saw Ghana's quest for self-government as a turning point for the movement.

So many people had descended on the country to be part of the historic occasion. My uncle Henry Osei Asibey, who had been Dr. Nkrumah's Secretary, knew most of the public figures, some of whom had arrived from the United States and the Caribbean nations. Together with my uncle Kofi Darko who was serving as Deputy Protocol Director to Dr. Nkrumah at the time and had lived in the United States and also knew many of the foreign guests, he was tasked with organizing a lunch at my family's home.

The jubilation in the streets of Accra on 7 March 1957 was not much different from the sheer delight in our house. I was a little girl, but the smiles on the faces of the guests were enough to let me know that Ghana had indeed crossed a golden threshold. One after the other, they introduced themselves and cheered. People like George Padmore, Martin Luther King Jr., Lady Humphries, Lord Kitchener and Harry Belafonte laughed and sang. They spoke among themselves and enjoyed an amazing afternoon of music, and a variety of Ghanaian dishes. Many other senior civil service personnel including Mr. and Mrs. Adu, Mr and Mrs. Elliot, Mr. and Mrs. E.L. Quartey, Mr. and Mrs. Ribero-Aryeh, Mr. and Mrs. Tachie-Menson, Mr. and Mrs. Gardner, Mr. and Mrs. Quist Arcton and Nat King Cole were in attendance also. Out of nowhere, American singer Louis Armstrong burst into a song that seemed popular to most of the men and women in our home that afternoon, and they joined in. It was such a proud and striking occasion.

One young lady seemed especially nice as she engaged me in conversation. I was fascinated with a hat she wore, and I tried not to disturb her by fidgeting as she gently engaged in a conversation with my uncle Harry Asibey. Her friends called her Maya. She had me sit either on her lap as she listened to her friends, or make me sit on the footstool next to her when she wanted to taste the groundnut soup that my mother had prepared. She spoke of her own childhood in America, and it was as if Ghana's independence had become a moment of honour for a lot more people around the world. It was much later that I came to learn that the young lady was Maya Angelou.

The euphoria outside the walls of our home was not without its cracks and certainly not without detractors. Understandably, not everyone in Ghana shared the same vision that Dr. Nkrumah and his comrades were pushing for. Yet, the celebrations immediately after the declaration of independence had silenced every criticism, even if for a brief period, and painted a sense of achievement on the horizon that all Ghanaians, and indeed all Africans, could reach.

In both Africa and the Caribbean, Ghana became the first African colonial territory to regain its independence. Our new nation lit a torch, which became an inspiration for the rest of the colonial world still fighting for its own independence. For Nkrumah, liberation was only the first step. The next was advancing his Pan-African agenda of unifying the entire continent—a task that would prove much more difficult.

Later that same year, on Christmas Eve, I remember listening to a radio broadcast in which Dr. Nkrumah said: *"My first objective is to abolish from Ghana poverty, ignorance and disease. We shall measure our progress by the improvement in the health of our people; by the number of children in school and by the quality of their education; by the availability of water and electricity in our towns and villages... The welfare of our people is our chief pride..."*

Throughout Africa, Ghana's route to independence became the model for the rest of the continent. By the mid-1960s, over thirty African countries were independent, gaining their freedom from the

French as well as the British, and eventually the Spanish and Portuguese.

In spite of massive support for independence, the transition from colony to a nation (1951 to 1957) was a divisive one, and the threat of violence from the opposition remained a challenge for Nkrumah. In an attempt to quell the outbreak of violence and disorder especially along tribal lines, the government passed the Avoidance of Discrimination Act in December 1957. This outlawed all political parties based on ethnic, racial or regional grounds, and it subsequently forced all existing political parties to disband, including the dominant opposition NLM party and the less popular Northern People's Party. Determined to get around this, the two parties immediately merged forces to form a new and blended political party called the United Party (UP) under the leadership of Dr. Kofi Busia. United in their common purpose to oppose and destabilise Kwame Nkrumah, the UP became the only opposition party in 1957.

Fearing that the UP would seek all means to overthrow his government, Prime Minister Nkrumah introduced the Preventive Detention Act in 1958, which he stated was only temporary, but gave the government increased powers to detain any person, especially suspected assassins and saboteurs, for up to five years without a trial. In some cases, this led to what many judged as an abuse of power, as detention became a way of conveniently removing any opposition or critics of the CPP, even on mere suspicion, with no means of redress. Anticipating his own detention, Dr. Kofi Busia fled the country in 1959 and went into a seven-year self-imposed exile.

For all the fanfare surrounding independence, the three major instruments of government —the army, the police and the civil service—were still in the hands of British expatriates. Underneath this commanding framework of government was a stratum of Ghanaian professionals.

The British government had grown accustomed to obedience in its realm, so it was hardly surprising that Nkrumah's intentions to make

Ghana a republic, ending the parliamentary system with a prime minister at the helm of the executive, were met with stiff opposition from Her Majesty's government. Meanwhile, on the other side of the political divide, the UP was busy campaigning for Ghana to remain a monarchy.

Even as a little girl, the weight of history was not lost on me. It was a seminal moment, filtering down from the political class to the classroom. I remember being taught about this during our civics class, in parallel with the unfolding events being marshalled by our decision-makers. On the playground, my friends and I pondered what it meant for Ghana to become a republic or remain under Great Britain. It was not until July 1, 1960, that Ghana became a Republic with Kwame Nkrumah elected as the first president of the Republic of Ghana.

No longer would Ghana have to be led by leaders who did not resemble them, who did not share in their ethnicity yet shared their history and struggles but from opposite ends of the spectrum. The struggle paid off: presidential elections would take place for the first time in Ghana on 27 April 1960.

The promise of realised potential was infectious. The sense of change and excitement was almost palpable. But history had always been littered with examples of over-inflated expectations placed on the shoulders of leaders, the weight of which soon becomes burdensome to all when reality comes into sharp view. Nkrumah's tenure was no different.

From 1951, while Nkrumah was still prime minister, and then throughout his presidential tenure until 1966, Nkrumah's CPP government embarked on an ambitious, yet very costly, programme of rapid industrialisation. Their goals were lofty. Our spirits too were elevated and nourished by the call to action for the African man and woman to chart his and her destiny with pride, rather than be dictated to, as had been our reality for so long. These changes were structural, intense and driven by a vision of lifting Ghana to a position of greatness. Heavy investment was ploughed into Ghana's transportation infrastructure and port facilities, a new rail link was opened, and major roads were constructed, including the Accra to Tema motorway. A national airline company was established, Ghana Airways, as well as a national shipping company, the Black Star Line. The largest man-made harbour in Africa at the time, the port of Tema, was established.

Nkrumah ventured to set Ghana on a course that, even though was ambitious, was attainable if the people saw themselves as contributory pieces to an enormous development puzzle. Hospitals were refurbished and new ones built, including Korle Bu Teaching Hospital and Kumasi General Hospital, later to be renamed Komfo Anokye Teaching Hospital, where Ghana could train her own doctors. Nkrumah expanded education by building several more primary, middle and secondary schools to increase enrolment nationwide.

Two universities were also established: Cape Coast University and the Kwame Nkrumah University of Science & Technology. Teacher Training Colleges were built, and Nkrumah's government introduced free and compulsory basic education for all primary school pupils by abolishing school fees in government and missionary schools. By the late 1950s, Ghana's primary and secondary school enrolment rates were far ahead of average rates across West Africa.

Ghana's industrial and economic expansion required a sustainable and reliable source of power. Marrying this need with an understanding of Ghana's natural endowments of bauxite as well as the export market potential for aluminium, the idea was born to create the world's largest man-made lake, the Akosombo Dam, on the Volta River. Such an audacious plan would link various components of the supply chain: the Ghanaian people and their power needs, the significant natural bauxite reserves, the smelter to convert the bauxite into value-added aluminium and the dam itself to generate the power.

With financial assistance from the United States, the World Bank, and the United Kingdom, construction of the Akosombo Dam was completed in 1966 on the Volta River. The international interest in the dam was clear because it would guarantee power for Africa's largest steel smelting plant, the American-owned Volta Aluminium Company (VALCO). But this was also an example of conflicting goals. While Nkrumah's stated objective, and conceivably his real intentions too, were to provide Ghanaians with power, the United States and other international partners were more interested in ensuring their power needs were met.

I was too young to fully appreciate the implications of every signature, but in my adult years, I wondered if Ghana negotiated the best deal it could have. By official agreement, only 20% of Akosombo Dam's electric output would be provided to Ghanaians in the form of electricity. It would serve a fraction of national demand, while the remaining was to be generated for VALCO. Adding to this, an arrangement was made for Ghana to sell power to neighbouring countries, particularly during the energy crisis of 1973, which left much of Accra and other areas dependent on power generated by diesel generators.

A glaring reality that both his critics and supporters could agree made a remarkable impact was the fact that under Nkrumah, Ghana underwent a period of constant expansion and construction. One result of such rapid industrialisation was the increasing influx of foreign national workers, diplomats, and business communities. Ordinary citizens held on to the promise of a hopeful future, a dawn of a new day.

Accra, during my childhood and adolescent years, was a vibrant city with modern, commercial areas interspersed with green parks, luscious gardens, and tree-lined residential suburbs with unusual-sounding names like Cantonments, Ridge and McCarthy Hills. It was a city we were proud of. The city had some of the best schools, healthcare facilities and one of the finest universities in all of West Africa. I was growing up in a place full of life, and witnessing first-hand a city blossom and expand as the central hub for foreign companies, well-stocked shopping centres, and busy open-air markets.

Among the most famous markets was *Makola*, where traders and farmers from neighbouring countries and surrounding villages congregated to show off their wares in tightly-packed stalls. People from all over West Africa came to buy and trade there. It was beautiful watching men and women bargain boldly, in a trading centre where a person could find almost just about anything. Run by powerful women traders, all wares were beautifully displayed, from fresh oranges stacked in colourful pyramids to pots and pans arranged in neat tiers. Around the market in the area we called Opera Square, there also, were the glittering jewellery displayed in glass showcases which I found to be completely enthralling as a young girl.

My mind often travelled to when I was about eight years old, roaming through the aisles in Makola while trying hard to remember the long list of grocery items that Maa said she needed for the house. "*Konadu, listen: I need yams, two tubers... milk, three cans... Exeter corned beef, one... sardines, four tins... tomatoes, two. . .*" Refusing to write anything down—wanting to test our mental agility, I suspect—Maa would call out each item verbally just before we left the house. As an educator, she always saw a teachable moment in everything she did with us. In turns, she would send one of my siblings or me on the market-run, with only a short memory and a strict budget in tow.

Anxious not to forget an item on the list, I would whizz through the market with dogged focus. Without even knowing it, at the age of eight, I was already making responsible buying decisions on a tight budget, and I learned very early the useful art of negotiation from shrewd market women. The overflowing aisles of Makola market abounded with tempting distractions. "Oh, my friend! Come and buy from me!" I would hear as I walked through the market. "Come and taste my *waakye* (rice and beans), or *red red* (fried plantain and bean stew), or *bofroot* (doughnuts) or *kelewele* (fried plantain with ginger and hot pepper).

The intoxicating aromas and persuasive calls from food sellers was a strong pull on a young girl's attention. I loved going to the market, and without giving it much thought, it would be here that I would learn the art of making any amount of money buy as many things as possible, so I could save just enough to visit my favourite food vendor, the plump *Ga* 'maame' who sold hot rice cooked in margarine and trotters stew. *Mmmm*, delicious! I savoured every bite in its entirety before returning home.

Unfortunately by my mother's rules, buying food prepared by 'outsiders' was strictly forbidden, especially street food from the busy markets or roadside. I had to find a way to bend my mother's rule because, for me, rice and stew at the local market had become the one delicacy which was always number one on my shopping list.

When my family moved to Accra, it did not take long for me to adjust, or to feel embedded in the Ridge community. Soon after we settled, the Ridge Church requested the participation of neighbourhood children to take part in a newly-developed program called "Bob-a-Job". It was about fundraising for the construction of a school, which would become an extension of the local Ridge Church. As part of this program, we were each given little notebooks and individual financial goals. We were then sent door-to-door to seek out jobs we could do for hire, ranging from polishing shoes and silverware to weeding, gardening, and washing floors. Our neighbours would log the work we did and the monies they donated in our notebooks.

After several weeks, we raised enough money to build the first three classrooms. The opportunity I and the other children had, to lay down the building blocks for the school, symbolised the cementing of the fundamental values of education for my own life. Our naming of the school, Ridge Children's School, was a proud moment for all of us. The lesson that education had to be the foundation of everything I was to embark upon in life was impressed upon me, both in my immediate setting, from my mother, as well as from my neighbourhood and community.

I could not have fathomed how much of my personality and value system was being shaped slowly in these environments. My sense of being rooted in the community also coalesced around Arbour Day when the children went around the neighbourhood to plant trees. It was a big event for us, one that brought the children of Ridge together, supervised by a British public works official. We planted "our little trees" all along the road from the Military Hospital to Ghana International School and all the surrounding areas of the Holy Catholic Cathedral. As if to symbolize the birth of our own ambitions, we hoped each tree would reach high into the sky someday. The same trees were to beautifully line the roads that led to the Castle.

One of the high points of my childhood was going to watch children's films at the Rex Cinema in central Accra. For good behaviour, my parents rewarded us each week to a children's matinee on the big screen. Newly-released films such as *Hansel and Gretel, Tom Thumb, Snow White & the Seven Dwarfs, Robin Hood, Red Riding Hood, Jack and the Beanstalk, Bambi, Dumbo* and the first series of *Superman* were featured. In the late 1950s and 1960s, going to the cinema appealed mostly to the expatriate community and a handful of emerging crop black civil servant families living in Ridge area, and other well-to-do residential communities of Accra.

My youthful consciousness had not associated the arts with wealth or a social fault line. Watching classic films from such a young age simply sparked my imagination and encouraged my early love of playacting. It also influenced my love of organising neighbourhood children to create our own productions. I was about nine when I began mobilising peers in our community—Canadian, American, British and a few Ghanaian children—to put on plays, dances, pantomime shows and even sporting events in our community.

I grew to love writing and directing many of our performances, encouraging some of the close-knit neighbourhood children to re-enact play versions of the movies we watched, such as *Red Riding Hood*. We would invite our parents to performances on a Friday or Saturday evening and charge door fees to raise money for the expansion of the Ridge Church. I always made sure our staging area was appropriately set apart from that of the audience, with plenty of room for props to indicate a forest and a small cottage.

The stage was my expression of channelled emotions, observations, and thoughts, where I felt at ease in taking on different characters, whether in plays put on by our school or church. Thankfully, I did not suffer from stage fright and memorising lines came to me with little effort. It was thrilling to move outside of myself and my environment into a world I found even more exciting.

After only one year at Osu Progress School, my mother convinced the program was inadequate and that we were not being challenged enough, decided it was time to try another approach. Maa spent a lot of time that year teaching us from home as we shuffled between schools in Accra, before landing in the clutches of a private school: Mrs. Sam's School, Accra, near an area that had come to be known as Ministries.

Sadly, the two years I spent at the school must have been the lowest point of my early school years. It was the first time I ever felt or experienced any kind of discrimination. Up until this point, I enjoyed going to school and taking an active role in school activities. A different reality reared its head in this school where the children with lighter skin complexion were clearly favoured over those who were darker in complexion.

It was the strangest feeling, and I dreaded going to school every day. The headmistress, Mrs. Sam, was herself of mixed race—Ghanaian and, probably, British. She had a daughter who was also a teacher at the school. Coincidentally, one trait they both seem to share in my young eyes was their bias and a rather awkward kind of prejudice.

The mixed heritage of the school leadership was reflected in the diversity of students on the compound. I recall most of the children seemingly being of a mixed race. Some were half Ghanaian and half Lebanese. Others were half Ghanaian and half Caucasian, with their parents having settled in Ghana from either Europe or the United States. As luck would have it, this was the first place I ever came into close contact with a young boy, Jerry John.

I loved the arts until my experiences at Mrs. Sam's school found a way of curbing the fervour. I remember vividly how anytime the school staged a play or any artistic production, the dark-skinned pupils with obvious African parents would be shoved aside in favour of the bi-racial or lighter-skinned children.

Occasionally, there would be a few insignificant roles needing pupils to fill, and that was the only time we were given a chance to be seen or heard on stage. As a child who loved to participate in school plays, I found this environment disheartening and utterly demoralising. There were several moments when I felt I could sing or act better than the lead girl on stage, but I never got a chance to even be considered. This propelled me even more into the neighbourhood productions. That was my way to fill a void and make up for the neglect I often felt inside this school. Sadly, most of my memories of Mrs. Sam's school were so negative that I did all I could to block most of them out.

One day stands out vividly in my mind. It was late afternoon during a routine school day when I was playing with my best friend, Violet, a Ghanaian girl whose father was serving as the Minister of Finance in Nkrumah's government, and other classmates Miazor and Zorher, half Ghanaian and half Lebanese girls.

I don't remember much about the game we were playing, but I do remember being caught off-guard when I suddenly turned and accidentally tripped another girl in our class over. Not only did the girl fall and hit the ground, but the impact from her fall split her lips open. Her mouth instantly started to bleed. My heart sank, and I felt horrible. When I caught a glimpse of her face and bloody lips, my empathy quickly turned to fear as I realised she was one of Mrs. Sam's favourites. Sure enough, within seconds, all hell broke loose!

"Dear God! What happened?" Mrs. Sam exclaimed as she darted

over to us. A hush came over the playground and all children stopped playing as they narrowed in on the scene of the accident. "Sweetheart, let me see your face," Mrs. Sam said anxiously to the girl as she knelt beside her.

"I'm sorry," I blurted out, quivering in fear. "It was an accident," I quickly added for good measure. Turning in my direction, Mrs. Sam glared at me with hate filling her eyes.

"YOU DID THIS?" she hissed, staring me down.

"I did not do it..." but before I could finish my sentence, she hauled off and slapped me hard across my face with enough force to cause me to stumble, and so too did my last word, *purpose-poly*" instead of "purposely." Dumbfounded, I stood there feeling dazed and humiliated as the whole class broke into raucous laughter at my blunder. From that afternoon, the pupils began teasing me with an inadvertent nickname, "purpose-poly," a constant reminder of that horrific day.

After two years at Mrs. Sam's school, I was ecstatic to leave and go to a public school called the Experimental School in Accra New Town. Any place would do. I spent a short time there before I was enrolled in another private school, Ghana International School (GIS) in 1958. I was ten years old.

GIS was located in the Cantonments area of Accra and had been established in 1955 originally for the children of foreign nationals, such as diplomats, Baptist missionaries, foreign construction workers who were working on the Akosombo Dam and employees working for American companies like VALCO and Kaiser. The curriculum at GIS adhered to the international standards of education so that foreign children could easily transfer their credits to continue their education back home. Two-thirds of the class was American, while the other third was British, Indian, Greek and a few Africans.

At the time, I was one of only a handful of Ghanaian students attending the school. The tuition fees were prohibitively expensive for most Ghanaian families, such that my parents never enrolled more than two of us in the school at any given time. By the time I enrolled, I was fortunate to be in the company of my older cousin, Afua Achia, whose father, Harry Agyeman (my father's younger brother and former secretary to Kwame Nkrumah), was abroad studying at Columbia University. My parents, steeped in Asante culture where uncles supported their nieces and nephews, made sure Afua Achia had the same opportunities as they gave their own children.

Some of my fondest memories at GIS are of the close friendships I made. I became especially close with two girls, in particular, both American, named Florine Hazel and Lynn Erstein. Florine was one of two daughters of a Baptist Missionary, and Lynn was an extremely bright, yet very quiet, the only child of an American diplomat. I spent a lot of time at Lynn's home during weekend sleepovers. Kibrah Dalwit, an Ethiopian classmate, and daughter of the Ethiopian ambassador became my best friend. Life had turned out to be a stark contrast to the gloomy experiences at Mrs. Sam's school.

The routine at GIS was quite different from the other schools I attended. School opened at 7:30 a.m. and closed at 12:45 p.m. After school, activities like ballet, music or sports started at 2 p.m. and ended at 4:30 p.m. Every student brought a snack to school, and unlike the other schools I had attended, lunch at Ghana International School was always at home.

One afternoon, I had two of my American friends over to our house for lunch. After we ate, we sat at the table and giggled and laughed amongst ourselves before changing our attire for our weekly ballet lesson. My father had opted to drive us all back to school that afternoon. Wrapped up in chatter, the three of us mindlessly jumped in the back of his car, engrossed in our world of conversation all the way back to GIS. Regrettably, my mother later brought it to my attention that none of us had the decency to say thank you or goodbye to my father as we jumped out of his car. I was completely oblivious to this oversight and, more so, to how much I had offended my own father that day until I got home that evening.

Boy, did I ever get it! Maa made me apologise profusely to my father for not showing appreciation. "I am very sorry, Dee. I honestly did not mean to be disrespectful," I pleaded, but it did not get me very far. From that day forward, as a lesson, my parents registered me to start taking the bus each day, to and from school. It was a necessary scolding, indeed, but also very eye-opening. My parents had to inject a clear reminder that nothing in my life ought to be taken for granted because even the seemingly simplest of acts come at a sacrifice of another person's time and effort. Eventually, I began enjoying the daily commute. The only adjustment was that I had to wake up much earlier each morning to be on time for the strict bus schedule.

Attending GIS had to be a highlight of my early education. I had always loved sports, but at GIS I realised that I had a knack for athletics. In my Junior 3 class, I came in first across the board in the long jump, high jump, relays and the 110- and 220-yard hurdles. For indoor sports, I learned how to swim, and I joined gymnastics. I also enjoyed performing arts, took voice lessons and learned classical ballet. I often reminisce on how we would put on beautiful productions of "The Nutcracker," "Swan Lake," "Hansel & Gretel" and "Snow White and the Seven Dwarfs" as part of the ballet program.

My active involvement in sports and the arts was encouraged just as the school placed tremendous emphasis on academic excellence. In the end, the new chapter spurred me on to immerse myself even more into opportunities to develop my talent and interests, and strive to excel. It was empowering at the time, one that many decades later would give me a greater sense of self, both in worth and in confidence.

Around 1962 my father decided that French would eventually become an important part of Ghana's life, or even on a world stage. I remember he would travel and come back home with French records which he took his time playing and having each of us children recite the French words. My father was insistent on us learning French, and although he did not understand a word of the language, in his own way, he wanted to prepare his children for an oncoming future that could arrive with a string of uncertainties, one of them probably being the fusion of the French language into our Ghanaian society. He imagined we would need it because we were surrounded by Francophone countries, and learning another language might serve to an advantage.

We memorized and repeated each word and sentence as the record played. At the end of each month, he would conduct a test and send it to his friend, Mr. Newlands, who understood French to review our progress. So gradually, I learned a lot of French words and even though we could not speak the language, that exposure had given us some confidence to explore the world around us at a very early age.

The French lessons gave me one of the most unforgettable memories of my early school years. The tuition at GIS was expensive and my parents were doing all they could to afford what they were convinced was an excellent education. My mother did not let an afternoon go by without asking for our homework and making all of us sit down to finish every one of the questions we had brought home from school. One such afternoon, I was not interested in going through the same routine. My mother called all of us, one after another, to bring our homework for her usual inspection. My brother was first, with his homework tucked in a bag, so he pulled it out.

"How about you, Nana Konadu?"

I did not want my mother spending the rest of the afternoon asking me what seemed like an endless list of questions.

I thought quickly.

"Maa, today my homework was in French."

She sat up.

"French?" She did not have any ability to review French homework, so she said I was free to leave and hoped I had done it well. Maa did not even ask for the French book; she reasoned that she could not read it anyway. She had to trust me.

The next day she called us to review our homework again, and I gave her the same reason for not having to show it. "Today also, all my homework is in French."

I got away with this lie for a whole week. My mother, being a teacher, knew that couldn't be right. One thing was certain, she had not paid all that money to GIS for her children to be learning only French.

My mother showed up at the school one morning and asked to speak to the headmistress, Mrs. Webb. The only thing more haunting than the image of my mother walking to my classroom with Mrs. Webb was her watching me from the corner of her eye as Mrs. Webb asked me politely why I had lied to my mother. I was shaking like a leaf.

Even before my mother could say a word, Mrs. Webb jumped in again and assured my mother that this would not happen again. Maa left the school compound quietly, but my afternoon at home left a permanent imprint on my mind, the kind that was to forever remind me of the consequences for dishonesty. I can never forget it.

A truth rose to the foreground that anything worth achieving was worth conscientious devotion, sacrifice, and effort. In the end, the integrity of a passion and the sense of duty even when no one watched, became the bedrock of other character traits I was nurturing, even unconsciously.

CHAPTER EIGHT

FIGHT 'TIL THE END
Young Pioneer

I was about twelve years old when I experienced something that intensified my anxieties about death. I was home one afternoon when I overheard fragments of conversation between my parents about the declining health of my father's aunt, Afua Konadu. I could not make out the details of the conversation from where I stood, but whatever they said, it was pretty evident that my grandaunt was not feeling very well. From the hushed tones echoing from their room, I could tell something was wrong.

Before illness set in, I used to love it when Afua Konadu would spend long stretches of time in our home, caring for my siblings and I, and helping Maa balance her household duties. Her narration of bedtime stories to us about our family history was incredible. Now, too weak to walk, she was losing her vision in both her eyes and was bedridden in her village home. Due to her condition, I had not seen her in a long time. When my father emerged from his room, his face looked drawn and distressed, and he immediately came to speak to me.

"Misewaa, you know Auntie Konadu has been sick for a while now."

"Yes, I know."

"Well, I need to visit her, and she's always asking about you. So tomorrow, I will take you with me to visit the old lady." I did not protest. I loved spending time with my father, especially when I got his undivided attention. So the next morning, my father and I set out on a five-hour journey that took us from Accra into the heartland of the Ashanti Region, just beyond Kumasi and into a small town, *Wiamoase*. Almost as soon as we crossed the town limits, I witnessed the stark images of poverty in the faces and dwellings surrounding us.

"Okay, Misewaa," my father said with a heavy sigh, "we are finally here." His car came to a halt in front of a small house with decaying walls and peeling paint on the exterior. Behind it stood my grandaunt's house, it seemed like it was the only nice built house in the area.

"Dee, are these the only homes they have here?" I questioned, feeling apprehensive to get out of the car.

"Come on," he said, dismissing my question, "let's go and see the old lady." Upon entering her home, my father called out to his aunt, announcing our presence as we slowly made our way back to her room. Soon my eyes caught sight of my grandaunt's frail body, lying in the centre of a single bed. Feigning cheerfulness, my father greeted her in a voice choked with tears.

"Auntie! Good morning-ooo!"

"Morning," she replied slowly.

"Auntie, guess who is here?" Dee asked, eager to deliver good news. "It's Konadu! I'm here with Nana Konadu," he repeated. Her frown slowly disappeared and her face brightened. Dee looked at me expectantly to say something, but I couldn't. Raising her hand, my grandaunt beckoned me to come to her bedside.

"Konadu, come. Come and sit by me. I want to tell you something," she said softly. Terrified, I was unable to move. My father raised his eyebrows and gestured for me to move in closer. It felt a bit painful for me to see the same woman who had once been so full of life now weak and unable to even smile as broadly as the woman I had always known. It took some coercion on his part, but I eventually went to sit at her bedside.

"Konadu, listen." she started, visually impaired, but still sound of mind. "Continue working hard in everything you do. Always stand tall. Never give up... or give in... do what you know is right. Do you hear me?" she asked, her breathing laboured.

"Yes, Auntie."

"Never compromise your values. That is why you and I are called Konadu, 'Ko-na-du'," she emphasised slowly. "Like the queen mothers of the past, we 'fight 'til the end'. That is the meaning of our name," she said in Asante. "Do you understand?"

"Yes, Auntie, I do." Her words dissipated my fear and sadness suddenly engulfed me.

"Good." She paused between thoughts, then added, "Look after your siblings. They are not as strong as you and they will need your guidance. Keep them in check. Take care of them. And be a good girl. Okay?"

"Okay," I replied.

The gentle sound of my grandaunt's voice flooded my mind. Watching her speak brought tears to my eyes, blinding me. I sat there feeling helpless and heartbroken. Her genuine nature moved me, and her last words both saddened and emboldened me. That afternoon, Dee and I made the drive back to Accra, both of us sad, pensive and barely uttering a word. A few weeks later, we received news that my grandaunt, Afua Konadu, had died peacefully in her sleep.

When I was a young girl, my father's cousin, Baffour Osei Akoto, who became chief linguist to the Asantehene, and later, a founding member of the National Liberation Movement, NLM was a man who would visit us often. At one point, he lived with us for a period of two years. And politics was never lost during the frequent visits of my father's long-time friend and schoolmate from Achimota, Dr. Kofi Busia. Dr. Busia would later become Prime Minister of Ghana, 1969-1972, and also a staunch opponent of Nkrumah. I recall the men's devotion to governance, how Dr. Busia would spend hours in our home drinking tea and discussing the hot-button issues of the day, mainly Nkrumah's politics and the future direction of Ghana.

My father and Dr. Busia shared a strong bond of brotherhood. Their many personal memories, from being at the same place the day my parents first met and years later, Dr. Busia having a wedding reception in my parents' home, overrode any political differences. For them, the unpretentious friendship that had brought them together forced them to think as independent scholars and men and be willing to challenge each other's ideology and politics. But as the nation's political scene changed, so too did the faces at home.

By the time I entered Achimota, it was pretty evident that Dr. Busia's visits had tapered off. They eventually stopped. I never knew why. I did not ask questions. I was to find out much later that Dr. Busia had fled the country into exile in 1959, fearing his own detention under Nkrumah's government.

In 1961, President Nkrumah offered my father a new position within the government. He moved my father from the Ministry of Commerce to be in charge of a newly-established state-owned company called the Ghana National Trading Corporation (GNTC). Earlier that same year, Nkrumah had paid a visit to the Soviet Union and had been very impressed with Russia's rapid pace of industrialisation.

President Nkrumah did not disguise his enthusiasm, "We must try and establish factories in large numbers at great speed." Nkrumah wanted Ghana following the same blueprint. Nkrumah was dissatisfied with the British stronghold on the Ghanaian economy and probably believed that the continued presence of the large British-owned UAC in Ghana prevented the development of an indigenous consumer goods industry.

This motivated Nkrumah to dispatch a small team of business experts, which included my father, on an exploratory tour of Hungary, Czechoslovakia, the Soviet Union and Poland to study the economies of the Eastern-bloc. Nkrumah was well aware that political independence was often granted in name only.

Even though Western European powers granted colonies their political freedom to self-govern, they often continued to control the economies of the newly-independent nations, as if nothing had changed. Nkrumah called this condition *neo-colonialism,* where in theory, independent African nations possessed government or state power, but in reality, the economic system and political policy were still being directed from the outside by multi-national corporations. Thus, new nations possessed political power, but without economic emancipation, which in essence, was meaningless because they failed to achieve the goal of true self-determination.

Even as I got older, I could not help but wonder how modern-day Africa seemed to be undergoing this same phenomenon—too dependent on the economies of the developed world and less focused on the sustainable development of our own nations driven by our own citizens. In many respects, Nkrumah's ideological perspective was to be a train of thought that was destined to be relevant in any modern day, and one that perhaps had to be at the very forefront of every African leader's mind.

Nkrumah's ideology became known as *Nkrumahism* – a new breed of socialism adapted to the African condition. *Nkrumahism* was a reflection of Kwame Nkrumah's personal philosophy of nation-building, opposing all manifestations of colonialism, neo-colonialism, and external interference. As he saw it, neo-colonialist control is most often exercised through economic or monetary means. In Ghana, the essence of neo-colonialism was the continuation of the economic model of British colonialism after achieving political independence.

In a move to change this, Dr. Nkrumah appointed my father and other key experts to begin drafting the new Seven-Year Development Plan, a broad national plan that would serve as the blueprint to transform Ghana into an industrialised, socialist economy and society. Among other initiatives, the plan was designed to break the monopoly of multinational corporations in the Ghanaian economy through nationalisation policies.

My father and the team were to embark on an ambitious outline that would become the reconstruction and development agenda, from 1963 to 1970. The members of the National Planning Commission were Mr. V. Adegbitey, Mr. J.O.T Agyeman, Mr. L.K. Akpaloo, Mr. K.K. Apeadu, Mr. S.C Appenteng, Mr. K. Amoako-Atta, Prof. E.A. Boateng, Mr. B.A. Brown, Mr. J.E. Cudjoe, Mr. C.A Dadey, Prof. Jan Drewnowski, Mr. G,K.B. de Graft-Johnson, Dr. C.O. Easmon, Mr. A.K. Kwateng, Mr. S. La Anyane, Mr. J.H. Mensah, Mr. H. Millar-Craig, Mr. H.P. Nelson, Mr. S.T. Nettey, Mr. E.W. Omaboe, Mr. E.J. Prah, Mr. E.A. Quist-Arcton, Mr. J. Riby-Williams, Mr. F.T. Sai, Mr. J. Thereson-Cofie, Mr. P.N.K. Turkson, Prof. K. Twum-Barima, and Mr. E.A. Winful.

Nkrumah believed that only a socialist and a centrally planned economy could achieve his goals. Thus, in this new economic order, the state was to dominate the economy, which meant that all trade would gradually be taken over by government resulting in the "socialist transformation of the economy and the complete eradication of the colonial structure." As part of this plan, the Ghana National Trading Corporation (GNTC) was set up with 43 branches spread throughout the country to become the main importer and distributor of consumer goods.

In what seemed contrary to the core values of Nkrumahism, the eponymous leader appointed an Englishman, Sir Patrick Fitzgerald, who was on the verge of retirement as the chairman of the UAC, to be the first Managing Director of GNTC. Next in line to Fitzgerald was my father, who was appointed General Manager.

"Dee, why weren't you made Managing Director?" I asked my father soon after he was appointed.

"Misewaa, so much pressure is on Nkrumah right now. We've had a long discussion, and I completely understand. He has a good reason for his decision," Dee replied, as he looked down at me.

The discussion he was referring to, took place soon after Dee's appointment. One evening, President Nkrumah had called on Dee to come to Flagstaff House, the office and official residence of the president, for a private meeting. It was there that Nkrumah clarified the reason why he could not make Dee the managing director was that members of his own party would strongly oppose it. They would not understand why an "outsider," like Dee, who had nothing to do with the formation of the CPP, would be given such a high position. On the other hand, if he puts a white man on top, most would not question his decision.

A strange truth, but the reality remained that Ghana at the time was still living in the shadows of a British Colonial empire. The opportunity, however, would be that my father would get to study the programme that both Dr. Nkrumah and Fitzgerald were setting out to establish. With time, Nkrumah assured Dee, Fitzgerald would be phased out, and he would be next in line to take over as the Managing Director of GNTC. Though Dee appreciated Nkrumah's explanation, my father was not worried about his own position. He understood, all too well, the pressures that encompassed Nkrumah.

My first inkling of my father's prominence came the day we were invited as a family to accompany him to Flagstaff House at a gathering hosted by Nkrumah. It was an exciting day, and I remember being in awe at the sight of the president. As I noticed, Nkrumah's first qualities were his magnetism, his confidence, and his vitality. It was not difficult to feel the energy of his presence from across the room. He was of medium height, graceful and assured. When he noticed my father, he turned to greet him and my mother with a boisterous welcome. Then, to my surprise, he greeted each one of us individually, attentively asking our names, our ages and the schools we attended with a genuine smile and sincerity. I felt myself being immediately taken in by his charm, his jovial sense of humour and his ease of manner.

From this point forward, I began to notice the respect Nkrumah held for my father. It was not long before my father's status as an "outsider," a non-partisan public servant, actually drew Nkrumah closer to him, as a confidante.

I was a young girl and fortunate enough to witness for myself some of both the admirable and challenging moments of a person's life devoted to public service. My father would often have to leave home late in the evenings to sit with Nkrumah for long hours, burrowing through the details of policy issues and international partnership that affected millions of people. The frequency of these meetings grew in the years of what was becoming Nkrumah's biggest challenge with his own party leadership and the apparent mismanagement that seemed to plague his own government.

As state-owned companies mushroomed throughout the country, unfortunately, so too did mismanagement and corruption within the CPP. Anxious to use state power to channel the economy's initial surplus in their own direction, critics asserted that many CPP officials began to abuse their positions of trust by enriching themselves.

Blindsided by the selfish ambition of party officials, Nkrumah seemed to have quickly become a victim of the opportunistic people around him. The very evils of society that he fought desperately to prevent were growing around him, and some of the men and women he would have counted on to fight the crisis, sadly, had become the architects of dishonesty. Some were high-ranking officials who, in spite of the nation's economic situation, openly lived lives of opulence. These men formed the core of the self-serving Ghanaian bourgeoisie who exploited socialist institutions to stockpile private capital.

As corruption inside the CPP grew, Nkrumah was forced to address it publicly. In April 1961, he delivered a dramatic "Dawn Broadcast" on the radio, in which he lashed out in a call to action to end "self-seeking" and "corruption in high places." Individuals and families shivered at the thought of hearing their names bundled with any suspicions of corruption, or embezzlement. Even an allegation could unravel a person's life in an instant. In response, some of the leading personalities fled the country into exile to avoid possible imprisonment under the Preventive Detention Act. Soon there were political arrests and deep resentment throughout the country.

Also disturbing, but no less significant was what appeared to be Nkrumah's growing cult of personality. It was impossible for anyone to miss his glaring parade of authority. Dubbing himself *Osagyefo*, "the Redeemer," he attained cult figure status that began with give-away pictures bearing his photos that were to be framed or nailed or scotch-taped in every home. People wore shirts emblazoned with Nkrumah's picture, his name, and his slogans.

Printing presses began turning out booklets and brochures with Nkrumah's ideas and teachings. Street signs, statues, and landmarks sprouted all over Accra bearing his name or image. On postage stamps, Nkrumah was featured alongside the other "Great Emancipator," Abraham Lincoln. Nkrumah's portrait was engraved on all currency and coins and his birthday, September 21st, was to be observed as a national holiday and celebrated in grand style as "Founder's Day."

He did his best to convince the world that he had not suddenly turned into a dictator, and certainly was not power drunk. One such intriguing presentation of his powerful persona happened when he was asked about why it was important to replace the image the Queen's head on Ghana's currency with his own. In the *Daily Sketch* newspaper, President Nkrumah explained "Why the Queen's head is coming off our coins:"

"Many of my people cannot read or write. They've got to be shown that they are

now really independent. And they can only be shown by signs. When they buy

stamps they will see my picture—an African like themselves—and they will say

"Aiee… look, here is our leader on the stamps, we are truly a free people."

This was June 1957, some four months after Ghana had celebrated our independence.

While I was still attending GIS, I became one of the thousands of students who were mobilised into action through the Young Pioneer Movement, a nationally-established youth movement set up by the Nkrumah government to train youth leaders. Nkrumah saw the mobil-isation of the youth as an important part of nation-building. So, in June of 1960, he launched the Young Pioneer Movement to give primary and middle school students a political education according to CPP ideology.

As Young Pioneers, we had special ideological training sessions after classes, where we were taught slogans and jingles, among other things. The aims of the Young Pioneer Movement were to instil in the youth of Ghana a high sense of patriotism, respect, and love for country while pledging allegiance to Osagyefo. At GIS, I volunteered to join, before it became compulsory for all school children in 1963.

Much like Boy Scouts and Girl Guides organizations in many parts of the world, we learned useful things such as work ethic, discipline, moral integrity and their role in national and continental development, first aid, sewing, drama, singing and drumming, and community ser-vice. We also had the enormous privilege of learning about African his-tory and Africa's founding fathers and leading personalities, protection of state property, and the Young Pioneer's code and pledge, which we recited to open every meeting:

"I sincerely promise to live by the ideals of Osagyefo Dr. Kwame Nkrumah, Founder of the State of Ghana and Initiator of the African Personality. I promise to: safeguard by all means possible, the indepen-dence, sovereignty and territorial integrity of the state of Ghana from internal and external aggression; to be always in the vanguard for the social and economic reconstruction of Ghana and Africa; to be in the first ranks of men fighting for the total liberation and unity of Africa, for these are the noble aims guiding the Ghana Pioneers. As a Young

Pioneer, I will be a guard of workers, farmers, co-operatives and all other sections of our community. I believe that the dynamic Convention People's Party is always supreme and I promise to be worthy of its ideals."

Immediately following the pledge, Young Pioneer organisers who had become CPP-trained activists led us in a chant:
"Nkrumah does no wrong.
Nkrumah is our leader.
Nkrumah is our Messiah.
Nkrumah never dies."

Although I was young, I was mature enough to recognise some of the bizarre tactics employed by the government to engender loyalty and youth support for Nkrumah and the CPP government. And bizarre they were.

In one such extreme and very odd ploy, one afternoon a youth organiser asked us all to close our eyes and pray to God to give us toffees. When we opened our eyes, naturally, we found nothing. Everything had remained the same as before we prayed. Then, the organiser told us to close our eyes, except that this time we were to pray to Osagyefo Nkrumah for the same toffees. As if by magic, when we opened our eyes, toffees appeared on our desks. Our eyes instantly grew big, and our childish hearts filled with joy. The organizers had sent their message clearly: when it came to providing for our needs, Osagyefo could be relied upon, perhaps even more than God.

For good reason, the aims of Nkrumah's youth policy began to raise serious doubts and concerns across the country. This was especially true among parents of school-aged children who feared, among other things, that their children were being taught to deify Nkrumah. Moreover, we were asked to make loyalty to the state our primary objective, even ahead of loyalty to our families. In order to do this, we were taught to report our parents, teachers or any others we heard expressing anti-government opinions. One of the biggest criticisms, therefore, was that the Young Pioneer Movement encouraged children to spy on their parents.

At home, I remember hearing my mother unconsciously whispering her concerns to my father. "Dee, what these people are teaching our children is serious indoctrination. On the ground, people aren't happy with it."

Equally frustrated, my father responded, "Felicia, I know. I am aware, but what do you expect me to do about it?"

"Dee, tell Osagyefo to stop, or at least reduce the cult-like behaviour of his CPP activists. It is dangerous! People are saying that they are trying to replace God with Nkrumah."

My mother's concerns were not only valid but widely felt. Her sentiments represented a growing number of Ghanaians who denounced the idolisation of Nkrumah, and who criticised the youth movement as a forum for indoctrination. As the political climate in Ghana grew more fearful and repressive, tensions around the Young Pioneers came to a head. Like other parents, my mother felt the youth movement was beginning to do more harm than good and she felt my father was one of the few people who could let Osagyefo know.

By the early 1960s, Dr. Nkrumah's socialist inclination and oppressive tendencies began to earn him many enemies both in and outside of Ghana. Attempts on his life increased. In August 1962, he was attacked by a grenade in the northern region village of Kulungugu. In what was later dubbed the Kulungugu attack, Nkrumah was injured when a hand grenade was thrown at him at close range, missing him, but killing a small girl offering him a bouquet of flowers. While arrests were made, it was never discovered who threw the hand grenade.

Nonetheless, several CPP party leaders were put in jail under preventive detention. Curfew was immediately established and roadblocks were set up along roads leading into Accra. In the weeks to follow, Ghana became restless and angry supporters of the outlawed NLM party went on the rampage in Accra, throwing grenades in the streets and killing up to thirty more people.

Another attempt on Nkrumah's life happened in Accra in January 1964, a shooting at the Flagstaff House. As Nkrumah was leaving his office and walked through the gardens towards his residence, a policeman opened fire on him, but missed him and ended up killing his bodyguard instead. The shooter was caught, but it was never discovered who was behind the assassination attempt. These events heightened Dr. Nkrumah's suspicion and mistrust of both the police force and, sadly, the people in his inner circle.

No longer trusting the regular army, he set up his own special presidential guard of elite soldiers housed in the barracks opposite his residence at Flagstaff House. A direct repercussion of the 1964 assassination attempt was Nkrumah's decision to dismiss several senior police officers and to detain even more opponents of his government.

But most significantly, in that same year, Nkrumah banned all opposition political parties and declared Ghana a one-party state. In doing so, he made himself president-for-life and assumed absolute control of the CPP, which, by legislation, was now the only political party in the country. From this point forward, there was no constitutional way to change the government without physically removing Nkrumah from office.

In the face of this mounting trepidation and chaos within his own government, perhaps, Nkrumah's declaration of a one-party state was an honest attempt to address a potentially explosive situation, a boiling cauldron. Faced with violent opposition and severe economic problems, Nkrumah was desperately looking for a way to maintain order.

In light of the serious threats to Ghana's national cohesion, Nkrumah must have believed that the multi-party system was more of a divisive force—one that undermined national unity, deepened ethnic divides and triggered the political and social disorder. In Ghana, political parties seemed to form primarily along ethnic lines, and perhaps, through the lens of Nkrumah, a newly independent nation like Ghana, required the energy and enthusiasm of a united people to move forward in all aspects of nation-building. Unfortunately, his opposition would stop at nothing to undermine his efforts.

With the growing challenges, Nkrumah seemed to be determined to make Ghana the economic showpiece of independent Africa. He was a staunch Pan-Africanist, and therefore, his vision stretched way beyond the confines of Ghana's borders. He was often criticised for his interests in the political development of Africa more so than Ghana's. More important to Nkrumah was his Pan-African vision of continental unity in a politically united Africa.

As he saw it, the only way to achieve true economic and political independence among newly-independent African states was through the creation of a United States of Africa with a centralised union government. By making Ghana a model of economic success and development, Nkrumah hoped to obtain the reverence of the continent's newly-independent leaders, and ultimately, the political leadership of Pan-Africa.

During the height of the Cold War, Nkrumah began to implement a new approach to foreign relations. In dealing with the world's two great superpowers, the United States of America and the Soviet Union, Nkrumah played a leading role in steering Ghana and all of emerging Africa on a course of non-alignment between the East and West. He formalised this position in 1961 when he became one of the founding fathers of the Non-Aligned Movement (NAM) alongside world leaders, such as India's first Prime Minister, Jawaharlal Nehru.

In his 1965 book, *Neo-Colonialism: The Last Stage of Imperialism*, Nkrumah wrote:

"Non-alignment, as practised by Ghana and many other countries, is based on co-operation with all States whether they be capitalist, socialist or have a mixed economy. Such a policy, therefore, involves foreign investment from capitalist countries, but it must be invested in accordance with a national plan drawn up by the government of the non-aligned State with its own interests in mind."

In spite of most foreign investments coming from the United States and Western Europe, Nkrumah openly opposed foreign control of Ghana's economy and political policy. To break the monopoly of foreign-owned companies, my father, and his boss, Sir Fitzgerald, were busily overseeing the opening of state-owned GNTC shops around the country, which were set up to provide "essential" food commodities, such as flour, rice, maize, sugar, and vegetable oils at discounted prices. Moreover, to reverse the long-standing practice of capital flight, Nkrumah implemented a policy requiring all foreign investors in Ghana to re-invest at least 60% of their profits back into the economy.

Nkrumah became increasingly suspicious of the U.S.' motives, labelling their activities "imperialism" and even suggesting that some Peace Corps volunteers in Ghana were there as a front for the U.S. Central Intelligence Agency (C.I.A.). As Nkrumah became a champion of the NAM, and openly demonstrated his independence from Great Britain and the United States, the Western powers began to shun Ghana's industrial hopes.

As tensions rose between the East and West, the capitalist West began viewing the bilateral economic agreements between Ghana and socialist governments of Eastern Europe, the Soviet Union and China with intense suspicion and distrust. In subtle ways, outside pressures started mounting as the West began flexing its muscles over Ghana.

First, western economies stopped buying Ghana's cocoa—the main revenue base of Ghana's economy and the single largest foreign exchange earner. This had an immediate effect. With no storage facilities, Nkrumah had no choice but to burn off the excess amounts of cocoa. As school children, we naively rejoiced at the overwhelming scent of cocoa in the air. "Nkrumah is making chocolates!" we declared. But in reality, the price of cocoa had suddenly taken a sharp dip, one-third of what it had been ten years prior, and by 1965, Ghana was producing twice the volume of cocoa that was produced in 1958 but earning far less money for the output.

With no buyers, the national economy suffered from the sudden loss of cocoa revenues, and national debt soared, resulting from Nkrumah's heavy spending on large infrastructure development projects. Adding to the squeeze, US foreign aid was cut and Western countries stopped supplying Ghana with imported food products like flour, sugar, milk, medicines, shoes, matches and auto parts. This led to immediate short-ages, and Ghana took a turn for the worse.

Faced with little room for manoeuvre, Ghana turned to the Soviet Union for flour, Italy for Fiat cars, the Czech Socialist Republic for more cars, and Hungary, Yugoslavia, Poland and China for factory goods and spare parts. From 1962, Ghanaians began standing in long lines for everything from bread to sardines, corned beef, milk, and sugar.

We had abandoned our local ways of providing local foodstuffs. It seemed we had become increasingly reliant on foreign imports for our survival so much that even the basic tools we needed for our farms had to be brought in from other countries. The sudden shortages, then, un-dermined the country's ability to feed itself and for the first time, Ghana became a net importer of food. Under such conditions, basic consumer products were disappearing from store shelves in Accra and inflation soared to thirty percent.

Life in Ghana was clearly on the decline, but it taught all Ghanaians, and perhaps even more so, an entire young generation full of curiosity and aspiration to serve, some very biting lessons.

CHAPTER NINE

BRACING FOR A TURN
Awakening

Dr. Aggrey wrote: "The surest way to keep people down is to educate the men and neglect the women. If you educate a man, you simply educate an individual, but if you educate a woman, you educate a nation."

In a society where a girl's pursuit of any academic accomplishment was widely considered irrelevant and fruitless, the dissenting voices had to fight long and hard for what they truly believed would transform a nation and its people. Their philosophy led to life-changing opportunities for girls like me, who directly benefitted from early access to a world-class education.

Achimota Secondary School was located just outside the centre of Accra, Achimota. The institution had quickly made its mark as a prestigious co-educational boarding school spread across a vast compound. Though the school was established by the British in the 1920s, one of its three founding fathers was an African — a Ghanaian — Dr. James Emman Kwegyir Aggrey. He was a distinguished scholar, missionary, and intellectual. Dr. Aggrey was educated mostly in the United States, earning his Ph.D. from Columbia University. Upon returning to Ghana, he was appointed as Achimota's first assistant vice principal until his death in 1927.

Long after his passing, Dr. Aggrey's work and legacy impacted me and countless other girls who would walk the halls of Achimota School.

He had campaigned vigorously for women's education at a time when the idea seemed to be tucked away from what the country considered worthy of national attention. He was able to successfully persuade the British Governor, Sir Gordon Guggisberg, also a co-founder of Achimota, that the school was indeed pivotal to social and economic progress, and that it should be co-educational.

Equally fascinating was Dr. Aggrey's advocacy for racial harmony. On a mission to develop the African continent through education, he was widely celebrated for a speech in South Africa in which he illustrated the importance of racial harmony with the keys of a piano: "You can play a tune of sorts on the black keys, and you can play a tune of sorts on the white keys, but for harmony you must use both the black and the white."

These words, along with his beliefs in equal education for boys and girls, inspired the crest of Achimota—black and white piano keys with the motto *Ut Omnes Unum Sint,* meaning "that all may be one," a reference to the founders' philosophy that all people, black and white, male and female, should work together harmoniously for the good of all.

It was in late September 1961 when I entered Achimota Secondary School. I was twelve years old. The transition to Achimota, my father's alma mater, required that I move away from home and into a dormitory. As it was with many students, my transition to boarding school was both nerve-racking and full of childlike, giddy excitement.

On the first day of school, the compound was buzzing with the usual frenzy of a new academic year. Among packs of nervous newcomers, I roamed the compound in total awe of my new surroundings. I recognised a few familiar faces from previous schools.

A short distance away, six girls and I stood huddled in a circle, each of us in our first year, form one. We were some of the newest residents of Kingsley House, an all-girls house on the compound. Smartly dressed in our new school uniforms, my friends and I laughed and giggled nervously amongst ourselves in the courtyard until a loud shout in our direction scared us into silent submission. It came from one of the boys.

"You! *Nino* girls! What are your names?" a senior boy demanded, closing in on us with his friends close behind. His name was Marcus, a tall and lean boy who moved with an air of confidence. Stammering, we took turns:

"Rosemary DeGraft Hayford."

"Eileen Djoleto."

"Eileen Mills."

"Marjorie Quist."

"Gytha Nunoo."

"Nana Agyeman."

Then the same boy bellowed, "Okay! Now you *Ninos* bring your grimy faces closer and show us how you wash them every morning." Obviously looking for mischief, it was clear these boys took pleasure in harassing students whom they called "Ninos," a nickname given to first-year students in a sort of initiation process, carried out on an unsuspecting *Nino*, or newcomer.

Jerry and his friends had chosen us as their target for the nose pinching and face brushing with their palms swiftly down my face. I was defiant. I resisted this supposedly routine 'rite of passage' by hiding my face between the two pillars in the corridor, and as soon as I got the opportunity, I took off running to the classroom. My friends begrudgingly underwent the ritual. I did not take any time to imagine if I could outrun the older boys, but I was not prepared to subject myself to that ordeal. My gutsy escape managed to ensure that at least, I suffered less mistreatment to my face than my girlfriends did.

Just about an hour later, I walked into class looking for my desk, only to find the same Jerry John seated in the next row towards the back. *Oh no,* I thought. My eyes quickly shifted, and I pretended not to see him.

What is he doing in here? Isn't he supposed to be a senior? I was beyond surprised. As I sat in my seat, I struggled to maintain my composure and forced my gaze away from his. Then I thought, *if he's in this class, then he must have been held back,* I quickly concluded. *He's probably not smart enough to be with his mates.*

For a moment, my quick assumption gave me some comfort, and I dismissed him as unintelligent. Perhaps this overly poised "senior initiator" was not that impressive after all. I was confident I had uncovered the truth behind his apparent overconfidence, but I was in for a surprise.

Sure, he, Jerry John was in the same class year as I was, but he was also extremely bright. I found his circle of friends at school were not a reflection of his age, but of his personality. Then it began to fit, at least in my young mind, why he seemed to be liked by children much older than he.

I could not get past the initial encounter on my first day in Achimota School. Nothing could convince me that Jerry and I would become friends. I resolved to stay clear of him. I had slowly come to a point where I disliked him, even reporting his behaviour to the headmaster. But it seemed the more effort I put into staying away from him, the more frequently he reappeared.

I remember vividly how the chapels at Achimota had separate provisions, one for Catholic and another for Protestant worship. Since I had been raised Protestant, I joined the Protestant church choir. Jerry, who had been brought up Catholic, naturally attended Catholic worship. But when we were around 15, I remember him suddenly showing up one day to join the Protestant choir. A look of confusion crossed my face as I thought, again, *what is he doing here?*

Unfortunately, before I could find out, I got into trouble together with some of the other girls for disrupting the rehearsals. Mr. Ian Hall, the choirmaster, asked one of the girls to sing a particular song, with the right notes, in an alto tune. The poor girl was doing her best, but nothing she did seemed to bring her close to the perfect pitch that Mr. Hall was hoping for. It was amusing in the moment, equally frustrating for the choirmaster. Most of the choir chuckled quietly to themselves and turned with straight faces when Mr. Hall looked in their direction. A few of us could not hold our giggles.

Fed up with our antics, the choirmaster abruptly kicked us out of choir for unruly behaviour. "Students here must be serious!" Mr. Hall bellowed. "If you refuse to be serious, then you are not permitted to stay in this choir." We were asked to gather our belongings and leave. It was particularly disappointing for me because the choir had been rehearsing from the beginning of the school term for a performance at the Flagstaff House in just a few weeks' time. I was crushed. At the time, I had no idea that Jerry—the new choir boy—had only joined the group to be closer to me.

It was much later that I found that Jerry had no interest in even being a part of the choir in the first place. Now that I was kicked out, his motivation and apparent desire to learn Protestant hymns suddenly went out of the window! His only thought soon became how to make a quick exit himself. For the moment, the self-assured boy had trapped himself in an otherwise noble undertaking, one that all his clairvoyance and alluring attitude couldn't help him escape easily.

One rainy afternoon at Achimota, I was making my way to Kingsley House after class without an umbrella. As I hopped over puddles in an attempt to find cover so my books would stay dry, Jerry spotted me from a distance. Hoping to catch my attention, he snatched an umbrella from another student and rushed over in my direction. Just as I reached a street crossing, he appeared, seemingly out of nowhere, smiling broadly and holding the umbrella steadfastly over both of us.

Without expression or uttering a word, I crossed the street, inwardly happy to have a cover, but outwardly determined to be stubborn as he provided shelter and proudly acted as if he had saved me from the rain. Upon reaching the other side, I made a speedy departure towards a dry, covered area under a veranda. I saw a flash of disappointment cross his face, followed by his demand for my acknowledgement.

"Umm… excuse me?" he questioned.

"Yes?" I answered.

"Haven't you forgotten something?"

"Like what?"

"Shouldn't you say thank you for my taking you across the street under the umbrella?"

Later in our lives, Jerry insisted that I looked at him and said, "You should be honoured to have walked me under that umbrella." And with that, I walked away. I cannot remember being so brazenly curt, and even harsh, especially to a young man who had done his best with a kind gesture. Nevertheless, this moment began the cat-and-mouse game that marked our young friendship in Achimota School.

The school grounds at Achimota were vast and spacious and kept spotlessly clean. They spread across 950 acres of land, with large shade trees lining the roads around the compound and neatly trimmed hedges bordering the paths that ran between airy, whitewashed, colonial-style buildings. There were the teaching and administration blocks, ten boarding houses - seven for boys and three for girls, a dining hall, assembly hall, a school farm, a swimming pool and chapels, one designated for Protestants and the other for Catholics.

The grounds were well-equipped with a sizeable athletic playing fields, including a cricket oval, a football and hockey pitch, volleyball and netball courts and a huge arboretum with trees from all over the world. There was also a gymnasium for indoor sports like table tennis and gymnastics, which I personally enjoyed, and each sport was taught by a host of specialist teachers. If injuries occurred during sporting events, they were quickly taken care of at the fully staffed and equipped school hospital.

Achimota was renowned for its high academic standards, at par with some of the best schools in Europe. It was staffed mostly by expatriate teachers from countries like Great Britain, Canada, the United

States, Ireland, India and the Soviet Union. We also had excellent local-ly-trained teachers from Ghana and other parts of West Africa. What I loved most about Achimota was the wide scope of learning. The curriculum was designed to create a well-rounded student with leadership abilities and broad knowledge.

In the classroom, we studied standard courses like maths, the sciences, geography, history, English language and literature. Additionally, we were able to choose from courses like astronomy, beekeeping, agriculture, and sewing. Daily activities ranged from farming at the school farm to swimming to working in the arboretum to gardening, sports, and daily prayer. Evenings were spent in prep study, a period intended for doing homework or preparation for the next day's classes.

Interestingly, some of our art courses, such as pottery, wood carving, weaving, and sculpture were taught by local artisans who had expertise in their craft, but no formal education. I remember one incredibly accomplished pottery teacher, Mr. Mosla, who could barely read nor write. He was a master craftsman who was gifted in ceramics and earned all of our admiration as we watched how effortlessly he went about his work. One day, he was exceptionally proud of a pot I had created in his class. It had been very challenging running my fingers through the slippery clay to make something that would resemble what he had shown us. He joyfully commented that I had done very well. The awkward moment happened during my practical exam when I was so sure I could easily recreate the pot. I was quite pleased with the outcome. Mr. Mosla, too, seemed very impressed.

Then I received my report card while on vacation at home, only to find my score: "F". Why would Mr. Mosla give me an "F" when he had told me only a few weeks before that I was a "very good student", and done so with such a broad smile on his face?

When school resumed for the next term, I rushed back to the Pottery Department to question him about my grade.

"Mr. Mosla, did I fail my pottery exam?"

"No. Nana, you did very well," he said, smiling.

"But sir, why did you give me an 'F'?"

"Yes, 'F' is the highest. So those who didn't do well, got 'A'."

Mr. Mosla was just as calm-mannered and respectful as he was a masterful craftsman. He patiently listened as I tried to explain how the grade should have been reversed. Realising his mistake, he passed a light-hearted comment, we laughed, and he went on his way to make corrections to the grades for the entire class. It was at such moments that Achimota made a young girl appreciate the worth of every person, regardless of how different their life's path may have been. We were fortunate to learn from the people who were the best at their crafts, but what made the biggest impression on our young minds was the humility with which they carried themselves.

Each of the boarding houses had a mix of students, ranging from the first year to the sixth-year students. The students came from different ethnicities, even from different countries and socioeconomic backgrounds.

When I moved to Kingsley House, there were four dormitories to a house, and each dormitory had about twelve to eighteen girls. As part of our training, we were each assigned rotating cleaning duties—scrubbing the bathroom floors, cleaning the toilets, sweeping the halls, dusting the common room and maintaining the house grounds and garden. Each assignment was reinforced by daily and weekly inspections by the house prefects and house mistress, who usually doubled as teachers too.

Life at Achimota was about diligent work and exciting play. Every waking hour had been mapped out for us—a full timetable that compelled obedience to it. Our mornings started with cleaning duties that had to be completed before 6:45 a.m. Then a bell sounded for morning inspection which was our cue to stand to attention and line up straight for Miss Harbourne—a strict, no-nonsense British woman who would file past, while pedantically peering at us from head to toe.

Miss Harbourne was our senior house mistress. Her checklist to pass inspections was long and thorough. Not a single, rebellious strand of hair, a lacklustre pair of shoes, a misaligned pillowcase in our living areas or a nervously-bitten down nail would escape her checks. If any of these fell short of her expectations, we were immediately called out to correct our mistakes. If we had the good fortune of making it out of the line of purgatory, as we saw it, what felt like paradise, by comparison, waited: morning worship at 7 a.m., but we were expected to be there five minutes beforehand.

After chapel, the entire student body moved to the dining hall by 7:30 a.m. for breakfast before classes began at 8:30 a.m. It would be much later in my life that I would come to truly appreciate the foundation of this regimen. It had been designed to shape our younger minds. It built character and instilled the discipline that travelled with us beyond the classroom.

One of my favourite house duties was gardening. Each of the boarding houses had a beautiful flower garden and hedges, to be maintained by the students. Once every term, there was a garden competition between houses and the judges were local professionals brought in especially by the school. Achimota encouraged a lot of inter-house competitions. There was inter-house swimming, inter-house music and performing arts shows as well as inter-house sporting events. In the same way that sports and the arts were taken seriously, so too was the maintenance of our house gardens. I liked the peacefulness of working outdoors. Before Achimota, I had learned quite a bit about caring for Maa's flower garden at home, so the love for gardening came easily to me.

Inspection for garden duty did not take place before morning chapel like most other duties. Due to the morning timetable, it was usually reserved for later in the day when we were in class. If you passed inspection, you heard nothing. But if you failed inspection, you were likely to be called out of class, as was my experience one horrific day.

I sat at my desk during Miss Coleman's English class, listening to her attentively when the class was interrupted, and she was called outside. After a brief moment, she returned, paper in hand, and announced, "Nana Agyeman, please come forward." In unison, all eyes turned to me. My heart raced, my eyes grew big, and I could not help but wonder, *What did I do?* I walked forward slowly.

"Yes, Miss Coleman?" I asked nervously.

"Nana," she whispered, leaning into me, in an effort to maintain my privacy. "Miss Harbourne has asked to see you right away. She's waiting outside," she said, her eyes studying my face. "Nana?" she questioned. "Do you know what this is about?" her face filled with sympathy.

"No," I answered, my eyes wide with sudden dread.

"Okay, well, never mind. You're free to go. I've given her my permission to take you out of class, but please make sure to complete your assignment for tomorrow."

"Yes, Madam," I said, only partially paying attention to that dialogue. My stomach grew queasy. Miss Harbourne's file-past routine was just a microcosm of her general modus operandi: to rule by fear and ridicule. If you fell out of line or misbehaved, she openly regarded you as an outcast and made sure everyone else harboured the same feelings towards you. She became famed for her use of public shaming to correct behaviour. As a consequence, everyone seemed to have a healthy dose of fear when it came to dealing with her.

As I stepped outside the classroom, Miss Harbourne's eyes, bulging with fury, met mine. Her lips were pinched like clenched fists, and her face wrinkled into a frown. She looked me up and down as I shifted uncomfortably under her gaze.

"Good morning, Miss Harbourne. Miss Coleman said you sent for me."

"Yes, I did. Nana," she started, "why didn't you do your work before going to class?"

"But... I did..." I replied, confused by her allegation. Her face darkened. Her eyes narrowed.

"You *did?*" she questioned in a tone of disbelief.

"Well, you better follow me." She turned and stormed off, as I followed, nearly skipping to keep pace, before I reached Kingsley House a few moments behind her, breathless.

As we reached the house, Miss Harbourne charged into the garden, leaned forward, and pulled out a shiny piece of metal hidden between two shrubs. "If you did your house duty, then *What is this?*" she hissed as she held the evidence high in the air. At first, I could not make out what she was holding, and then I realized it was an empty sardine tin can. I looked at it; then nervously at her, and then my eyes shifted back to the can. I stood there defenceless—unable to give an answer.

It had been a simple oversight on my part, but inexcusable neglect in her eyes. As my punishment for this offence, that afternoon, she made me give up my rest hour, and instead, I had to spend most of the afternoon working in the garden, watering the plants and cleaning the house grounds. From that day, I could not help but meticulously check every inch of my housework to be sure it never happened again. Perhaps in Miss Harbourne's eyes, what defined a person's character is the commitment to the details even in the seemingly routine moments of our lives.

Boarding school had become a real awakening. It stretched my mind intellectually and forced me to think in ways I never had before. It expanded my world—and as my world grew, so did my outlook on life. At Achimota, I formed friendships with students from all over Ghana and beyond. These relationships led to unique encounters with a myriad of worldviews, all of which were to shape my own, and challenge my assumptions. I remember how in those days, the determining factor to study at Achimota for the majority of students had been the Common Entrance Exam.

There were, however, a small percentage of students whose admission process differed. They were high-achieving students from rural schools across the country that underwent a rigorous interview process and were subsequently granted admission based on the results of their interviews and their academic performance. Often, due to their socioeconomic backgrounds, some of the students were offered academic scholarships to waive the tuition fees. Ultimately, Achimota became something of a melting pot, blending together students from various regions, faiths, ethnic backgrounds and to some extent, social strata. The school brought to life the motto, *ut omnes unum sint*,that all may be one, and that was to leave a lasting impression on me in my adolescent years.

Still, it was not until I had a chance encounter with a woman from a rural part of the country on the compound that my conscience was awakened to the harsh realities of poverty, class differences and female oppression in our society.

One afternoon while I was strolling around the compound, I met a weary woman just outside Kingsley House. She was doing her best to set a basket of food atop her head, struggling to keep her balance. She wore a traditional blue and white *kaba* (a cloth blouse), wrapper (skirt) and matching headdress. Her flat, worn slippers were caked with enough mud to tell of the distance they may have covered in the afternoon rain showers. She was medium height, her skin was leathery and sun-drenched, and the whites of her eyes were visibly yellow. Footsore and weary, she forced a smile and called out to me.

"My lady, please," she paused. "Help me put this down," she request-ed, referring to the large load balanced on her head.

"Oh yes," I replied and swiftly complied. As I helped her lower the basket, my eyes quickly scanned the wide variety of fruits and other items inside—oranges, pineapple, *kenkey,* fried fish and hot pepper.

"Oh, thank you, my lady. Thank you very much," she said, looking relieved. "Umm, I'm looking for Mercy and her sister Dinah. Do you know them?"

"Mercy? Yes, I do," I replied, as it occurred to me that Mercy bore a fleeting resemblance to the woman.

"Can you call her for me? And Dinah too? They are my daughters," she said proudly and then flashed a warm and lingering smile. "Tell the girls their mother is here to visit them."

"Yes Madam," I said and flew through the front door and up the steps of Kingsley House to the first floor and into dormitory "B", where Mercy lived. I found her sitting on her bed, relaxing and sewing by hand what looked to be an apron. Two other girls sat on her bed conversing with her while a third lay reading.

"Mercy" I shouted, "you have a visitor!" Mercy looked up and smiled, wide and radiant.

"A visitor?" she said expectantly.

"Yes, it's your mother" I replied, proud to be the bearer of important news. "She's waiting for you in the front yard, so you better hurry."

Her smile died as quickly as it appeared. Mercy dropped her sewing on the bed and shot a quick glance through the window. Looking startled, she froze as if all life was sucked out of her while the four of us stared at each other in confusion.

"Mercy?" I called out. "What is it? Has your mother left? She was just there a minute. . ."

"Oh, leave me alone!" she shot back, cutting me off mid-sentence.

"I need to find my sister Dinah, quick!" She jumped up, ran past me and stormed out the door.

"Did you see how she behaved?" I asked the other girls, feeling slighted. "All I did was tell her that her mother was here. It's as if I brought her bad news."

"I'm surprised too," added one of the girls. "She's never like this."

"Well, whatever she's like, she has no business behaving like this towards me."

"Ah, I wouldn't worry. I'm sure she'll come back thanking you after her mother leaves," put in the other girl.

Just then, I peeped through the same window Mercy had and was shocked to see the woman still alone where I had left her. Visibly hot and tired, she was now sitting on a short flight of steps, resting her weary head on her right palm with her basket of food items faithfully keeping her company.

"What is going on?" I shouted. "Where are these girls? It's nearly 5 o'clock. Very soon visiting hours will end."

One of the girls then suggested that we should check Clark House, where Mercy's sister, Dinah, lived to see if something was holding them up. When we arrived, neither of the girls was there, nor had anyone seen them. I was at a loss. I suddenly felt a tremendous weight of responsibility on my shoulders. I thought to myself, what was I going to tell their mother? That her daughters suddenly vanished? How could I even fathom the thought that they bolted because they were too ashamed of her?

While they made every effort to avoid her, I was left with the unenviable task of going back to deliver the bad news. "I am sorry Madam. I tried, but I can't seem to find either of your daughters."

A look of dejection crossed the woman's face as if she knew the circumstances that prompted my white lie. Her broad shoulders suddenly drooped in resignation. And though she said no more, I could tell she knew the truth—that her daughters were hiding behind a wall of shame. She stooped to collect her belongings like someone collecting the pieces of a shattered dream. It had to be a bitter disappointment. I was saddened by the scene that day and appalled by the arrogance and posturing of the sisters. The situation left me feeling heavy-hearted. Nonetheless, the image of their mother, an authentic picture of rural Ghanaian womanhood, left a powerful and enduring imprint on my mind.

When school was over for long vacation, I was always excited to return home to Maa's home-cooked meals and Dee's insightful talks. I could not wait to test some of my newly-acquired knowledge from the classroom on anyone who would listen, who, by default, was usually only my parents.

Feeling almost entitled to some rest and relaxation after an arduous term in school, I was soon reminded that the romanticism of home-life was slightly more ethereal than real. In our home, in spite of the holidays, some things never changed. Saturday mornings were always reserved for general house-cleaning: sweeping, washing, gardening, kitchen chores, tidying the dining room, sitting room, and bedrooms. Each of my siblings and I had our own area of responsibility. By Maa's rules, there was no time to laze around until all work was done.

On one of these Saturday mornings, the doorbell rang. Before I could answer the door, my mother skilfully intervened and made her way to the front entrance. It was Jerry. I tried to eavesdrop and watch from a distance as best as I could.

"Good morning Madam," he said, greeting Maa with a pleasant smile.

"Morning," Maa replied, her expression straight-faced and forbidding.

"Sorry to disturb you, Madam. My name is Jerry John. I attend Achimota, and I am looking for Nana Konadu. We are friends from school, and I just want to say hello... please." His charm, usually disarming to the student on Achimota compound, had no effect on Maa. Although he was respectful, his confidence seemed to slightly irk her. As a mother of six girls, she was unsurprisingly suspicious of every boy who appeared at her front door, but especially one who seemed as full of confidence as a young Jerry John. She had no way of knowing Jerry had left Achimota after we finished our fifth year, and had enrolled in the military academy.

"Young man, Konadu is busy doing her housework. You wouldn't want to disturb her, would you?"

"No, no Madam, not at all."

"Good. Then I'll tell her you were here," she said as she gestured to close the door.

"Madam... Please... can I wait?"

"*Wait?* For what?" she snapped, visibly taken aback by his determination.

"For her to finish," he smiled, pleading with his eyes.

"Young man, in this house, there is no time to chat on Saturday mornings."

"Yes Madam," he replied, and then quickly added, "Madam, I can also help clean around the house."

His persistence surprised Maa.

"Young man, what did you say your name was?"

"Jerry John... Madam."

"Remove your cap!" she ordered and walked him outside around the house.

When Maa recalled the story years later, she said, "I told him to clean all my French windows, which he did—and cleaned them beautifully. After he was done, he asked politely for permission to leave, knowing Konadu and her sisters were still working. But he came again."

On his second visit, he came on a Sunday. Maa answered the door and once again, he greeted, "Good morning, Madam."

"Morning," Maa replied, noticeably annoyed that he had returned so soon.

"Madam, please, I would like to see Nana Konadu."

"Young man, it's Sunday, and on Sundays, we have church service."

"Yes, Madam."

"But, you can go and wash my car," she told him. And without hesitation, Jerry enthusiastically complied.

While he was washing Maa's car, her cousin, Mr. Owusu Afriyie, who at the time was serving as the Conservator of Forests, drove in for a visit. As he parked his car, he noticed the light-skinned young man busily working. Mr. Owusu Afriyie came into the house, greeted Maa, and could not keep his thoughts to himself. Half-jokingly he said, "Ei! Sister, so you now have *oburoni* (white man) to wash your car? If so, then let him wash my car too." Jerry washed both cars clean and afterward, politely asked for permission to leave. But he was sure to return again.

Before granting him any visiting rights, Maa certainly made him work for it. Peeking through the windows, I giggled as I watched him wash Maa's car. But Jerry seemed happy just to be around our home. It appeared that the more often my mother saw him, the more she made sure to find chores for him to do around our house. Her intention was probably to keep him occupied and minimise the time he could spend with me. There were some days he would pass by the kitchen and see me polishing Maa's kitchen floors, or her silverware, or the wooden tables. What must have been intended to be a deterrent for young Jerry had gradually become his excuse to visit. So long as he could come to the house, he did Maa's chores with enthusiasm.

Interestingly, the one person in our home who caught Jerry's imagination and seemed to have earned his highest respect was my father. Jerry was fascinated by my father's demeanour and commitment to family. Dee embodied the many things he expected in a father figure, and eventually, he would become an important role-model in Jerry's young life.

CHAPTER TEN

The Last Page of History
What We Leave Behind Leads the Way

It had to be a painful journey for my father, seeing all of the promises the country held in its grip slip away one moment after another. It was as if the politics of the day had overtaken the heart and common sense of the men and women who held the reins of power and not even the most obvious turning points eluded them. Gradually, the CPP had been fixated on fulfilling campaign promises to such an extent that any voice that raised a contrary viewpoint to what they were bent on achieving had to fall by the wayside. My father somehow believed that a country could reset its priority and still become the shining example it had set out to become at the dawn of its independence.

By 1965, there were several United States' CIA operatives active in Accra. As Nkrumah prepared for his second state visit to China, this time to try to negotiate an end to the Vietnam War, he composed his last will and testament, which began, "I Kwame Nkrumah of Africa," as if he sensed his own end was near.

The night before his departure, Nkrumah called my father, as he often did, to come to Flagstaff House for a late night meeting. Dee never told me what was discussed that night, but he did remark almost quietly to himself that Nkrumah was a very lonely man. The following morning, on February 22, 1966, my father went to see Nkrumah off at the airport, not knowing that would be the last time he would ever lay eyes on Osagyefo.

Two days later, in the early morning hours of February 24, 1966, a group of senior army officers of the Ghana Armed Forces in collaboration with the British-trained Ghana police overthrew Nkrumah's government in a well-organised coup d'état, with the backing and funding of the CIA. The CIA denied any involvement at the time and its decisive role in the "coalition coup." Perhaps it was not until a 1970's memoir, *In Search of Enemies* by John Stockwell, who was now a retired CIA officer that the strands of the clandestine operation that crippled a country unravelled. Stockwell had become critical of the United States government's policies after serving in the Agency for thirteen years.

In his book, Stockwell provided first-hand testimony of the CIA's role in the overthrow of Nkrumah. He detailed how the agents at the CIA's Accra station had been instrumental in outlining the framework with the plotters in order to ensure success of the mission. In a 2002 interview, Stockwell spoke of his friend and colleague, Howard T. Banes, another American who had operated undercover in Accra as a political officer in the U.S. Embassy but had been the linchpin in the greater undertaking to oust Kwame Nkrumah.

Decades later, declassified CIA documents confirmed that the United States, with the help of Great Britain and France, masterminded the coup that overthrew President Nkrumah in 1966. Despite varying opinions over the extent of American involvement, one thing that was painfully clear was that the coup had been very well-planned, with skilled military precision and strategic execution. For a nation that had never had any military overthrow, the high degree of intelligence involved in the ouster of Nkrumah left the world, and surely Ghanaians, certain about the significant outside influences that had been the architect of this significant event.

Nkrumah's President's Own Guard Regiment (POGR), his presidential guard and intelligence apparatus, made it impossible for the plotters to strike from Accra. So, when Nkrumah left Accra on Tuesday,

February 22, 1966, the coast was clear. Lieutenant Colonel Emmanuel Kwasi (E.K.) Kotoka, who was then in charge of troops in Tamale, and his adjutant, Major Akwasi Amankwa Afrifa, mobilised their troops, a group of 600 soldiers stationed in northern Ghana, from Tamale to Accra on the pretext of going for a military exercise code-named "Operation Cold Chop". The journey took two days since they moved only under the cover of night and avoided the road during the day. Major Afrifa may have been especially motivated to see the coup succeed, as he was scheduled to face a court-martial the next day, on February 25, 1966, for insubordination.

As they moved south, the soldiers were divided up and led to the capture of various government buildings. When the commander of the Ghanaian army, Major-General Charles Barwah, refused to coop-erate with the coup, he was reportedly shot to death in cold blood by Lieutenant Colonel Kotoka. Time was of the essence and resistance of any kind was not to be tolerated.

Units of the army were ordered to occupy key installations in Accra and other major cities. State Broadcasting House and international communications buildings were captured fairly quickly and early in the morning of Thursday, February 24, 1966, Lieutenant Colonel E.K. Kotoka announced the coup to the nation in a radio broadcast that control now rested in the hands of the military, the CPP was banned, and Nkrumah's government was overthrown.

I was 17 and in my fifth year at Achimota when I was awoken by noisy disturbances coming from outside my room at Kingsley House. We had a radio in our common room which would typically broadcast news and radio programs daily from 5 a.m. to midnight, but on this particular morning, the volume was unusually loud. Concerned by the confusion, I got up to see what was going on. By the time I reached the common room, I saw several girls, some of them wide-eyed, gathered around the radio, listening attentively to the radio announcer.

"What is it? What's going on? Why is the radio so loud?" I questioned nervously.

"Nkrumah has been overthrown," one girl solemnly replied.

"What? Overthrown? By who?" I responded, incredulous.

"The military... they're saying the Ghana army has taken over the government."

I could not believe what I was hearing, and I immediately thought of my father.

That morning, the army immediately suspended the constitution and soldiers went round arresting CPP ministers. But the coup was not without resistance. Fierce fighting broke out at Flagstaff House when the army, led by Major Afrifa, attacked President Nkrumah's presidential guard of roughly 200 men. For several hours, heavy fighting persisted between the troops and the president's security guards. Neither side showed signs of caving in. By the time Nkrumah's guards surrendered, at least 20 of them had lost their lives, and 25 were severely wounded.

Meanwhile, that same day, President Nkrumah's plane landed in Peking, the first stop of what was scheduled to be a grand Asian tour on the way to Hanoi, North Vietnam with the aim of adding his voice to broker peace in the Vietnam conflict. He was accompanied by a 70-person delegation, including Mr. Alex Quaison-Sackey who was serving as the Ghanaian Foreign Minister. In Peking, Dr. Nkrumah was officially welcomed by President Liu Shao-chi and was later informed of the coup, which at first, was not publicized in China to preserve the dignity of the Ghanaian president.

In a statement read by Mr. Quaison-Sackey the following day, Dr. Nkrumah declared that he was still the head of state of Ghana and that he would return home soon, with the full knowledge and hope that the people of Ghana would be loyal to him. On the same day, President Ahmed Sékou Touré of Guinea condemned the coup in Ghana and offered President Nkrumah political asylum in Guinea. On February 26, the North Vietnam News Agency stated that President Nkumah's visit to Hanoi had been postponed.

Tragically, the first coup in Ghana was very bloody—the bloodiest coup d'état in the history of the nation. Hundreds of Ghanaian citizens were killed for showing support or loyalty to Nkrumah. For one full week, hundreds of innocent men, women, and children were shot dead. Unconfirmed reports put the death toll as high as 1,600 across the nation. Nonetheless, as Nkrumah's biographer June Milne said, "Whatever the death toll, it was far from a 'bloodless coup'."

Dr. Nkrumah addressed the unprecedented violence in the country in his February 28 statement and left Peking for Moscow that same day in a Soviet aircraft. He continued from the Soviet capital to Conakry, Guinea, where he was welcomed by President Sekou Touré on March 2.

In his absence and following the overthrow, Ghanaian soldiers and police began to govern the nation through a new military regime called the National Liberation Council (NLC) with Major-General Joseph A. Ankrah as chairman and head of state, Police Commissioner John W. K. Harlley as deputy chairman and senior army officers Major Afrifa and Lieutenant Colonel E.K. Kotoka (promoted to major-general) as commander of the Ghanaian Army. It became well known that many of the coup plotters within the armed forces promoted themselves to higher ranks and eventually all had earned the designation of general, for one reason or another.

Not surprisingly, the agenda of the new government revolved mainly around the undoing of Nkrumahism. The NLC banned all political parties and declared that the aim of the coup was to end corruption and change the constitution in order to get Ghana back on a democratic footing. This was the first time a military junta took the sweeping measure of scrapping the entire constitution after seizing power.

As the regime tried to establish its legitimacy, there was widespread jubilation as Ghanaians pulled down Nkrumah's statue and spat on CPP officials as the new NLC government hauled them off to jail. The government also renamed various streets and institutions by removing

Nkrumah's name and set out to "re-educate" the public by launching a massive public relations campaign with the aim of destroying the image of Nkrumah not only in the urban centres, but also among people in rural areas. To this end, the Ministry of Information deployed many vans over several months to villages promoting the new government.

In the case of my family, we did not go through these turbulent times unscathed. Though my father was a leading official in a government-owned institution, he had maintained his status as a 'political outsider' and his integrity as a business professional. So even after the coup took place, my father continued his obligations without too much interruption as the general manager of GNTC. It was his long-standing service and commitment to GNTC which protected his employment there and our livelihood through successive coups and counter-coups until his eventual retirement in 1972. But at every turn, the CPP leaders threatened that they would rather their own man, a party loyalist, hold that position.

In moving the country away from socialism, the military took specific measures to purge the government of any individuals who had left-wing tendencies. In the first week of its rule, the NLC expelled all Russian technicians and teachers and all Chinese technical workers from Ghana. They then set out to erase all symbols and imagery of "Nkrumahism," even declaring a campaign to eliminate the "myth of Nkrumah."

All traces of Nkrumah went up in smoke: the military staged a ceremonial bonfire of his books, pamphlets, party literature, photos and historical records. The new leaders ordered all schools to do the same. Since the soldiers had guns, civilians had no choice but to comply.

I distinctly remember a radio broadcast announcing that anyone—irrespective of age, gender or social standing—who was found carrying a picture, book, printed material of Nkrumah or a CPP party card, would be subject to arrest and imprisonment without the option of a trial. Upon hearing this, I asked myself if these were not the same people who were opposed to the same injustice, the detention without a trial, under Nkrumah's Preventive Detention Act. It was sad and rather strange that they had become the same men and women who were now imprisoning Ghanaians for possessing photos or literature of Nkrumah. How could they conceivably call themselves stalwarts of democracy?

At the beginning of the coup, the NLC spoke of "democracy," yet the wave of book burnings became symptomatic of just the opposite—a harsh and oppressive regime seeking to censor or silence a critical part of our nation's history. This was perhaps an inherent flaw in the NLC agenda—their direct attempt to erase Nkrumah's legacy from Ghana's history.

Adding to our anxieties at Achimota, a number of Russian teachers were rounded up and presumably shipped away to their home countries. I remember feeling frightened and uneasy at the time of such drastic change in our country. Suddenly, we were all following orders to burn any books, pictures, literature or artifacts that bore Nkrumah's name, image or ideology. From one dormitory to the next, we took down Nkrumah's pictures. If we wanted to keep any, we did so at our own risk.

What I found most disturbing, however, was the sight of the newly appointed United States Ambassador on Achimota school grounds to supervise our book burning exercise. Many of the students, even in our naiveté about politics and the political wrangling, could not fathom the sight of an ambassador from the United States, a country which boasted its love for freedom of speech and one that diligently preserved its own history, helped turn ours into ashes. The imagery was stunning, and we struggled to piece together why anyone from the United States would openly oversee the destruction of our written history, irrespective of the current tide of government.

From the little I knew of the men around Nkrumah, I immediately felt a deep sense of betrayal for him, and imagined he would too. The new ambassador was an African-American who coincidentally had been a former classmate of Nkrumah at Lincoln University. His presence at Achimota felt like an unwelcome visitor sitting in on a family quarrel. It unnerved me to see him at our school at such an unstable moment in our country's history. His supervising the burning of our own literary works and anything even remotely associated, but many of which have no relation to Nkrumah, felt repulsive.

As I flung my collection of books, photos, and pamphlets into the fire, I had an overwhelming feeling of sadness watching the leaves flap as they flew into the hottest parts of the blaze. Collectively, our whole student body stood there until all our books smouldered in the raging flames.

I recalled the days as Young Pioneers when we were indoctrinated to believe that "Nkrumah never dies"—a phrase many of us did not fully grasp. Understandably, as I grew into a young adult, I came to find that it was not a literal death that we were to believe, not Nkrumah's immortality. Of course, *people* die, but ideology and teachings never die. Without a doubt, Ghana benefitted tremendously from Nkrumah's foresighted investments in education, healthcare, and infrastructural developments. But one of the most important contributions Nkrumah made to Africa was a deep sense of pride in our own heritage, - what was known and propagated by Dr. Nkrumah as the *African personality*.

The truth remained, irrespective of the limitations of Nkrumah's ideology or even the integrity in the hearts of some of the people who occupied influential positions in his government. There was a legacy that would take much more than fire to wipe from Ghana's story. No army, no matter how aggressive and deliberate, could erase Nkrumah's ideology or achievements from Ghana's collective memory. We were young men and women staring at the reality that it would be impossible for any man to rid the world of books that embodied Nkrumah's eternal fight toward a drastic paradigm shift for all of Africa.

The certainty was not lost on us that Nkrumah's legacy was to live on, long after he had said his last goodbye to his motherland. He had been a prolific writer and one of the first African leaders to leave behind published works for posterity. So, in a way, his supporters had been right; Nkrumah never died.

As part of the agenda of the military government, the coup paved the way for Dr. Kofi Busia's return to Ghana, only a month later in March 1966, after seven years of self-exile. The NLC adopted the political tradition of Dr. Busia's former party, the United Party (UP), and soon appointed Dr. Busia as the Chairman of the government's National Advisory Committee. Sending a clear message to the West, the new government ceased all diplomatic relations with Russia, China, and Cuba, closing their embassies in Ghana, and withdrawing Ghana's embassies from their countries, in addition to North Vietnam and five other nations in Eastern Europe. The West viewed it all as a positive new direction in Ghanaian politics and economics and immediately rewarded Ghana by restoring food aid and relaxing policies designed to isolate our country.

Suddenly, world cocoa prices began to rise, and relations with Great Britain were restored and normalised.

Nkrumah would never return to Ghana, though he never gave up hope of one day returning home to continue his duties as president. To that end, he continued to write and publish books and make regular shortwave broadcasts to Ghana from his home in Conakry, Guinea, where he remained in exile until his death in 1972, at the age of 62.

I often wondered how much of my father's work had been futile or derailed by party politics. I admired, more than anything, how he forged ahead amidst the chaos. When I was a young girl, every one of his words and actions painted indelible images, many of which made clear that life in our beloved Ghana had taken a different turn.

CHAPTER ELEVEN

SHAPE OF A DREAM
The Climb to Great Expectations

Halfway through the year 1966, both Jerry and I finished our Ordinary level (O-Levels) at Achimota with a General Certificate of Education. I opted to stay and complete my Advanced level (A-Levels) in the Sixth Form to prepare for university. Jerry, on the other hand, had decided to pursue his life-long dream of becoming a pilot, even though his mother wanted him to go to university to study medicine. Thus, she was bitterly disappointed when he left school after O-Levels and moved out of the family home to apply to the military academy. In 1967, he enlisted as a Flight Cadet in the Ghana Air Force.

Meanwhile, life for me as a sixth former was a transformation which forced me to grow in several ways. For one, my class sizes were smaller and teachers pushed us harder and expected more from us now that we were older and more mature. Since Sixth Form was focused on preparing us for a university, I had to adjust to the increased academic rigour and rise to the challenge of being a student leader.

At Achimota, I held two key leadership positions. One was as dormitory monitress in Lower Six, and later as a house *prefect* in Upper Sixth. Both roles profoundly impacted me and further shaped my character. A house prefect was an appointed senior who was given extra authority and responsibility to supervise other students and keep the house in order. Each prefect was supported by other students appointed as dormitory monitors (or monitresses for females). As a monitress, I guided younger students and made sure the house operated smoothly. When it was time to wake up, for instance, it was my responsibility to see to it that every girl in the house was out of bed and in the washroom getting ready.

By the time I was a dormitory monitress, Miss Harbourne had left Achimota and was replaced by Miss Elizabeth Halcrow, a wealthy English woman believed to be related to the family of Halcrow & Sons, a large British conglomerate. Miss Halcrow decided she wanted to spend some time in Africa and was appointed to run Kingsley House as our new house mistress. But unlike Miss Harbourne, whose strict order and demand for discipline *put the fear of God* in us, Miss Halcrow struggled to get students to even take her seriously.

One crop of girls proved especially troublesome. They were often caught smoking cigarettes or breaking lights-out rules and seemed to have no respect for any of the school's rules. Since punishments were not as severe and Miss Halcrow was lax on discipline, this unruly group of girls pegged her as weak and continued to test the limits of their freedom.

Late one night, after the house lights were turned off, this pack of girls took their mischief to a new level, as they ambushed Miss Halcrow in a dark hallway and cowardly began to beat her under the cover of darkness. I was in my room reading on my bed when I heard the scuffle and immediately jumped to my feet and ran in that direction. I switched on the house lights and there on the floor, I witnessed a shaken Miss Halcrow, flanked between two of her offenders. "What is going on?" I screamed and ran toward her and just as quickly, her offenders ran off.

Outraged, I took the issue into my own hands and went to report the incident to school officials and then identified the ringleaders to the school's security. Both girls were immediately punished and suspended for the long run. The incident drew attention to the misconduct of a few girls in Kingsley House, which not only stopped the harassment of

Miss Halcrow, but restored some much-needed discipline and order in Kingsley House.

The following year, I was selected house prefect when I entered the Upper Sixth Form. As house prefect, my responsibilities began just before the first day of school, at which time I welcomed and greeted first-year students who arrived in flocks, luggage in tow, accompanied by bewildered parents. "Welcome to Achimota. My name is Nana Konadu Agyeman. For those of you in Kingsley House, I am the house prefect, and I am here to help you. Now, if you follow me, I will lead you to your dormitory." It actually felt good knowing I was helping new students make the often difficult transition from home to boarding school.

In addition to monitoring student behaviour, I was also responsible for the safety and well-being of all students in Kingsley House. My mind often recalls moments when, if a student became ill, I was expected to get them medical assistance or, if needed, transportation to the school hospital. I was also in charge of assigning the house duties, with the help of the dormitory monitresses, who would assist me in preparing the duty roster for each of the students. Assigned jobs included maintenance of the house clinic, where we stored necessary first aid supplies; and running of the house shop, which included customer service and managing the daily accounts.

Students who ran the shop generated a daily sales report for my review. But before the report reached me, they turned it over to another sixth form student who reviewed the accounts for accuracy and then turned it over to me for final approval and signature. I then turned the report, together with all monies earned, over to the housemistress. Without a doubt, it was a cumbersome process of checks-and-balances, but in the end, it taught some invaluable lessons in accountability, management, and leadership.

One Sunday afternoon in late 1967, I was in my room when one of the girls came to tell me I had a visitor. In Sixth Form, I especially looked forward to Sundays. That was our rest day. While I still had responsibilities, we were all given free time to receive visitors or to engage in our own activities. After church service, Maa would always pay me a visit, with some provisions and home cooked food to last throughout the week. After a long week, I always looked forward to seeing her. Knowing Maa had arrived, I put on fresh clothes, quickly fixed my hair and tidied myself up before going down to meet her. I hurried to the front room; however, Maa was nowhere to be found. To my astonishment, Jerry and two of his friends stood in the waiting area, - the Common Room. I was stunned. I stopped dead in my tracks.

"Aren't you happy to see us?" he said, smiling broadly. "We haven't been back here since we left in '66 and you don't even say hello?"

He held his arms open for a hug. I was lost for words, steeped in surprise and trying to contain my composure. Seeing him made me realise how different life in school had become, and the absence of boys and girls like Jerry, Eileen, Marjorie and others have changed the nature of our class student body and lost some of its character.

Before I could utter a word, he moved over toward me, held me in his embrace and turned both of us around in a full circle. We sat down and talked, laughed and reminisced for a while before he headed off. Our friendship had clearly changed. It had matured, just as we had. But for the first time, there was an attraction. I kept my feelings to myself. Soon after, in early 1968, he asked me to be his girlfriend and our relationship began—a few months before I left Achimota. As our love life swung from one end to another, Ghana's political pendulum seemed to also swing along, between 1966 and 1968.

Although successful, the coup of 1966 had several unintended consequences. Under the NLC government, military and police officers were increasingly appointed to public positions that were previously held by civilians. This not only politicized the Ghana Armed Forces, but it also led to a fragmented military. Barely a year after the overthrow of Nkrumah, there was a counter-coup on 17 April 1967, led by junior officers of the Ghana Armed Forces who wanted to overthrow the NLC government and return Nkrumah to power. That was what we heard on the radio.

Though the attempt was unsuccessful, the NLC government suffered some casualties. One, in particular, had been E.K. Kotoka, then Chief of Defence, who was shot and killed during heavy fighting at the Ghana International Airport. A towering figure of heroic status in the NLC, Kotoka was best known as the leader of the coup against Nkrumah. In his honour, the same airport would be later renamed Kotoka International Airport, and a life-size memorial statue was erected at the site of his death.

Shaken by their loss, the military government was determined not to let the attack go unpunished. In retribution for Kotoka's death, the NLC, led by Lt. General Afrifa, decided to carry out death sentences. This drastic turn of events was to be without any trial and was to be characterised by public firing-squad for the first time in Ghana's history. On Tuesday, 9 May 1967, the NLC government set a precedent by having the leaders of the coup, two junior officers convicted of treason, executed by firing squad before a crowd of thousands at the Teshie Military Range, in full view of the public road between the port city of Tema and Accra.

As news broke of the military's actions, I remember the wave of shock that came rippling through Achimota. In the classrooms, teachers were busily trying to calm a mixed bag of anxious and excited students, but in Kingsley boarding house, it was up to me, as house prefect, to maintain calm and a sense of normalcy.

Admittedly, I was nervous, but I had to put on a brave face for the younger girls. As a diversion, I focused more than usual on house duties, but below the surface, I was fighting to swallow my own fear of an increasingly divided military government. Without a doubt, uncertainty hung over Ghana like a menacing cloud with no sign of passing.

It was clear that despite initial expectations, the removal of Nkrumah did not solve Ghana's problems. In spite of the vast political changes, it did little, if anything, to improve the economic standards of the people. From the onset, the military government promised to restore a democratic government as quickly as possible, yet the ban on forming political parties remained in force more than two years later—even after I graduated from Achimota in July of 1968.

I was 19 years old and preparing to leave Ghana to attend a university in London. At the time, my sister Yaa Achia was studying and working in Geneva, and my brother was studying in London. My father thought it would be a good experience for me to live and study abroad, too, while earning a degree in economics, though economics was not my field of choice. I was more inclined towards art and graphic design, but I was willing to curb my ambitions for the opportunity to travel.

Admittedly, I was caught up in the novelty of going to school in Europe, even though I had been admitted into Ghana's two leading universities, the University of Ghana in Accra and the University of Science and Technology (UST) in Kumasi. Due to strike actions, however, the University of Ghana had suddenly closed its doors, sending all enrolled students home until further notice. While the strike was a setback, the timing worked in my favour.

My father had plans to travel to the UK on business, so with this development, he quickly arranged for me to travel with him. "We don't know how long this will last," he said. "So I will take you with me to London to register you at the London School of Economics. We'll get you settled into a boarding house, and then I'll move on to attend my meetings. So start packing."

Filled with excitement, I spent my final days in Ghana saying my last goodbyes to friends and family. I said goodbye also to Jerry, who was at the time stationed in Sekondi-Takoradi, where he was training to become a pilot officer with the Ghana Air Force. Although I was nervous to leave Ghana, I was quietly elated at the thought of my relatively good fortune. Many of my friends could only dream of such an opportunity, and here I was embarking on it.

Up until the last day, family members bid me farewell with loving words of advice and encouragement. "Konadu, don't get distracted, you hear?"

"Yes Auntie, I hear you," I replied.

"Focus on your studies and make us proud, ok?"

I was deeply touched by the show of love in my last days in Accra, but nothing moved me more than the surprise send-off party organised by friends in my honour. We danced and celebrated late into the night with lots of laughs. Jerry came, leaving his post for a couple of days, to come and say goodbye.

The night before my departure, I spent the evening in my room sorting out some last minute packing when my Uncle Harry, my father's younger brother, dropped by the house unexpectedly. He knew Dee and I were traveling the next day but requested an urgent meeting with my father in his study.

As busy as I was, I thought nothing of it and kept packing. However, in the course of that meeting, the unthinkable happened. Uncle Harry, who was working as a senior Economics lecturer at the University of Ghana, convinced my father that it was not wise for him to pay for the education of what would now be a third child overseas. In his opinion, I could go to school in Ghana for free on a full scholarship. "My brother, why would you pay fees for another child to go to school in Europe when the Ghana government will pay her full tuition here? Think about it," he said.

With great conviction, my uncle reasoned with my father using an old Akan proverb, *"If you send one sheep to graze and it doesn't come back, you don't send a second, or a third, because the first may have been eaten by a wolf."* With those words, my dreams of travel were crushed. The entire plan was scrapped, and my father, convinced of my Uncle's logic, travelled the next day without me.

I was devastated. I sat in my room, surrounded by overstuffed suitcases, crying inconsolably for hours.

To make matters worse, my Uncle Harry promised my father that he would take personal responsibility for getting me registered in school in Kumasi at UST. Making good on his promise, he arrived early the next day to take me to Kumasi by public transportation. I was in disbelief. Instead of sitting next to my father on a plane to London, I was sitting next to my uncle on a bus to Kumasi. I thought to myself, how did this happen? Sulking in disappointment, I sat quietly the entire journey, with dark thoughts swirling through my mind. I wish this bus driver would lose control and have an accident on the road—anything to get me out of starting school in Ghana, I thought foolishly to myself. We arrived safely in Kumasi later that day, though I was late for registration as lectures had already started.

Wasting no time at all, my uncle took me straight to the registrar's office, where he used his influence as a university lecturer to plead on my behalf for them to take me into the School of Architecture. Again, that was not my subject of choice, but one both he and my father considered more practical than Art. At the urging of my uncle, they bent their rules barring late registration for unclaimed scholarships, and I was granted entry and enrolled without incident into the School of Architecture on full scholarship—an enormous feat in those days in the usually slow and bureaucratic system of higher education.

For housing, I was given accommodation in Africa Hall, the only all-girls housing unit on campus. Uncle Harry saw me to my room and handed me pocket money. "Here," he said, extending his arm, and gave me twenty *cedis*. "Your father instructed me to leave this with you."

"Thank you," I said solemnly, still wallowing in self-pity.

He let out a sigh, and said, "Well… I believe that's everything. Are you all right?" he asked, anxious to catch a bus back to Accra.

"Yes, I'm fine," I replied, eager for him to go.

"Well, if nothing else, then I will leave you now, so you can settle into your room."

For much of my adult years, I looked back at this incredible turning point in my life, and regret that I was unable to recognise my uncle's efforts.

As soon as my uncle left, I made up my mind that I was not going to study architecture. I thought, if I was going to stay in Ghana, then I might as well study something I enjoy. So the next day, I marched back to the registrar's office to put in a request to change my course. They were not happy.

"Why are you changing your course?" the registrar angrily demanded. "Just yesterday, Mr. Agyeman was here with you and said you are here to study architecture. So why the change today? And where is he?"

"Sir, he had to return to his work in Accra at the University of Ghana. So he asked me to come to see you to please make the change for us before it is too late," I said, my voice quivering.

Naturally, after my uncle's efforts the day before, the registrar was confused and therefore, resistant. But without any means to verify with my uncle, I was able to convince the office that it was a joint decision. So they granted my request and I was officially moved from the School of Architecture to the College of Art and Social Science.

Making this change not only boosted my morale but gave me a much-needed sense of independence. Just knowing that I was able to take charge of my own destiny without any pushback from my family helped me move past the disappointment and begin moving forward. I cannot remember ever going back to tell my parents that I was studying Art while I was pursuing the degree. They might as well find out for the first time on the day of graduation.

What was most important was how much of an incredible footing UST was to become in my life.

CHAPTER TWELVE

FOG AND MIRAGE

Student Activist: Confronting Corruption (1969 – 1972)

In April 1969, a bribery scandal forced the resignation of Ghana's head of state and leader of the military government, Lieutenant General Joseph A. Ankrah, Lieutenant General Akwasi Afrifa replaced him. He had become an intimidating personality, at least to many young people, following the raids he led on civilians in the weeks after the 1966 coup. Under his orders, General Afrifa unleashed a wave of violence on Nkrumah supporters. His grip on power as president was short-lived after a national election was held to replace the military government.

After three years of military rule (1966-1969) and a deteriorating economy, the NLC government was eager to return Ghana to civilian rule. So the military lifted the ban on multi-party politics in 1969, at which time Dr. Kofi Busia and his politically-minded friends and colleagues formed the Progress Party (PP) out of the former United Party.

From Dr. Busia's previous powerful position as Chairman of the military government's National Advisory Committee, there was no doubt that the military was paving the way for his rise to power. Leading up to the elections, the NLC assured Ghanaians that in spite of the winner, Ghanaians would enjoy more of the freedoms that democracy afforded because each of the candidates that was allowed to run in the 1969 elections was a proponent of Western democracy.

Nonetheless, with the backing of the military, Dr. Busia was given a clear advantage over his opponents. To ensure victory, he continued the military government's anti-Nkrumah rhetoric and played on ethnic loyalties to appeal to the Asante vote, and the Akan-speaking population, in general. This strategy worked. With the sole exception of the Volta and Greater Accra regions, Busia's Progress Party won the parliamentary election handily.

Following the victory, General Afrifa gladly ceded to Dr. Busia, who was sworn in as Prime Minister of the Second Republic of Ghana on September 3, 1969. However, presidential powers were still partially vested in Afrifa until August of the following year, when Mr. Edward Akufo-Addo, Chief Justice of Ghana, was elected the ceremonial president, replacing Lieutenant General Afrifa.

When Ghana returned to civilian rule in 1969, the parliamentary system was restored. The new constitution of the second republic was approved and introduced in August of 1969. Under this liberal arrangement, the president acted as a ceremonial head of state. The prime minister was the head of government and had the power to select his own ministers. A house of chiefs was also approved. In all, powers that were formally held by the president became broadly distributed. So when the second republic began in September 1969, many agreed that a parliamentary democracy had again been established in Ghana.

We watched carefully and hung our hopes for a bright future for our country on the promises we wanted so desperately to be honoured. A return to civilian rule was seen as a triumph for democracy. Ghanaians believed that since Dr. Busia and his parliamentarians were considered intellectuals, their decisions would be particularly forward-thinking and also reflect the general interests of the entire nation. But it was not to be. Ghanaian optimism soon turned to bitter disappointment when things took the opposite turn.

By the middle of 1971, Dr. Busia faced intense public criticism on a number of fronts. In his first year in office, he fired over 500 senior civil servants on suspicion that they had worked for the opposition during the election. Then in an attempt to solve the rising unemployment problem, he ordered the expulsion of all foreigners without valid residence permits out of Ghana. He had only been in office for a month and had promised to create more jobs by opening up the private sector to citizens.

Known as the "Aliens Compliance Order" of November 18, 1969, this drastic initiative led to the mass deportation of over one million Africans—including over half a million Nigerians—who recall being driven out of Ghana like cattle to the neighbouring countries of Upper Volta (present day Burkina Faso), Ivory Coast, Mali, Niger, Nigeria, and Togo.

The expulsion of aliens dealt a devastating blow to the Ghanaian economy. There were fewer labourers on the cocoa farms and fewer sanitary workers to clean the streets and perform some of the other vocations that had kept the country's wheels churning. In some towns where the citizens did not have the necessary capital to establish the type of small shops that had once been operated by "African aliens," commerce suffered. Subsequently, items that were once easily available became scarce or even impossible to acquire.

At the same time, the widespread reports of alleged corruption and mismanagement at the highest levels of Busia's government, and coincidentally Dr. Busia and his cabinet members had suddenly earned the highest salaries for public officials in the country's history. One headline that became characteristic of the chaos that plagued the era was when Ghanaian taxpayers sought to understand why the Prime Minister was receiving a housing allowance, for example, when he had decided not to live in the Castle but in his own home at Odorkor, in a residential area in Accra. The discontent deepened.

University students and young people coming of age were not the only ones voicing their displeasure at the government that had once promised a democratic society, only to witness those aspirations, like smoke, vanish into the thin air. It came without much surprise to many, the prevailing sentiment in the country was turned to one that saw

Dr. Busia as just as dictatorial as Kwame Nkrumah had been accused of being. He fired newspaper editors who disagreed with him. He dismissed the editor of the *Daily Graphic* for being critical of his views on the Apartheid regime in South Africa. Soon, Dr. Busia sacked constitutionally-appointed judges and used his power to interfere with the independence of the court system. Every one of these actions was met with little support.

As the world prices of cocoa and gold rose, so, it appeared, did the level of corruption in his government. In 1970, when Ghana had a boom cocoa harvest, there was widespread criticism that Dr. Busia had spent most of the proceeds on imports of luxury consumer goods to satisfy the urban bourgeoisie. Throughout Accra and parts of the country, it was rumoured that the Progress Party was diverting gold from Ghana to neighbouring Cote d'Ivoire in exchange for Peugeot cars for the Party elite.

It was in the middle of all this economic turmoil that many Ghanaians wondered how much of the promises we clenched to at the birth of our nation had been empty. How much of our pain had been our own doing. The series of unfortunate turns of events in individual homes had left unsettling feelings in the hearts of so many across the country. Meanwhile, the majority of Ghanaian citizens were grappling with crippling inflation, rising unemployment, and shortages of basic goods in local shops.

At the height of this pandemonium, in July 1971, the government introduced an austerity budget that called for the removal of employment-based benefits to civil servants but raised taxes. As part of the austerity budget, Busia's government cut down the number of military personnel to supposedly save public funds. For those who remained in the force, their benefits were also reduced, and soon after, taxes were imposed on the military.

This aggressive economic strategy included a significant reduction in expenditure for the country's armed forces, and the military was expected to pay taxes on items and replacement parts from overseas. For the men and women whose sole commitment was to sacrifice their own lives to protect the country, some of the basic benefits they once had during Dr. Nkrumah's years were, henceforth, obliterated. These cuts resulted in agitations at the barracks.

Ghanaians had come to understand the collective sacrifice that would be required of all of us to move the country forward. The tumultuous years had not eroded the underlying sense of our identity, and increasingly, we hoped our shared discomfort would yield brighter years ahead. But while the government was calling for austerity measures, Ghanaians believed that members of the administration were still indulging in corrupt acts and leading opulent lifestyles.

By December 1971, when the economy was on a grim downslide, the government took a desperate decision to devalue the currency, *cedi*, by more than 40 percent, and imposed a five percent national development levy on the people. This led to an immediate spike in the price of imports, and a further rise in inflation.

Life in Ghana had become unbearable for many. Against all expectations, Busia's government had created a country in which corruption was rife, and power lay only in the hands of a few powerful men and women. It had become evident that the nation's political stage had turned into one with exclusive circles of corrupt business and political elites who were handing power back and forth.

For a government that had once frowned upon foreign nationals as an integral part of the Ghanaian society, a growing number of Syrian and Lebanese business people had found opportunity in the political landscape and an avenue to exploit for commerce. Many of the businessmen and businesswomen who had become part of the elite group were retail store owners and importers of commercial goods and were able to excessively maximize profits in a mismanaged economy.

Occasionally my friends and I spent much of our afternoons recounting the events making headlines in Accra. On the university campus at

UST, we also learned about how the culture of corruption had seeped deeply into the administrative arm of the university. It became an open secret, although probably we were supposed to understand that it was the order of the day.

Many departments, including the registrar's office, were rife with bribery and the staff stole university funds, without any concern or consequence. They did not have to; no one uttered a word of protest. Everyone in the administrative offices seemed to have turned a blind eye. The same apathy that indirectly endorsed the sleaze and dishonesty of Busia's government seemed to have become the hallmark of the university too. Agitated, I became active in student politics.

Until this moment in my life, I had never really been interested in activism of any kind. I had seen the sacrifices my father, his family both in the CPP and the UP and his friends had to make ever since I was a little girl, and lived through the agonizing choices they had to endure to effect change in the destiny of a nation. I had seen how much of their genuine efforts were met with disdain and indifference and was not sure I wanted any part of it.

I could not stand aside for long. Soon, I found myself deeply engaged in student-led movements to address the growing culture of corruption on campus, and even beyond. It all happened so quickly, and every waking moment was to be consumed by making a difference. In 1969, I stood for student elections and was elected to serve on the Students Representative Council (SRC), a collective voice for the student body at UST.

As elected officers, one of our first initiatives was to open formal discussions with the Vice Chancellor. The goal was to address the blatant mismanagement by some employees on the UST campus. To our surprise, not only did he welcome us, but following the talks, both he and the university President granted us permission to hold peaceful demonstrations against campus corruption.

As the SRC secretary, I wasted no time in drafting plans to organise the event. The timing was right. It was well attended, but more importantly, the demonstration provided a major outlet for the widespread anger and frustration that was brewing on campus. That day, our SRC executives addressed a sea of angry students, some of whom carried placards and chanted in unison on the campus lawn. It was a peaceful protest and drew attention to the indiscretions of many university staffers. After all was done, we felt empowered to do more.

Less than two years later, I was elected to serve on the National Union of Ghana Students (NUGS), the largest and most important student organisation in the country. As a NUGS executive, I was to be part of the national governing board, consisting of student leaders from all over the country and from three major universities. We shared the same aspirations and brought together perspectives from the different parts of the country where we attended university.

One of my fellow board members from UST was a young man, Paul Victor Obeng, a mechanical engineering student who went by P.V. Obeng. We were both required to travel long distances together to attend national board meetings in other regions of Ghana, by public bus. P.V. Obeng and I became good friends due to our common obligations to NUGS.

Our first big meeting was the NUGS Congress in Accra in early 1971 on the campus of the University of Ghana. During the Congress, the overriding issue concerning all students was the growing atmosphere of corruption in Busia's government. What fascinated me was that we were no longer local. This had become a turning point in my own life. Once I had watched events unfold; now I had the opportunity to be part of them. We were now addressing concerns on a national level. I observed with keen interest as student leaders like Kan Tamakloe and other leading figures of NUGS led discussions.

The Busia administration and its officials living in opulence while the rest of Ghanaians struggled to survive a day, and violating the constitution by not declaring their assets, quickly became the sticking points.

"Moreover, let us not forget that, to this day, Dr. Busia and his Members of Parliament have refused to declare their assets as required by the Constitution of Ghana," yelled one student as he rose to his feet.

"This, my fellow students, is a clear breach of the constitution, and for this reason, I say that we expose them and hold them accountable by making Ghanaians aware…!" the student bellowed amidst deafening shouts of applause, which continued for several seconds.

I was in awe at the proceedings and the sheer excitement and passion that filled the room.

After the student spoke, his motion became the substance of a draft resolution that was drawn up during the Congress. It stated, in part, that:

"… as required by the Constitution of Ghana, Dr. Busia and all members of the Progress Party (PP) government must – as a matter of urgency – declare their assets to the people of Ghana."

—National Union of Ghana Students (NUGS)

In that resolution, we also called for the amnesty of political exiles, namely Kwame Nkrumah, so he could return home. There were reports that Nkrumah had become terminally ill with cancer while in Guinea, but Busia refused to allow the ailing former president to return home in his final days. Before the closing of the Congress, all NUGS executives were expected to sign the resolution before it could be delivered to parliament. As a representative of UST, I was happy to add my signature.

We sent a copy of the final resolution to Parliament and to the Prime Minister's office, as well as a formal letter to Parliament requesting an audience to present the resolution to members of parliament. To add pressure, we created mass awareness among the public by distributing copies of the resolution to the media, including GBC Radio and the only state newspapers available at the time, *The Ghanaian Times* and the *Daily Graphic*.

To prepare, NUGS carefully selected two groups of students to hand-deliver the resolution. The first group were the speakers, who would present the resolution in Parliament, and the second group was those who would accompany the speakers in solidarity. I was part of the solidarity group.

It was no secret that the parliamentarians were, as they put it, "fiercely opposed to students daring to complain" about them. What we did not anticipate, however, was the hostility we would encounter on the day of our presentation. Before our speakers could utter a word, Members of Parliament (MPs) began grumbling with strong disapproval at, of all things, the way we were dressed. This caught us completely off guard, as many of us were dressed in our best African attire.

"What are you people wearing?" yelled one MP with apparent disgust.

"Why aren't the men in suits and ties?" yelled another. "Don't you know this is Parliament?"

"Yes! This is no place for *batakari*." He referred to the traditional smock worn by a young man.

It never occurred to us that our attire could become a point of distraction, or much worse, an excuse to reject our resolution that day. As murmurs of disapproval swelled into an angry uproar, a well-dressed MP in a Western-style suit stood to his feet and quieted the audience. He then turned to explain why they were not willing to accept our resolution.

"Young men and women, as you can see, my colleagues and I feel you are not properly dressed to address this body. This is Parliament. You have to show respect. We will not accept any documents from anyone dressed in this fashion. No smocks are allowed in the parliament. So you will have to go and come back when you are properly dressed. To be clear, this means wearing suits, ties, dress shoes with socks, similar to how you see we are dressed today." Determined to humiliate us, they thanked our group for coming and abruptly ended the meeting.

We were insulted by the baseless rejection of our resolution, and their refusal to hear what we had to say. In a country where the majority of people could barely afford regular meals, this group of new elite were more interested in our dress code than the substance of what we carried in our resolution. We were clearly disappointed, but *not* discouraged. Since they would not listen to us in parliament, we decided to air our grievances outside of parliament.

We ended up in the streets, in a public protest on that same day. We protested the stealing, corruption, and injustices taking place in government circles. At that moment we were convinced that was the only way our message would reach the men and women who were insulated from the crisis, while the masses felt the sting of it.

The next day, our visit made the front page of the *Daily Graphic*, but it had not been portrayed in the best light. A photo appeared of the Progress Party Parliament rebuking our NUGS representative, accompanied by a story that highlighted their refusal of our resolution. It did not end there. The MPs had been so upset by the negative publicity surrounding our demand that they declare their assets that they summoned every one of us who signed the resolution to report to the Castle a week later for a mandatory meeting with the Prime Minister.

I had returned to the university when I received the notice, addressed to me and titled *"To All Executive Members of NUGS,"* so I knew right away that, P.V. Obeng, my fellow board member, must have also received the same notice. Before I could find out, he came looking for me on campus. "Nana, did you see the notice from the Castle?" he asked wide-eyed and breathless from running.

"Yes, I just got mine," I said, pulling out my notice, "and I was wondering if you got one too."

"I did. Look, it says they are calling for everyone who signed the resolution. We're supposed to report at the Castle at 7 a.m. prompt."

"So early! How do they expect us to get there?"

"Look at the bottom," he said, directing my attention further down the letter. "To make sure everyone is present, we are arranging for your transportation from your institution directly to the Castle." For a brief moment, we both stared blankly at one another, our eyes filled with questions. The following week, we arrived at the Castle, as instructed, promptly at 7 a.m. We were met by security at the entrance and asked to sign a roster next to our names in print. Castle security then escorted us down a long hall and into a waiting room, where we were kept under surveillance for the next seven hours, with no sign of when our scheduled meeting would begin. Sitting and waiting for hours was torturous.

Finally, our wait ended as a group of senior members of the Progress Party, Mr. R.R. Amponsah, Mr. DaRocha, Mr. K.G. Osei Bonsu and a few of their colleagues stormed in. Then, in a very hostile tone, the meeting began. "Good afternoon," started one MP with a clipboard in hand from which he read. "Since all of you feel you can challenge the government and protest random issues at any time you like, a few changes are going to take place." I don't know what we expected to be walking into, but I could imagine no MP, certainly, no person, would roll out the red carpet for our arrival and treat us to a glowing reception when we had just openly called them corrupt, thieves and at the very least, dishonest public officials. He continued, "Going forward, the government will cut back on subsidies on your university education. Which means you will have two choices to finance your education: you will either need to take a loan to pay for your school fees or, if your parents can afford it, they will need to pay your fees directly."

At that moment, we were all startled. Completely blindsided. By this announcement, which was to soon become policy for students nationwide, the changes we demanded seemed to have backfired against us. University students, who had formerly enjoyed free tuition and board under Nkrumah's liberal education policy, were soon required to pay for their schooling directly. The MP continued, "Perhaps when your parents are paying for your tuition from their own pockets, they won't sit to allow you the luxury of wasting our time protesting and challenging your government when you should be at the university studying."

That became my first reality check at confronting government machinery on issues that stripped away monetary benefit. In essence, they made their point to us that no one had the right to criticise or even question the government's actions or how they ran the country, even if they went against the constitution.

"Furthermore, as punishment for your behaviour, none of you will be allowed to work in any government institution when you leave the university." He paused and looked up from his clipboard, eyes peering over his reading glasses, scanning our faces for reactions.

"Any questions?" he asked.

Naturally, no one had any questions, nor was it expected. The goal of this meeting was to tame our rebellion by promoting fear and distraction from our collective agenda to one of self-preservation.

With a look of satisfaction on his face, the MP continued, "Very good. Now... we will need the following information from all of you: *one*... your parents' names, *two*... where they work, *three*... what they do for a living..."

While he was reading out the instructions, the Prime Minister, a bespectacled man in a dark suit, made a sudden entrance with a small delegation following closely behind him. His entrance took everyone by surprise. The discussion came to a halt as all eyes turned to him.

Caught off guard, our student group and I stared in the Prime Minister's direction from our seats. "Stand up when the Prime Minister is walking into a room!" yelled one MP. Astonished, we sprung to our feet as the Prime Minister was greeted and shown to a seat. After he sat down, we began to slowly take our seats, until another MP barked, "Keep standing and introduce yourselves."

We stood up straight, eyes fixed forward, shoulder to shoulder, and began introducing ourselves. P.V. Obeng spoke first.

"Afternoon, Your Excellency, my name is Paul Victor Obeng."

"Obeng?" the Prime Minister clarified.

"Yes, sir."

"Which of the Obengs? The CPP Obeng?"

"Yes. Sir."

"Hmm. No wonder," he replied, unimpressed, and moved on to the next student.

"Afternoon, Your Excellency, my name is Kan Tamakloe."

The introductions and dialogue continued like this with the Prime Minister, who was particularly interested in our family backgrounds and who our parents were, as if that would explain the reason for our behaviour. The more he questioned my peers, the more nervous I became.

Then it was my turn.

"Good afternoon Your Excellency, my name is Nana Konadu Agyeman." His eyes narrowed, and he leaned forward at the mention of my name.

"Agyeman?" he repeated.

"Yes, sir."

"Young lady, which Agyeman is your father?" When our eyes met, my mind suddenly filled with images of Dr. Busia in our home when I was just a little girl, drinking tea with my father and discussing politics for hours on end.

"Mr. J.O.T. Agyeman, sir." A look of surprise and familiarity crossed his face.

"Mr. Agyeman's daughter is getting involved in this?" he asked in an exaggerated tone. "Maybe we should report you directly to J.O.T." I stood quietly, feigning confidence, but inside I was trembling. He stared at me in quiet contemplation and then moved on to the next student.

After introductions were complete, Dr. Busia repeated the announcement of the MPs. "Our government has taken some decisions. Soon, you will no longer receive subsidies from the Ghana government to finance your education… "That's all I heard because that's all that mattered. At that point, I knew that this change would not only affect us, but more so, our parents.

Sure enough, later that same year, in September of 1971, Busia's government introduced the Student Loan Act, which abolished Dr. Nkrumah's policy on free education in Ghana and introduced university fees for the first time in the nation's history. This began the shift of educational costs from the state to families. Not surprisingly, the public fiercely resented the introduction of a student loan scheme. For one thing, it placed students from lower-income families at a greater disadvantage than those from wealthier families. This, in turn, made it harder for lower-income students to gain access into higher education.

That evening, I was supposed to return to Kumasi, but I was so afraid that I decided to go straight home instead. When I arrived home, my parents were startled. "Nana, what are you doing in Accra? Why aren't you on campus?" they asked. I gave only half the story, of being kept in a room at the Osu Castle for seven hours, and being blasted by the Progress Party gurus for daring to send a resolution to Parliament the week before. I did not, however, make any mention of losing my scholarship. My parents were angry enough with me for being involved in student-political activity, so I did not want to add to the bad news. I figured they would find out soon enough. In their anger, they sternly warned that I was sent to the university to study, and *not* to do politics.

My father insisted that I return to school that evening. The only way that was possible was for me to travel by air, so he bought me a Ghana Airways ticket, and I flew to Kumasi and then took a taxi back to campus. From that point on, I convinced myself that I did not want to even think about getting involved in student politics ever again. That was until I heard that Dr. Busia and the Progress Party had been overthrown in early 1972.

Just a few months before I could make it past the finish line for my university education, there was another coup. On the morning of January 13, 1972, I woke up in shock at the rumour of a military coup. By 6 a.m., there was frenzy among the girls in Africa Hall, where I lived on campus. Gathered closely around the radio, my hallmates and I anxiously listened to the pre-recorded words of Lieutenant Colonel Ignatius Kutu Acheampong in a radio broadcast that was first aired at 6 a.m., followed by military band music played repeatedly throughout the day.

Prime Minister Busia was out of the country on a medical trip to Great Britain when Colonel Ignatius Kutu Acheampong overthrew his government in a military coup. Citing mismanagement of the economy, Acheampong declared, in part, *"Even the few amenities and facilities that we the armed forces and the police enjoyed under Nkrumah's government have been taken away from us by the Busia Government".*

All around me, I could hear shouts of joy. On the campus of UST, the coup announcement was met with open and spontaneous jubilation. Students rejoiced and danced in the streets for more than three days. I joined in the student street demonstration to show our appreciation for the new regime, though many of us knew nothing about it. Still, our joy had everything to do with the end of the Busia administration. It had to be arguably the best street demonstration the students ever held.

Dr. Busia, who was diabetic and needed treatment for his failing eyesight, was in London at the time of the coup and was forced into exile for the second time. With immediate effect, Colonel Acheampong made himself Head of State and Chairman of the National Redemption Council (NRC), which promised improvements in the quality of life for all Ghanaians through the implementation of programs based on nationalism, economic development, and self-reliance. Not surprisingly, they arrested Lt. General Akwasi Afrifa, former head of state and staunch supporter of Busia who overthrew Nkrumah's government with the late Lt. Colonel Kotoka. Upon arrest, Afrifa was held in detention for more than a year.

Acheampong won immediate support by reversing the fiscal policies of the previous regime. He took measures to abandon the Student Loan Scheme and restored student grants, winning him favour among university students across the nation. He also cancelled the five percent development levy and revalued the Ghanaian *cedi*.

Acheampong echoed the sentiments of many around the country when he set out to repudiate many of the country's foreign debts and gave voice to a popular cry *'Yentua, yentua'* which translates to mean "We won't pay". While these measures definitely won him popular support early in his campaign, many of these decisions were not economically sustainable. The wild effects of flawed economic policies were inevitable, and it appeared everything he was busy hatching was more likely to worsen the economic situation in the long run.

In the midst of my jubilation, I found it curious that my father remained sober and sceptical. He did not like partisan politics because he felt it deepened the divides among the people, rather than unify them. But as much as he suffered under the Busia administration trying to lead the GNTC as Managing Director amidst a weakening economy, I could not understand his lack of excitement. His calm, placid composure disturbed me, until the day he brought a letter to my attention that Dr. Kwame Nkrumah wrote in response to the coup that toppled Busia's government.

Prior to his death in 1972, Dr. Nkrumah weighed in heavily on the coup with a scathing letter to his former political rival, published in *The Black Scholar*, and which included the fact that the same accusations that had once been levelled against Nkrumah and his government, surprisingly, became a huge part of the downfall of Dr. Busia's regime.

Further, he criticised Busia for having relied on the same colonialists, imperialists, capitalists, and neo-colonialists who sought his demise, rather than displaying a political maturity and keeping the welfare of the Ghanaians as his utmost priority. Apparently, the two men had met in Monrovia, Liberia, at which a skirmish ensued at the funeral of the late President William V. S. Tubman. Perhaps Nkrumah's striking disapproval of Busia was that he had given the dignity of the "African Personality" to the racists on a golden platter.

Reading this letter amazed me. It opened my eyes to the somewhat strange twists and unpredictability of power and politics in Ghana. I suddenly began to appreciate the wisdom in my father's non-partisanship. There was a reason why he had been so focused on being a businessman with intentions that rested on facts and reason, rather than on political aspirations and campaign rhetoric. Certainly, he knew that his position would come with the frustrations, but he could not trade in his ideals for a political handout.

It is refreshingly amazing to uncover how when a person opens his mind to nonpartisan thinking and is focused solely on what is best for Ghana, he cannot help but see the wisdom in places and moments where he had not seen it before. I got to look back and recall an enduring characteristic of my parents' home, which was the constant flow of political leaders from different eras—from Nkrumah's era to General Ankrah's, from General Afrifa's era to Busia's and into Acheampong's era.

With the exclusion of Acheampong, all of Ghana's heads of state seemed to have called on my father in one way or another. Several ministers from all regimes also visited my parents' home, making it one of the most politically versatile and tolerant homes of their time. Because my parents had family members and good friends on both sides of the political divide, my father stayed clear of partisan politics as much as possible.

After multiple coups and a failing economy, my father retired from his role as Managing Director of GNTC later that year in 1972.

On the death of the Osagyefo in exile in April 1972, Acheampong earned the people's sympathy when he negotiated for the return of Nkrumah's body to Ghana from Conakry, Guinea, where he was first buried and gave him a full state funeral in Accra. As a student, I must say I found Colonel Acheampong's early approach to governance inspiring, even if only for a fleeting moment.

In his early years, Acheampong's primary focus became Operation

Feed Yourself (OFY), a national programme aimed at achieving food self-sufficiency for the country. By undertaking some form of food production, OFY encouraged all Ghanaians to focus on becoming self-reliant in agriculture and the production of food crops, like vegetables, rice and maize. Initially, the initiative seemed practical, because in one form or another, every Ghanaian was affected by increasing food shortages and long queues for bread and other items. So, Operation Feed Yourself inspired a renewed sense of hope and was a way to channel our youthful energy towards something positive.

Like many students in Ghana, I volunteered with other young women from Africa Hall to join the early efforts of OFY. It energised all of us to know that we could make a difference by getting involved. On a daily basis, I started taking the bus for student volunteers from UST campus to the rural farms on the outskirts of Kumasi. Feeling energised and enthusiastic, we would arrive at the farms, marching, and singing, our sleeves rolled up and our hearts and minds ready to join the workers in the field. We were bursting with enthusiasm and it was exciting. OFY created a powerful union between students and community.

In a short time, almost every household in Ghana had a backyard garden to supplement their food needs. Sure enough, within months, the country saw an increase in food production as a result of infrastructural investments that had been made during the previous Busia administration. Some of those initiatives included the implementation of new approaches to farming, and the construction of access roads to market centres which were now paying huge dividends for the new administration. But before long, a number of unforeseen challenges proved difficult for Acheampong, starting with the oil crisis of 1973 which increased the price of oil and affected the importation of vital goods. Adding to that, a drought hit Ghana, affecting farmers and leading to a fall in cocoa production.

So although OFY ushered in a brief period of increased food production, the program's success was short-lived. Instead of being a systematic and strategic program to ensure long-term economic growth, OFY was an ad-hoc and poorly designed program that was unable to solve the country's underlying problems.

Later that same year in July of 1972, I graduated with an Honours Bachelor of Arts degree in Graphic Design. My Uncle Harry and my parents, still under the impression that I was studying architecture, were understandably shocked when I received my degree. At that point, they had little choice but to trust in my decision and celebrate this milestone with me, which thankfully, they did. But my father was not completely happy. Dee wanted me to continue school and pursue a master's degree right away to strengthen my credentials coming out of school. While I understood this, a master's degree was not in my immediate plans. I was eager to start looking for work, earning some money and learning how to be responsible on my own.

So I moved back home to Accra and started looking for a job. But since I refused to do a master's degree, Dee refused to assist me in my job search. My father, at the time, knew everyone who either owned a business or was a decision maker in some of the leading companies in Accra. All he needed to do was to make one phone call to any of these people, and I would have had an opportunity. Instead He looked at me and said, "The essence of your university education is to be self-reliant". He advised that I start sending applications to any company that I was interested in working for, just like any other graduate. He added that it would be in my own interest to actually go to every one of those companies in person and follow up on the progress of my application.

So on my own, I took my portfolio from one company to another and eventually had a choice of four different offers. But it did not come easy. In the process, I turned down several offers from opportunistic men asking for sexual favours in exchange for career opportunities. It was a brutal wakeup call.

University had certainly become a time of personal growth. I had enjoyed learning in the halls; taking part in several sporting activities and representing the university in netball, tennis, athletics and swimming; learning to act and perform by being in the theatre club and singing in the university band; and engaging in prolonged discussions under the hot sun. Four years of my life in the university had transformed me into a woman with colourful perspectives on leadership, politics, and power.

I walked onto the campus in 1968 unsure of what my voice ought to be, and left in 1972 having discovered my strengths and experienced a closer connection with the world around me. Perhaps being a student activist made me politically aware of what was happening in our country and fostered my love for civic engagement.

If nothing else, every one of those encounters would have nudged me to think more critically through the fog of politics, and independently about the mirage in the issues I cared about most. And they had become many.

CHAPTER THIRTEEN

WHIRLWIND
A Young Career Woman: 1972 – 1976

In 1972, I was hired by the Union Trading Company (UTC), a large Swiss trading firm, where I found a golden opportunity to put my graphic design degree to work. As an interior decorator, this was supposed to be a dream come true for a young woman who had set out in pursuit of what I genuinely had a passion for, even though deep in my heart I had every reason to be unsure what the next chapter was to bring. My work included transforming UTC showrooms, adorning window displays and take care of the interior décor of more than a hundred corporate housing units throughout Ghana. At the time, I was one of only a handful of Ghanaian women working among the professional ranks at UTC.

In the latter part of 1973, I made arrangements to move out of my parents' home and into my own place—a final snipping of the proverbial umbilical cord. I was a recent graduate and more than a year into my first job with UTC. While my father supported my decision, my mother wholeheartedly objected. Even at the age of twenty-four, my decision ignited a heated debate under my parents' roof. From every possible angle, my mother tried reasoning with me.

"Konadu, you've only been working for one year. What is the rush?" she demanded.

"Maa, there's no rush. I just want to feel some independence, to learn what it's like to manage on my own. Under your roof, I don't pay for lunch. I don't pay for rent. I don't even buy food… *nothing*! I just want to learn to be responsible. What is wrong with that?"

"Take your time Konadu! If you, a small girl who's not even married, moves into her own flat, what will people think? I'm telling you, it does not look good," Maa protested.

"Maa, I'm not worried about what people will think. I have finished the university. I have a degree… and a steady profession! What more, Maa? What more do I need to prove to anyone? So long as you know me, Dee knows me, why should I worry about what others think?"

"Konadu, people will talk! And people will think you are one of those bad girls. And I don't want that. I'm not for it, at all."

On the other end of the spectrum, Dee sat quietly, but in favour of my decision. In the beginning, however, because of Maa's strong protest, he did not express his support, at least not openly. He was always one to let the dust settle, especially with Maa, before he chimed in.

At the time, the idea of a young unmarried woman doing all she could to move out of her parents' home was still too new. But in my mind, and in my plans, all was practically said and done. There was a long waiting list for the French-owned Compagnie Francaise de l'Afrique Occidental (*CFAO*) company bungalow in Accra. My older sister, Yaa Achia, had been a bilingual administrative secretary, having studied French in Geneva during her school years, to the company's Managing Director, so she was able to guide me through the process of securing a bungalow. I had committed to sharing the place with a colleague, who graduated with her master's degree from UST in 1973, a year after I had. With rent at 100 *cedis* a month, between two of us, we could split the cost evenly down to 50 *cedis* each.

With plans firmly in place, we moved into our new bungalow without delay. Maa eventually came on board and helped me furnish the place with curtains, bed sheets, plates, and glassware. The CFAO building was just behind the Parliament House in the heart of Accra, Osu.

By this time the relationship between Jerry and I was unsteady. Our on-again, off-again status was taking its toll on me. He would surface, sometimes after a long morning jog from the Burma Camp Military Headquarters, and my house would be his resting place. We might be together daily for one week, and then just as quickly, he would disappear for two months or more. While my feelings for him had become strong, I imagined he could have another young lady on his radar. My mind raced occasionally. I had fallen in love with a man whose heart perhaps was crawling at a snail's pace to get to me.

I wondered some more. In university, I had been devastated when a letter arrived from a friend telling me about Jerry apparently living with a white woman. She was a Swiss teacher at the Swiss school, in Accra, and the letter did not bring me any comfort by insinuating that whatever relationship Jerry had with this woman was probably a serious one. I shrugged it off.

By the time I was in my third year in university I had come to grips with the reality that our young love was heading to a dead end. I told myself that I was going to write him off. As hard as it was to live past the disappointment, I could not ignore the fact that there had never been any certainty in the relationship. Frustrated, I concluded that our relationship was not going anywhere and Jerry was just wasting my time. Sure he might have been an intelligent and charming man, but he would be that for someone else. I decided to let go and move on.

There was a genuine friendship that was effortless. The years had passed and taken both of us through life in Achimota, and each of us plunged into different paths after secondary school, but somehow our worlds seemed to find their way back together. Even when I had done all I could to walk away, serendipity had a beautiful way of pulling our lives back onto the same track. Every time I found the courage to move on and to date someone else, Jerry would surface and sabotage any attempts at a new relationship.

Once, I accepted an invitation for an evening out with a former schoolmate and friend from UST. He was popular by his nickname, Jimbo Jimbo. I had first met the young man in Kumasi on UST campus and he must have spent much of his time in university pursuing me, but I never showed any interest. After graduation, Jimbo Jimbo relocated to Accra to work at a food research company he'd found, and suddenly I would run into him almost daily.

On the night when we were going out, Jimbo Jimbo arrived at my place neatly dressed to pick me up. As I finished getting ready, he waited patiently for me in the sitting room. Slipping on my heels and adjusting my earrings, I was suddenly startled by the sound of the front door opening. I was not expecting anyone.

Who could that be?

I rushed to check. Without warning, Jerry pranced through the front door with the confidence of a homeowner. Startled, Jimbo Jimbo looked Jerry in the eye, and for a moment I imagined he wondered if there was something he needed to know. He seemed confused. Jerry did not even blink, stared at the young man without a care in the world, up and down in an almost arrogant manner, as if to say, *"Aren't you in the wrong place?"*

Jerry then walked straight into my bedroom, plopped onto my bed and casually asked, "Oh, are you going out?"

"Yes! I'm going out. Don't you see I'm getting ready?"

"Oh, so where are you going that you can't take me?"

"That's none of your business," I snapped. I was angry and still upset by the relationship that seemed to have come to a screeching halt, and that Jerry did not seem to care.

And just like that, poor Jimbo Jimbo, who arrived with confidence, now sat with the posture of a wilted flower. It ruined the evening for both of us, and I felt bad for the young man who had been caught up in our emotional roller-coaster. I never had the courage to kick Jerry out. My heart would not allow it. Sadly, the pattern with Jerry didn't stop.

I tried to turn my attention to my work and any distraction I could find in the hopes that someday, soon, I would run into the love of my life, and perhaps shake off the dust left behind by Jerry, the man whose affection I wished I did not have to scramble for.

After a while, I tried to start a relationship with someone else. He was Nii, a young man I had known for many years from our days in secondary school, in Achimota. Nii had come to visit at my residence, and even though I was not sure there was any future or love interest in store, perhaps anyone with whom I could hold a decent conversation could be a beautiful distraction and a chance to move on with my life.

Sure enough, Jerry reappeared. This time I kept my door locked. But that was not enough to keep him out. He stood outside with hand tools as if he was getting ready to go on an expedition, and before I knew it, there were crackling sounds from the back walls. Jerry carefully pulled apart the wall unit of my air conditioner that was attached to the building and crawled in. Again, I was in shock. He actually undid the screws, jimmied off the frame and pulled the whole unit out of the wall and wiggled his way into my bedroom! I did not know whether to laugh or cry, but laughter prevailed—howling, choking laughter at the absurdity of what I was seeing. I thought for sure this man was crazy.

Not surprisingly, so did my date, who did not find it amusing and quickly disappeared. I later learned that Jerry was able to keep tabs on me by making friends with the security guards and gatemen on duty around the townhouse where I lived. I thought to myself over and again how easy it would have been if young Jerry managed to always be there, so he would not have to go through outrageous hurdles to barge back into my life, and into my heart.

By 1974, the economy had, once again, taken a plunge due to many overriding factors. Industry and transportation suffered greatly as world oil prices rose, and the lack of foreign exchange and credit left Ghana without fuel. By 1975, public support waned, and it became clear to all that *Operation Feed Yourself* had run its course. After a promising start, disillusion with the government set in and accusations of personal corruption among the rulers also began to surface. The economy was moving into deep recession, and Acheampong clearly lacked the ability to solve the country's growing problems.

Faced with an emerging economic crisis, Colonel Acheampong's National Redemption Council, fearing that the military as a whole would be discredited, set out to restructure itself. In an effort to create a truly military government, the ruling council was reorganized into the Supreme Military Council (SMC) in October of 1975. Remaining the leader of the Council, Acheampong, who had now promoted himself from Colonel to General, restricted membership within the SMC to only a few senior military officers. The only people who would be in this inner circle were commanders of all the military services and the Inspector General of Police. Until this point, the NRC mainly comprised those middle-ranking officers who had staged the original coup of 1972.

The goal was to consolidate the military's hold over the government by putting senior officers in charge of all ministries and state enterprises.

When Acheampong came to power, all forms of political activity were banned. The constitution was suspended, the Supreme Court abolished, and the military tribunal was declared the highest court in the land. It did not take much for every Ghanaian to read the writings on the wall, that there was clearly no plan to return the nation to democratic rule. On the contrary, however, the government did not allow or encourage any input from the civilian sector, and there was no intent to return any part of the government to civilian control.

Unfortunately, the Acheampong regime quickly turned out to be even more corrupt than its predecessor. The inability to deliver on its promises cracked into the support they had garnered. The mismanagement and rampant corruption eroded any semblance of transparency and honesty, and left a black eye on the governance of the NRC-turned-SMC. As the economy fell apart, the military officers in positions of power began to help themselves to the country's dwindling coffers. Senior military officers now in charge of ministries and state corporations used their positions to look after their own interests.

The magnitude of the corruption ranged from diverting state funds and selling import licenses, to using army labour and equipment to build private houses for themselves. Moreover, military officers who headed state corporations allegedly conspired with some corrupt Syrian, Lebanese and Indian businessmen who made huge profits illegally manipulating contracts and hijacking the import licensing system to amass fortunes for themselves and their Ghanaian collaborators through capital flight.

With the country in such dire shape, the timing could not have been better for my boss to ask me to travel abroad for an extended assignment sponsored by my employer UTC. By this time, Jerry and I had parted ways, making it easier for me to embark on the trip and take full advantage of some much-needed time and distance between us. I could not truthfully admit that I was over him, but I relished the time away to think things through. Before I left, I moved out of the flat I shared with my flatmate, and acquired my own flat in another C.F.A.O. building.

In the early months of 1975, I was aboard a large commercial airplane that was preparing for departure to Switzerland at Ghana's Kotoka International Airport, when an air hostess approached me in my seat.

"Excuse me ma'am, are you Nana Agyeman?"

"Yes," I replied, a bit surprised.

"Ok. Just one moment please... there's someone outside who has urgently requested to speak to you before we depart. I'll let him in to see you, but only for a brief moment," she cautioned. "All right?" she asked, searching my face for quick consent.

I hesitated in confusion. "Um... yes... alright," I agreed, feeling a bit dumbfounded and without a clue as to who she was talking about.

As she retreated briskly back down the aisle, I watched past her direction with a burning curiosity. Seconds later, in walked Jerry at the cockpit entrance, wearing a jogging suit.

I gasped, and my eyes grew wide. *What is he doing here?*

"The plane is about to leave. Why are you here?" I demanded, masking all emotion.

In a jovial manner, he responded, "Why? Is there anything wrong with me wanting to say one *laaaaast* goodbye?" His smile then faded and his gaze intensified. "Nana, travel safe, ok?"

Softened by his sincerity, I replied, "Ok, I will. Thank you."

Though we were no longer a couple, seeing him that day left a lasting impression.

I arrived in Zurich on a cold and snowy day in the middle of February 1975. The ground was a blinding white, covered in a thick, blanket of freshly fallen snow and the weather was crisp and refreshing. At first glance, the world looked so different from here, so clean and flawless. The snow covered everything. There was no trash, no litter; it was all hidden by the clean white of snow. Everything looked so beautiful covered in snow, and all of the blemishes of the world suddenly seemed gone.

The cold, however, was a disturbingly different contrast from what I was used to. It was a wet cold, one that seeped into me. It made my toes numb, my fingers numb and my eyes sting. It was a possessive cold. Once it hit, I found it incredibly hard to stop shivering. No matter how much I covered up, it always seemed to penetrate the protective barriers of my winter coat, scarf, and gloves. Such a different landscape this was from the beaches, coconut trees and unrelenting heat of the African sun.

My travel to Switzerland was a thirteen-month assignment at the corporate home base of UTC. Working on attachment to Jelmoli, then Switzerland's largest department store, I was there to gain more experience in retail window display and decoration. At the same time, I was undergoing management training and certification courses.

The time away from the hardships of Ghana was both freeing and enlightening. A contrasting reminder of how a strong and vibrant civil society should function. There was order in the country and daily efforts to ward off repressive laws, to compel government accountability and to expose any kind of government corruption.

People moved about with a sort of freedom unfamiliar in Ghana in recent years. There was public confidence to risk dissent by opening up a debate, not closing it down. And it seemed it was important to the public to ensure the fair representation of all groups, interests, and ideas. Although it was not perfect by any means, life in Switzerland was undoubtedly a good reminder of a functioning society that was, in part, strengthened by the power of a decentralised government.

In contrast, however, I often found the Swiss people to be as cold as the outdoor air. Unlike Ghana, the Swiss seemed to live for their work and prioritised all the money they earned to support the next moments of their lives. I reasoned that this sort of life did not leave much room for social and communal interaction. It was very different to observe how people thought first in terms of money and placed a high priority on work and career. It took me a while to adjust to this mindset and organise myself to work effectively in this system. Each day before dawn, I had to report to work around 5:30 a.m., to prepare shop windows with attractive displays before the 8 a.m. opening to the general public.

Unlike back home in Ghana, where employees are paid overtime for the extra hours they put in on the job, this concept was unheard of in Switzerland. In spite of the gruelling extra hours we put in daily, we were simply expected to report to work as frequently as needed. In a strange way, I admired the unquestioning discipline with which the Swiss approached their work.

During this time, I was able to travel between Germany, Holland, and Switzerland and gained a new perspective on life and what mattered to me the most. After thirteen months of hard work, intense training and some leisure travel between Germany, Holland, and Switzerland, I arrived back in Accra in March 1976.

After the cold months living abroad, it was indeed good to be back on Ghana shores. Sadly, however, not only had the social and economic conditions worsened but now the country was in the midst of a severe two-year drought; a natural hazard which left the weather unbearably hot and heightened the tensions of an already treacherous situation. Again, the stark contrasts between countries took some time and effort for me to readjust to.

About two months after my arrival, Jerry appeared on the steps of my front door, eager to see me, and asking if we could spend some time together. But with a memory of his other girlfriends during our relationship, I was determined not to go down that road of heartbreak and disappointment again. I told him I was tired of that and I had no interest in resuming our relationship. But he pressed on, saying that the separation from me had given him much-needed time to reconsider his priorities in life and that our time apart had really opened his eyes to what he wanted in a relationship. He also expressed how much he wanted us to be together.

I was reluctant because I had spent the last thirteen months and more convincing myself that our relationship had ended and I was now focused on moving forward. He, on the other hand, expressed an urgent desire for us to meet, at a later date, so he could express himself. Grudgingly, I agreed and we arranged a time.

At that meeting, Jerry requested that we start spending serious time together and then he began pledging his love and commitment to me. I was a bit overwhelmed, confused and at times, lost for words. He begged for my forgiveness, saying the idea of marriage and commitment had at first terrified him. He said, knowing the home I came from and the way my parents provided for me had made him wary of whether he could ever measure up in the eyes of both my parents, but especially my father, who he knew adored me.

I felt swept up again in a whirlwind. Life had taken on a dizzying pace, and everything seemed so important, suddenly. Then Jerry added that he had been trying to deny his love for me by being distant and non-committal. Now, however, he was clear: he loved me and wanted me to be his wife. I was now struggling to fight back emotion. The sincerity in his eyes made mine swell up with tears. In all the years I had known Jerry he had never been this expressive, openly baring his heart and his soul, and he had never shown such vulnerability. I was deeply moved and had no choice but to take him at his word. I accepted his plea.

I loved him too.

CHAPTER FOURTEEN

BAREFOOT ON A CLOUD

Love, Marriage and Forever

"What was wrong with the white girl?

What has she done that you have to leave her?" she asked as if I was not in the room.

What I had imagined would be a warm reception had quickly turned awkward, and I felt odd standing in the middle of it. Perhaps it was due to Jerry's Scottish ancestry that his mother had so badly wanted her youngest son to marry a white woman. She made this abundantly clear the day we first met in 1976 when Jerry and I had decided to get married.

Informally, his mother and I had seen each other often and had even greeted one another on several occasions when I was with her son, but this time was different. I had recently returned to Ghana from working in Switzerland when Jerry excitedly took me to his mother's home to formally introduce me and announce our plans to get married.

Madam Agbotui, as she was known, lived in a tidy residential block of flats reserved for government employees in a well-kept area of Accra, Airport Residential. At the time, she had become the Chief Matron at the State House and had a noble history of cooking for every Head of State and President of Ghana from the time of independence, starting with Osagyefo. Her duties now included supervising a team of caterers at the State House.

To my surprise, our visit to her home that day became explosive. Hoping to get his mother's blessings, Jerry's brimming excitement was met by his mother's deep disdain and disapproval. Upon receiving the news, Madam Agbotui switched from speaking English to their native *Ewe* language, perhaps assuming I would not understand. As she spoke to her son, however, and he replied in English, I was able to piece together enough information to know what she was saying.

She asked about a white girl, and blurted out, "What has she done that you have to leave her?"

"I never thought of marrying that girl," Jerry snapped back, his voice rising with each word. "The person I want to marry is right here, the woman I have brought to you. If you do not want to give us your consent or blessings, that's fine. At least we have come to inform you and I am going ahead with my plans," he said defiantly.

His mother was neither moved by his words nor by our announcement. She showed no interest in learning more about me or my family. She simply disapproved of our relationship and our plans for marriage and made no attempt to hide her disappointment. Her wish was for her son to marry a white woman, plain and simple. To her disappointment, I was a dark-skinned black woman, who, unlike her son, was not of mixed race. Even worse, I was not even an *Ewe*, but rather an Ashanti, which did not seem to help the situation. Ironically, she, too, was dark-skinned with a wide nose, full lips, and a deep black complexion, no different from mine.

Taking no part in her son's excitement, she stood her ground and refused to even look at me. Her mulishness infuriated Jerry, and he exploded with anger. This was far from what I had envisioned such a day would be for me. Banging his fist against the wall, he yelled, "What did a white person ever do for you?" I felt I had driven a wedge between the man I fell in love with and his mother, and the longer the heated dialogue continued, the more the whole encounter seemed bizarre. There was nothing I could say or do. It felt odd.

Jerry could not hide his anger, and perhaps they both had deep-seated convictions that fuelled their fury. He continued, "What did a white person ever do for you? Look at me! What did a white person do for you… that you think I should marry a white person? You don't want to do it? You don't want to see her? Fine!"

Jerry asked me to leave the house and wait for him downstairs in the car. Startled, I left the room feeling horribly uncomfortable as if I had sparked a very sensitive and perhaps unresolvable family feud. Sitting in the car, I could hear Jerry's voice bellow with rage from the top floor. I could not hear the exchange, but within minutes he returned to the car, still huffing and puffing. "Let's go," he said, "I want to take you to go and see my aunt." That day ended my interaction with his mother until our wedding day.

We left her house and headed straight to the home of his mother's younger sister, Auntie Joyce, a contrastingly warm and bubbly, gentle-spirited woman who joyfully received both of us as well as news of our intended engagement. More importantly, she offered us her blessing and was willing to honour Jerry's request to represent his mother and the family. Jerry was relieved, and so was I.

The sad truth was that we lived in a Ghana that was choked by tribal splits. It was not unusual for parents and families to turn a blind eye to their son or daughter befriending a person of the opposite sex until they decided to marry, and then the glaring discontent suddenly jumped into the light. And in that instance, suitable life partners failed a litmus test simply on account of their name or heritage. And at every opportunity, those differences, no matter how subtle, reared their ugly heads.

It was not only Jerry's mother who fiercely opposed our relationship. My mother strongly disapproved as well. From the time I was in university, Maa would ask me, "Nana Konadu, who is this *wewereman* – (stiff looking guy) with a stiff face? My mother had arrived at her own conclusions about Jerry even before she had the chance to barely speak a word to him. "From his behaviour and the way he walks, he appears too arrogant," she said.

"But Maa, he's not arrogant. If you get to know him, you will find he's very respectful," I would try to steer her in that direction. But Maa wouldn't hear it. Everything I said seemed to fall on deaf ears, and perhaps it was much easier for a person to hold on to any stereotype that had coloured their own life's lenses than take a moment to stray from their own typecasts. She felt that Jerry was too pompous and that he walked with an arrogant gait.

She would protest and often hurt my feelings, even more, when she would say, out of nowhere, that, "Just by seeing him, I get angry." To erase the tension in my home, I had stopped having Jerry accompany me to my parents' house. As our relationship became more serious, Maa pleaded with me, "Nana, there are plenty of young men around with good professions. And there are even older, more mature men who are well established that would love to marry you. But your problem is you won't take your mind off that *small boy*," as she would call him. She could not help but be condescending as if that would change my mind.

My mother's sentiments hadn't been born out of hatred or even bigotry. It was what they knew, and what their worldview had forced them to comprehend. She would say, "I don't understand. Why him? If it's a fair-skinned person you want or a white person, then go with a white man. Someone with a profession! Not a soldier." Maa felt I should be in the hands of a doctor or a lawyer or someone with a presumably reputable career, not a soldier.

Her reality was not unusual. My mother had grown up in an era where only children with real behavioural problems were sent off to enlist in the military to become soldiers. Society assumed that would be a perfect way to make use of their aggression, hence a career in the military was not deemed by many families as something a young man sets out to pursue. It was no surprise that when she found out Jerry was in the military, it deeply concerned her. For Maa, there were two main issues of concern, the first being that Jerry was a soldier, and the second being that he was an ethnic Ewe, and not an Ashanti.

Jerry was aware of my mother's disapproval and my father's concern. So when he decided to ask my parents for my hand in marriage, he insisted on doing it without me. He neither wanted me present nor involved. So it was later that I learned that he first sent Dr. Reginald Addae, a middle-aged Air Force doctor who was a dear friend of my parents, to go and see them on his behalf to inform my parents of Jerry's wishes to propose and to vouch for Jerry's good character.

Dr. Addae was someone my parents highly respected. He was a soft-spoken man with a slightly heavy build who had been a long-time friend of our family's. On several occasions, he had cared for me at the Military Hospital when I had suffered from severe asthma attacks. If my mother had it her way, a man like Dr. Addae would have been her choice for my future husband.

Apparently, as Dr. Addae spoke on Jerry's behalf, my mother vehemently declared, "We don't know anything about this young man. We don't know his mother, or his house, or his hometown. We don't know anything about him. When you are putting your child into a marriage, you look beyond the person. Without knowing this, I cannot agree. If this is what Nana Konadu wants, we cannot stop it, but I will not be a part of it. And when there is a problem, I will not be a part of the consequences." She meant well and was not ready to shake off her convictions.

What turned the tide had to be my father's reasoning and having a logical way of pleading with my mother to reconsider her stance. "We may not know his mother," he said, "but I knew the young man's father. His father and I were both Freemasons, and we met each other often at the Lodge meetings. His father and I also worked for the same company. When I was working for the UAC in the General Goods Department, his father was with the UAC as a Chemist at Kingsway Chemist in Accra. So I knew his father well. And as for the way the young man walks and moves, I'm telling you, his mannerisms are just like his father's. I think if Konadu loves him and he also loves her, then it is really up to the two of them. They are the ones that matter. So, I don't think we should make it difficult for them. Let's support them and allow them to move on." It had to be that this turning point was what paved the way for Jerry's visit to go and see them and our plans to get married.

Before the wedding, as custom demanded, ours was a simple traditional engagement ceremony between the two families, which Jerry's mother predictably did not attend. Fortunately, his Auntie Joyce stood in her place as his parental figure, accompanied by Dr. Addae and a few of Jerry's family members. The ceremony involved the offering of gifts, much like a dowry, and words of advice from family elders and the desired blessings of both extended families. It was a simple affair, about ten people, mostly elders of the families.

The toughest hurdle had to be behind us, and it would be left to the two of us to prove to ourselves, and our families too, that there was more to a human heart than the cultural and ethnic derisions that we went to great lengths to endure. The most significant part of the engagement was when one of my uncles cited a piece of Ghana history to drive home his point. He stressed the fact that historically, the Ewes and the Ashantis have always had a long relationship.

Tracing it back to one of the ancient kings, he emphasised that there had never been a battle between the two tribes. So, as it was in our history, he expected the same cordial relationship between our two families, and especially the two of us as husband and wife. And if at any time, we thought there was a problem in the marriage, he advised us to bring it to the family and sit down and discuss it rather than dissolve the marriage. I found his words and his show of support inspiring.

On the eve of my wedding, I was in my parents' home when my father asked to speak with me in his study. Sitting pensively behind his desk, he said he wanted to offer me some words of advice. "Misewaa," he began. "Now that you have made your choice, and you are about to get married, I want to advise you on a few important matters about marriage. So please, listen carefully and remember what I am about to say," he pleaded. Then he paused for a moment, seemingly to gather his thoughts. "Misewaa, since you were small, I have always told you and your sisters that, no matter what, you should always remain independent of any man you decide to marry." He had a long lecture in mind and wanted to be sure I was paying attention to every word.

"Number one: You should never, ever, have a joint account with your husband. But if you do, then make sure you have your own money saved in a separate account. That way, you are not solely dependent on him, especially in times of emergency. Number two: Remember that your husband is not your pillow. Never let your guard all the way down and think that 'Okay; now I can sleep very comfortably on him.' Because the day he decides to move that pillow, you may bang your head so hard on the ground, it will not only daze you, but it could kill you. So it's fine to be in love, but do not lose your sense of self."

"Three: Your husband will always be your first born. You see, women are always able to see through a man as they see through their own children. So be patient. Don't be too quick to act. And be careful with how you deal with what you see."

I tried to think if there was an underlying thought that drove this intense warning. I had to be patient, and remember that he spoke out of love, and probably had assured my mother that he would do everything possible to send me off on my journey well. I almost wanted to find the courage to remind him that I was not embarking on a suicidal mission and he did not have to worry about every inch of my welfare.

"Number four," he continued, "while the man is always the head of the family, the woman is the neck, and without the neck, the head cannot stand. So wherever the neck turns, that is where the head goes. He doesn't have to know that, but you do. So don't be afraid to take decisions to determine the direction you want your family to go. Ultimately, that is where the head will go. In most homes, it takes a woman to determine the destiny of a family. So keep that in mind. And last, but not least: Never let him raise a hand to you. If he ever attempts to hit you, don't just stand there. Move! Don't go and tell your mum or your friends. Tell me. Right away. Do you understand?"

"Yes, Dee. I do."

"Good. That is my advice to you as your father."

"Thank you, Dee." The words of my father the night before I got married made me realise how truly blessed I was to have a man like him care so deeply about my happiness.

Our wedding date was set for Saturday, January 29, 1977. By then, both of us had advanced professionally in our careers. I was a Group Manager working for the same Swiss firm, the Union Trading Company, and Jerry was a Pilot Officer in the Ghana Air Force. We were both in our late twenties; Jerry was 29, and I was a year younger. We were eager to keep our wedding simple, low-key and within a budget we could afford. Jerry was adamant that my parents understood this. We did not want to rely on anyone, but ourselves financially, if possible. My parents, on the other hand, felt differently and were eager to have a hand in organising and helping to finance the wedding of their second daughter.

For them, it only made sense. We had every reason to suspect that they may have in mind a more lavish affair. My older sister, had gotten married a few years earlier and my parents planned and funded the wedding. Guests on that day numbered around one thousand people, and I was her maid of honour. Because our father was then still the managing director of the Ghana National Trading Corporation, hundreds of people poured in from all over Ghana, and even parts of Europe, to support the nuptials of his first-born child and eldest daughter. The event was truly grand and extraordinary at the time. The images were still new in my mind. They spared no expense.

I remembered how for my sister's wedding dress, my mother flew all the way to Switzerland to buy the finest Swiss materials she could find to have the dress custom made in Ghana. Even my dress had been so elegant that for a moment it felt as though I was the one getting married.

I wore silk gloves and my hair and make-up were professionally done by local stylists. My make-up was so elaborate that I thought I was barely recognizable in the wedding photos. Sparing no expense, my sister's wedding cake was a towering, tiered centrepiece surrounded by two smaller tiered cakes. At the reception, the bride and groom sat smiling at the decorated high table for everyone to see. The affair was grand and beautiful, but that was not the kind Jerry and I had in mind.

Jerry had convinced me on not making the wedding event anything elaborate and high-class, and I accepted it. Now I was sure that I wanted the exact opposite of what my parents had probably dreamt of for me. If I could have gone to the local registry to get married, I would have done so, and Jerry felt the same way. In planning our wedding, the first thing he said to me was, "Nana, I want you to inform your parents that I don't want our wedding to look anything like your older sister's."

"Don't worry," I assured him. "I don't want that either. As far as I'm concerned, we can invite just a few people, like fifty people each," I blurted, to which he agreed, and the two of us naïvely settled on inviting no more than a hundred guests, fifty for my parents and fifty between the two of us. When I delivered the message to my father, he was furious.

"What? You can't be serious. *Fifty* people?"

He reminded me of a small detail I had overlooked. Even the close relatives I had in my family were more than fifty. "So how can you ask me to invite only fifty family members? Impossible. Have you told Jerry that my brothers and sisters alone will be more than fifty people? And what about the Asantehene and his entourage?"

My father's reaction forced us to compromise. So we increased the number of total guests to 150, with the majority of invitations reserved for my parents. I then proceeded to print out 150 invitation cards. Yet, somehow, word-of-mouth easily mobilised more than twice that number, and we ended up with more than 300 people.

We managed to keep our wedding party small—no bridesmaids, no groomsmen, no flower girls, no page boys—just one maid of honour, my younger sister, Sefa, and one best man, Jerry's friend who was in the Ghana Armed Forces. If there ever was one person whose character I questioned from the time we first met, it was the same man. It did not take much for me to notice he was notorious for fabricating stories to make himself look good.

At the barracks, Jerry used to take me to visit him in his living quarters at Burma Camp. For hours, the two of them would sit and engage in in-depth political discussions that often lasted late into the night. In my mind, I could not get past what seemed to me as repeated contradictions, so I did my best to stay clear off his path. He was Jerry's friend, but he did not have to be mine too.

It did not surprise me in the least when Jerry told me before the wedding that his own friend who was to be his best man had warned him against me, that I was the wrong woman to marry. In the young man's mind, "Ashantis are not trustworthy, and an educated Ashanti is even worse." According to Jerry, his friend would carry on, denigrating "graduate women" and how they made bad wives. He would tell Jerry that he would never marry a woman who had been to university because university women have a chip on their shoulder. "You don't know these graduates," he would tell Jerry. "When they want you to marry them, they have a different style, and when you marry them, then you see their true colours."

Jerry's response was simple. "And you don't know this woman. I know her, and I am prepared to marry her." Needless to say, I was not happy that Jerry chose him to be his best man, but he was his friend so I didn't object.

As an Officer in the Air Force getting married, Jerry was entitled to some special amenities. These included two military vehicles reserved for his use on the day of his wedding, and, if he opted for a military wedding, the participation of his fellow officers to form the honorary "Arch of swords," or "sword crossing," for us to pass under as a newly married couple. I would have gladly embraced this protocol, as I've always loved watching the grandeur of how the military salutes newlyweds as they exit the building. But Jerry would have none of that. I was sad.

Much to my parents' chagrin, he wanted a simple, non-traditional civilian wedding with little fanfare. For this reason, our wardrobe choices were decidedly different. Instead of wearing any of the fancy white wedding dresses my parents bought me from Europe, I chose to wear a simple beige dress with a large, matching floppy brim hat.

My dress was long, but without a trail, and I refused to wear a veil over my face or gloves or even stockings because the humid weather was unbearably hot. And instead of professional hair and make-up artists, I chose to do my own. Similarly, instead of a western-style formal suit or a military uniform, Jerry wore a beige African-style men's two-piece outfit that somewhat resembled Muslim attire, popular in Ghana. His shirt had beautiful brown embroidery accents that matched his trousers. We were proud of our choices and eventually, my parents had to be okay with them too.

Not too far away, however, there was a high-profile military wedding taking place on the same day as ours with all the pomp and circumstance. Attending that wedding was Ghana's Head of State, General Acheampong, and a large contingent of military personnel and guests from all over Ghana. The groom was General Acheampong's personal aide, and unfortunately for us, the military had commandeered all military vehicles for this wedding—including the two that Jerry had reserved for our wedding, which naturally upset him. Not even one vehicle that Jerry was entitled to was made available to us on our wedding day.

Suddenly, we were left without the transportation we needed to convey each of us to the church. The only silver lining was that we no longer had to worry about a horde of soldiers showing up at our reception uninvited, as most of them would be attending the other wedding.

Stepping in to help, my father offered us his old-model Mercedes Benz and insisted on us using it for my transportation to the church. So we quickly put ribbons on Dee's car to get it ready for the wedding. Then one of Jerry's colleagues, a Lieutenant Colonel, offered Jerry his personal car for Jerry's transportation to the church, along with his best man and some of his friends.

Though Jerry had been raised in the Catholic faith, he agreed for us to get married at Ridge Church in Accra. It had been my home church since I was about seven years old. Moreover, I held on dearly to the memory that as a child I had been a part of the neighbourhood children who had helped build the church some twenty years earlier. While I was running about thirty minutes late, Jerry arrived promptly at 3 p.m. for the afternoon ceremony at Ridge Church. Jerry must have thought that I had changed my mind.

By the time I arrived, the church was full, and I was surprisingly calm. As the wedding began, a ceremonious hush fell over the audience. The music played softly. With measured steps, my father led me down the aisle to where Jerry was standing with Reverend Stevens. On cue, I felt my father's arm slip away from mine as the Reverend began to speak.

Before the wedding, Jerry and I had gone to see Reverend Stevens on two occasions for wedding rehearsals. During the rehearsal, he walked us through what to do. He taught us how and when to kneel, where to stand, where to place the ring and so on. After he finished, he asked us, "Do either of you have any other questions?"

Jerry replied, "Only one, but it is not a question, it is a statement. We don't want to hear any long sermons from you."

Flabbergasted, the middle-aged Reverend Stevens responded, "Pardon?"

Without skipping a heartbeat, Jerry continued, "I said we don't want to hear any long sermons from you. We are two adults who want to get married. You can give us a piece of advice if you want. But we don't want it to be longer than three minutes. And if you have anything to say, you should say it to us here and now, not in the church." Without my permission Jerry spoke as if we had discussed this specific demand. I was embarrassed, especially since my parents knew Rev. Stevens very well. The priest seemed a little baffled and looked in my direction as if to ask if that was what I truly wanted. I said nothing.

There was an awkward silence.

The priest said, "Oh, I see. Then I suppose I won't give a sermon."

Jerry confirmed by promptly responding, "Thank you very much."

So in church on our wedding day, following the singing and the reading of a Bible passage, guests were expecting to sit down for a lengthy sermon as was traditionally done in the Protestant Church. As they sat down, the Priest stood to his feet.

With a smile he began, "Well the Lord has brought these two young people together, and we pray that they will have happiness in their lives; and that no individual comes between them to create problems for their journey ahead. I would like the audience to know that, for once, we are not going to have a sermon after performing the wedding ceremony, because these two people have warned me, yes in the church, that if I give a long sermon they are going to get up and leave me standing in my pulpit talking."

This set the audience roaring with laughter. Astonished by the announcement, I looked at my husband with wide eyes.

Jerry leaned in and whispered to me, "Why does he have to announce this in the church? I thought we arranged this privately between ourselves."

Reverend Stevens continued, "So I cannot ignore the wishes of these two people. This is their day today, and we have to stick to their wishes. So on this note, I would like to propose that we sing a song for them, and then we can go and sign the register." As planned, the whole service that would typically fill an entire afternoon lasted no more than 30 minutes.

When Jerry and I went with our families to sign the registry, there was one outstanding feature that no one could ignore. Unfortunately for my new husband, my mother-in-law never came to terms with our decision to get married. Furthermore, she never forgave her younger sister, Auntie Joyce, for standing in as Jerry's mother during our engagement. She felt betrayed by her.

Throughout the wedding, Madam Agbotui sat in the church weeping, with a handkerchief in hand as tears streamed down her face. When it was time to sign the register, her whimpering became so conspicuous that one of my uncles could not help but ask her, with biting sarcasm, "Madam, are you crying out of joy for these two children?"

Caught off guard and looking embarrassed, my mother-in-law promptly responded, "Yes," as she wiped her tears away. It certainly did not help that in signing the registry, her son insisted that I keep my maiden name, Agyeman, and hyphenate it with his name. Upon hearing this, my father was elated. With six daughters and only one son, people had always told Dee that he would certainly lose his family name. So, Jerry knew this meant a lot to him, and he added that someday all of our children would carry the hyphenated name as well. This really endeared Jerry to my father. In my mind, I had initially thought that the hyphenated name was too long and cumbersome, but Jerry argued that the name "Rawlings" was so foreign that if I used it alone, I would lose a valuable part of my family background and the recognition that came with the Agyeman name. I became Mrs. Agyeman-Rawlings.

After signing the registry and taking pictures, we all proceeded to the Air Force Mess to join our guests for the reception. Because the economy was near total collapse, getting drinks for the reception was an uphill battle. No matter how much money we had, there was nothing available to buy in the shops. So we had travelled outside of Ghana to neighbouring Lome, Togo to buy beer, gin, brandy, whiskey and other special drinks and soft drinks in bulk.

After cutting the cake, Jerry was asked to give a speech, and he happily obliged. Standing to his feet, he spoke playfully about how he met me and how I had been a difficult girl in school. In his eyes, the sincerity in his heart shone brightly, as he spoke of how he admired the way I had carried myself because I would not allow any of the boys to place even a finger on my shoulder, let alone put their arm around me. I sat quietly, my breath taken away by a perfect moment. Jerry went on. Apparently, back then, he had made up his mind that he was going to protect me and later on marry me. As he spoke, our guests were enthralled by his speech.

He recalled the first time he came close to me and walked me under his umbrella. He told the story of how I was caught in the pouring rain, hopping puddles with my books tucked tightly under my arm as I desperately tried to keep them dry. Spotting me from a distance, he managed to snatch someone's umbrella, and like a superhero, he suddenly appeared and offered me the shelter of his 'borrowed' umbrella. Jerry joked that even then, as the rain beat down on me, I still did not want him to come near me. The guests burst into laughter, as every eye in the room seemed to have suddenly turned to look in my direction.

The day was long. After the reception, we went home to prepare for the dinner my parents were hosting in their home. It had been a very long day. We got back home that night completely exhausted. After carefully removing my gown and storing it in a safe place, I immediately freshened up with an evening shower.

By the time I stepped out ready to relive what had been the most memorable moment of our young lives, Jerry was fast asleep and sprawled directly across the bed. He was in a deep sleep. I decided not to wake him. Unfortunately, with him stretched across our bed, I was left with no other choice but to spend our first night together as a couple on the other side of the room on our single spare bed.

We had little idea of what life after marriage would become. I prayed it would be a magical ride, and maybe even the uncertainties that beckoned us welcome would be something we could live through. All my cards lay bare on the table; there were no regrets over the path I had taken to get here. Somehow, I found great comfort in the love that we shared. Having lived through what felt like fate, I was sure we would be fine. At least I hoped so.

CHAPTER FIFTEEN

The Shadows behind Us
A Nation under Siege

One of my younger sisters left Ghana for a post-graduate education at the University of California, in Los Angeles, in the United States, in 1976. She was getting a chance to explore a world where young people came from all over the planet with a host of ideas and experiences. I was sure she would enjoy the journey. The two of us wrote intermittently and spoke when we could. There was not much good news to share with her about the Ghana she left behind.

By then, Accra had become a place where the telephone system had turned into a mishmash of cables that lined the streets, and many of them not in any working condition. Sadly, if the rains did not wash away the telephone lines, people would steal them. When we were lucky enough to connect on the phone, our voices were cracking through the airwaves, our conversations broken and the line usually clicked dead before we had time to say our goodbyes.

It was just as irritating as the unpredictability of electricity and water services, each of which could be discontinued for several days at any time. All of us managed to slowly accept that reality as a challenge we had to live with, and even when it was unbearable through the nights, we could only hope for some permanent solution to this crisis. Much of Accra plunged into darkness at sunset. Sometimes in the evening, when the power was out and the night would be stark black, the only light

I could see from our doorway was from flickering candles carried by people walking by.

Standing at a distance, Ghanaians did not have to strain their eyes to see the hopes we hung on to shrivel with every passing minute. The government's handwork and day-to-day administration of the country had turned into an appalling display of service. At the time, the military government seemingly could not hide what had become a totally dysfunctional operation. With every passing moment, their work was undermined by incompetence, stifling procedures and dubious practices.

Incredible levels of corruption seemed to have permeated the highest echelons of the government, and the country was unravelling one moment after another. Most people tried to live their normal lives, as normal as they could make them and tried to ignore the ruins that seemed to be crumbling underneath our feet.

At the top of the pyramid was General Kutu Acheampong, whose political reign was witnessing severe inflation, political oppression, and food shortages. Adding to that was the police brutality and 'Union Government' scrambling to guarantee that the administration and the military had a permanent place in the government structure. It was swimming in a sea of unrestrained economic and political whims, and one that opened the door for the administration and its supporters to create loopholes to their benefit.

Rather than the clear turnaround he promised, Acheampong's regime only worsened the dishonest ways of the previous government whom he overthrew in the coup of 1972. General Acheampong could neither deliver economic reform nor any kind of political stability. As a result, the corruption heightened and economic mismanagement continued. It was painful to listen to the chatter in every street corner, with none of the frustration making its way to the administration's ear. The public's confidence eroded slowly. The country was in a downward spiral.

Before long, huge gaps in wealth seemed to be widening at every turn between the different segments of our society, and more and more people fell into utter poverty. In the rural areas outside of the major metropolitan areas, the sight was much worse. Families lived in dire deprivation.

In the capital, Accra's growing slum areas were filled with every sign of neglect on its filthy roads, and with no access to basic electricity services. Water pipes were dry, and people lined the streets with buckets, gallons and huge pans to fetch water in nearby areas. Sanitation had become an unfortunate afterthought.

Whenever I spoke to my sister on the phone, we would talk about some of the basic things one would expect any government to be able to provide for its people, or at least create an avenue to make the people support themselves. The present situation seemed so dreadful for so many, and the future did not look any brighter. Education had been devalued by the military government, and illiteracy rates ran high, especially among women and girl children. It felt as though the fate of Ghanaians born outside of the ruling members of government was confined to the squalor and devoid of any paths toward rewriting their own future.

In spite of this, Jerry and I were determined to make the most of the little we had. We were thrilled with our modest beginnings and the love we shared occasionally blurred the painful images around us. In early 1977, our married life had begun. We did all we could to make our first home together comfortable. After the wedding, Jerry gave up his single quarters at Burma Camp, and moved into the C.F.A.O. building with me.

As a young military wife, I was aware I could have joined him in the married quarters at Burma Camp, but Jerry claimed he would prefer to give up his residence altogether. His logic was that he would save on the monthly expense to be deducted from his salary for military housing. In my mind, keeping my flat was more cost-effective and convenient for my daily commute to work.

Like any young couple, we wanted to furnish our home, but we could not afford anything extravagant. We started out with the same cheap wooden furniture that came with the flat. I recall how, no matter how many times I tried polishing that furniture, the pieces still looked worn and badly in need of replacement.

Luckily Jerry was a good handyman and was determined to replace much of the furniture by building his own, mostly during the weekend. He started experimenting with different materials and began constructing furniture frames with scrap metal tubing we bought from a warehouse in town. He would spend hours at home on Saturday afternoons building chairs, a dining table, a living room table, the cabinets for storage, and wardrobes. Occasionally he would need special tools, and have no choice but to visit the carpenters whose shop was across the street from my parents' house. He would stay there, sometimes late into the night, until he got the chair frames perfect or the table tops levelled.

For my husband, being handy was an opportunity to find creative ways to provide eclectic pieces for our home. Once he came across a set of abandoned aircraft seats in an open yard near the Air Force station. He brought the torn and dusty seats home with plans to refurbish them. With new fabric, he re-upholstered the seats and converted them into living room chairs. This gave our room a unique look, and with time, our home became very comfortable with a lot of character. In these early years of my married life, the simple moments gave us memories to cherish. I would be cooking an afternoon meal in the kitchen, and hear the refreshing sound of Jerry pounding on wood and metal outside as our shortwave radio filled the air with music. It was enough being home together on Saturdays, knowing we were shaping our own future.

Our lives were far from picture-perfect. Soon after we got married, Jerry's mother would stop by frequently to visit her son. If I happened to open the door, Auntie Vic, as I later called her, would barge in, but would refuse to greet or acknowledge me. It was the strangest feeling, but I was careful not to disrespect my mother-in-law. It seemed very unusual to me, and I was sure that was not a normal practice in any culture.

Somehow, I had convinced myself that regardless of the sting of her antics, she would soon leave. As I held the door open to welcome her, Auntie Vic would launch straight into her native Ewe, addressing only her son. She knew I would not understand. Her blatant disregard for me infuriated Jerry and immediately spiked tensions in our home.

In one moment, we had been the happiest people on earth, and suddenly all joy would dissolve from Jerry's face as he fought hard to remain calm in her presence. Sadly, every time his mother came by, friction sparked the air like a storm. I felt it as well. From the second she entered, a knot tightened in the pit of my stomach. She spoke rapid Ewe in sharp, bellowing tones, but Jerry would reply abruptly, in English, "Auntie... wait! When you walked in I was talking to Nana about something. Let me finish with her. When I finish, then we can talk. Have a seat."

Auntie Vic would dismiss his comments, and start talking again. And again, Jerry would stop her. "No! Auntie... you will have to wait," he would say defiantly. On a few occasions, she would get angry, storm out of our flat and slam the door behind her. She had never gotten past the fact that her son had not married a white woman, and it showed.

It was agonizing for me to stand back at the times when she would barge in and start talking to Jerry, but he would stop her mid-sentence, "Auntie, when you entered, did you or did you not see another other person standing here?"

"What are you talking about?" she would reply, looking annoyed.

Then Jerry would have to explain, "Auntie, I'm asking you, did you see somebody other than me in here? If you did, then the least you can do is say good afternoon. If not, if you didn't see the other person, *then walk out*, because this is her flat and I don't think you have the right to come in and behave this way." Jerry did this a number of times to protect me from the harassment of his mother, which was helpful when we were both together.

But one afternoon she stopped by when I was alone. Auntie Vic would make her way to the kitchen to see what I was cooking. The moment she entered the kitchen, her gaze would zero in on the pot of soup or stew simmering on the gas cooker. Without hesitation, she would open the lids and take a spoon to each pot to examine the ingredients. "Oh, we don't eat this in our house."

"But Auntie Vic, this is not your house," I replied.

"My son doesn't like this type of food," she would say. "So why are you cooking this for him?" she demanded.

"Well, it was your son who asked me to cook this for him. And he is the one who asked me to put all the ingredients you see in there."

"Hmm," she muttered in disappointment. "So are you saying he has started eating pork?"

"Well, I don't know when he started. I just know that he always eats it with me."

It was sad to feel that my mother-in-law was doing all she could to fill my life with gloom. I always forced myself to maintain my composure. Inwardly, I felt anxious and tense around her. But outwardly, I tried not to show it. For years, our relationship remained icy and strained. Jerry saw this as well. On one visit when both of us were home, she took things too far. Perhaps, that day, she was irritated. Because out of nowhere, she made negative comments towards me and instead of responding, I quietly left the room and went straight into our bedroom.

But this time, her comments provoked Jerry to such anger that he picked up a chair and threw it at the window, causing it to shatter from top to bottom. I was in utter shock when I heard the sudden crash of the chair hitting the window and Jerry exploding in anger at his mother. I did not move. Still, in the bedroom, I sat quietly on the bed until she left the house. I felt sad for Jerry and sometimes was overcome with guilt that I had come between them.

After we got married, Jerry and I started spending more time together on the weekends, leisure travelling outside of Accra. We often drove up to *Sogakope*, a small town in the Volta Region, where we would go swimming, fishing, and camp along the Volta River. Jerry loved diving for oysters, so we would often borrow a small boat from the people he knew in the village and take it upriver, where Jerry spent hours diving in the water for oysters. At sunset, we gathered his catch, returned to the river banks and cooked the oysters over a hot fire. We savoured every bite. Our weekend excursions, as relaxing an escape as they had become, soon pulled back a curtain to reality.

The crisis had become too much for any of us to ignore. It was not until I travelled outside of Accra to places like Tamale and Takoradi on an assignment for my company, UTC, that I came face-to-face with the true horrors of poverty as it gravely affected our nation's women and children. The plight of the struggling mothers was gut-wrenching. The conditions in towns like Tefle, Sogakope, Mankesim, Anomabu, Suhum, and Enyinam were devastating, and not much different from the others.

In villages across the country, the situation for women was even worse as it seemed there was no semblance of any relief in sight for them. In the small towns, I worked in the gated communities of the beautiful UTC compounds, where I managed the interior design of all corporate housing units reserved for executives, mostly European, and their families. Each housing unit was fully equipped with luxury amenities in well-furnished, British-inspired architecture and bungalows. Though I worked within the compound, I was deeply affected by the local people who lived outside the compound walls. Their plight was impossible to ignore, and it was difficult to fathom what future lay ahead for them and their children.

It seemed it would take an eternity for them to taste some of the basic amenities that one would expect in a country, even one fraught with difficulties like ours. Malnourished children ran around barefoot and in rags, their eyes glazed and full of pain and confusion. In the distance, I was struck by the scene of women and young children seemingly working long days under the hot and unforgiving African sun. I heard inconceivable stories of women scraping to find a livelihood. Women in some rural areas would have to give birth in the morning and hurry back to work in the fields in the afternoon.

From the little I saw of the lavish lifestyles of the government officers, I couldn't often help but wonder if they felt any discomfort at the end of the day, knowing that for every resource they misused, many more people had to live wretched lives in such conditions. The women in the rural areas did not chant any slogans, nor did they demand better working conditions from their well-fed urban leaders. Instead, they simply stooped in their fields, from sunrise to sunset, tending to their crops, for any little money they could earn.

Adding to their misery, some of the young women were sold into marriage to older men. It was baffling to find an uneducated young girl who, by the age of 13, had been sold into marriage and given birth to multiple children within a few years. I could not imagine myself walking a mile in their shoes, yet they showed a strength and perspective that was almost unreal. For the preceding generation, the story had probably been the same, and they'd never had enough voices coming to their aid. Sadly, the marginalization and disempowerment had been a formula for the vicious cycle of poverty, and the women and children seemed to bear the main brunt of its ugly consequences.

My trips to Ghana's hinterlands became enlightening and equally crippling. It was as if so many people lived in a completely different world, one in which every hope was stripped away from them. In these small towns, some of the girls had been victims of cruel customs, such as *trokosi,* a female sexual slavery, and polygamy.

Other towns held on to traditions that condoned female genital mutilation, a practice which often resulted in excessive bleeding and the death of an infant or adolescent victims. It was as if the leaders of communities and the country had been too preoccupied with their own wealth to give any attention to some of these crises that had been brewing for years.

In my own mind, it seemed the weight of our local traditions was heaped onto the women, who were often regarded as the property of their husbands or fathers. They were commodities bought and sold between men. Over and again I saw how any attempt to liberate themselves was condemned or met with harsh ramifications. It was rather unfortunate, and one that would break anyone's heart. Yet, these women managed to become the backbone of the rural economy. They produced much of the food crops and bore the sole responsibility for raising the children, feeding their families and providing care for the elderly in their communities.

I was a young woman, fortunate to have had a life that did not face the same uphill climb these women and children had to endure. The national crisis in the country had magnified every challenge and the bitter sunburned even more. For the mothers, the scratches in their palms and dust on their bare feet with their children firmly tucked in the cloths on the backs told their story. None of their pleas ended up on the national agenda or were even prioritised as a part of the nation's development needs.

In a way, witnessing the total degeneration of women in our society strengthened my hostility towards the notoriously corrupt practices of an exclusively male-dominated political system. It was blindingly glaring and cruel. The women I saw in rural Ghana left an indelible mark on my mind, heart, and soul—one I could not ignore.

I often returned to Accra to much of the same contrasts of affluence and abject poverty I had just seen in the heart of the country. Jerry saw the same, and to get his mind off the poor social conditions of the time, he would spend time after work taking an aircraft out for aerobatic drills or going horseback riding at the *Recce* regiment, also at Burma Camp, riding stables. On other days, he would simply take his dog out and go swimming or fishing in the Volta River.

Still, the more he engaged in leisure activities to distract his mind from the despair in society, the more deprivation stared at him directly in the face. He would return home, clearly disturbed, a cigarette half-smoked and tucked behind his ear, and lament, "Nana, anytime I swim up-river, I become haunted by the hungry, lean and dejected looks on the faces of the fishermen, women and children at the riverside."

His restless energy struggled to find sufficient outlet in the outdoor activities he once relished. Now the images of poverty and misery that had become a permanent part of Ghana's landscape plagued his days and strengthened his resolve to act on behalf of the poor in our society. This started in our home.

As an employee of UTC, I was fortunate to be given employee access to a few essential commodities on a regular basis to keep for ourselves and take home for our families. But even with that privilege, Jerry's consuming passion for helping the poor constantly depleted our supplies faster than I could keep track.

Gradually I started noticing that our supply of food rations and other essential commodities that I bought soon disappeared. I realized that whenever Jerry left the house to go oyster fishing, he would carry with him whatever rations—soap, sardines, corned beef, mackerel fish— we had left in the house to the people at the riverside. At times, we'd be left with nothing, so I had to find a way of hiding a few commodities for ourselves. He became so obsessed with the poor living conditions of the ordinary Ghanaian that the two of us started working together to do whatever we could to help anyone we would come across.

One day a mentally-ill man paraded across the street from our house, and it was obvious he could use some help. "Nana, we must find a way to feed him something every day," Jerry insisted. "Look at the positive and beautiful way in which the man cleans the environment." The devotion of this man to cleaning trash from public streets while suffering from mental illness earned Jerry's respect and both of our sympathies. We did the little we could to make sure that he always had something to eat. We were a young couple with little of our own, but we soon found that the more we gave, the more overwhelmed we became. It seemed we could never do enough.

Like us, people's hopes lay bare, and the destitution had filled every cloud and sky. It felt like we were stuck in a nightmare, sinking slowly in a Ghana that was quickly becoming intolerable and hellishly hot.

CHAPTER SIXTEEN

A COUNTRY WITH NOTHING LEFT TO LOSE
The Silent Majority

Back in Accra, senior officers of the military, high-level corporate and government officials continued to increase their ill-gotten riches at the expense of the poor and starving masses. The *nouveau riche* 'friends' of Acheampong, including Lebanese and Indian businessmen, flaunted their newly acquired wealth with vulgar ostentation. Unlike those who were raised in wealthy homes or inherited family wealth, this *newly rich* class of people was conspicuous in their spending. They acquired lavish possessions they felt rich people would own, and bought everything they could find, to show that they had money.

This was happening in the same Ghana where most people could scarcely find a meal, yet anyone could see sprawling mansions were under construction in the most expensive areas in the city. The audacity of these men and women was nauseating. Most Ghanaians were outraged by the ostentatious display of wealth by the power elites and their total disregard for the masses. In a country as small as ours, no one could miss the close juxtaposition of a wealthy few and a poor multitude.

By 1977, the economic crisis had reached catastrophic levels. The standard of living for the ordinary Ghanaian had plunged to historic lows decades before. Inflation and every dire economic indicator pointed upwards. Men and women were leaving their daily jobs having earned only a few *cedis*. They needed much more to provide a decent meal for a family. Strikes and demonstrations spread throughout the country, from the breweries to the airport, to the post office, to the oil refinery. Medical doctors also went on strike to draw attention to the appalling hospital conditions.

While the few rich in Ghana managed to amass wealth in these turbulent years, healthcare facilities could not even boast of a trace of essential medicine. Supplies of bandages, syringes, needles and other essential medical supplies never found their way into the hospitals. Suddenly hospitals in Ghana had become the places where people went to die.

In plain sight however, people saw the government elites and their families completely shielded from the chaos that had engulfed the nation. Nurses, too, took to the streets in protest against the fact that they were being paid very little money each day at a time when they could barely afford a can of sardines and a bar of soap.

In the streets of Accra, organised mobs of angry students and skilled professionals — including doctors, lawyers, nurses, and professors — walked away from whatever wretched conditions were left behind in their vocations and took to the streets in protest. Many demanded higher wages to meet the prices of the basic foodstuffs that seemed to rise every day. Others carried placards and marched angrily for better working conditions. The overriding chant became a cry for the immediate resignation of General Acheampong and the SMC government.

For us, the crisis hit especially close to home. The degenerating state of Ghana had seeped into the Air Force. During Jerry's service, he witnessed the rapid deterioration of discipline and morale resulting from corruption and fraud within the military government. Jerry recalled how when he joined the military, he had hoped to find high moral integrity and a personal sense of purpose in military life, but even before he finished his formal training, he was quickly disillusioned.

Two years after Jerry joined the Air Force, he displayed what seemed to be a natural aptitude for flying, because he was recognised as the best pilot and commissioned as a Pilot Officer. He was promoted to Flight Officer in 1971 and became a Flight Lieutenant in 1978. However, like everything else in the country, the Air Force was quickly heading downhill through gross neglect.

As steady promotion through the military ranks brought Jerry in closer contact with the "ruling and privileged" classes, their social values and their reverence for the office they had pledged to uphold struck a loud discord. Jerry, much like some of his colleagues, developed a keen awareness and utter disgust for the injustices in our society. He became consumed by the sharp contrast between the affluent few and the impoverished majority of Ghanaians, many of whom were reduced to hunger and utter despair. Their plight was in plain sight.

In angry disbelief, he observed the corruption of the Acheampong administration and the contempt with which the senior officers of the military treated the lower rank and file. As the majority of Ghanaians' sufferings intensified, so did the public's hostility toward the military, the lower ranks bearing the brunt of their rage. The insults thrown at the ordinary soldiers were disgraceful. Out of anger, even some market women were reported to have thrown their urine on the soldiers walking through the market as a means to publicly humiliate the source of their suffering.

It was impossible to miss the chaos that had sunk to such filthy standards. The split remained in the military ranks. The men and women in the lower ranks were not given enough food to eat, and the same sense of abandonment was evident in the tattered uniforms some wore. Even their pride did not care to keep them company. These were the people who had the duty to protect the country and in many cases were sent out on duty without proper shoes or military training kits.

Equally neglected were the state of the police. At checkpoints and street corners, on-duty police officers and soldiers did all they could to enforce the law while wearing local *charlie wote,* flip-flops, on their feet, and they became the embodiment of the crisis of the time. The men and women were disgruntled, but they could only voice their discontent among themselves. None of the senior officers seemed to care.

Their faded uniforms pieced together from scraps left over by their predecessors made them look frail and unkempt. None of them had access to vehicles. Their mismatched and dishevelled appearance drew snickers from the public and ridicule from passers-by. Their emaciated frames reduced them to the image of boys attempting to look official, yet barely big enough to fit into their oversized uniforms. With hollowed eyes and gaunt faces, these men were a stark reminder of how quickly hunger and deprivation had depleted our population of strength and pride.

Such injustices made the soldiers of the lower rank and file an angry and embittered lot. Though Jerry was a middle-ranking officer of the Air Force, he had more friends and camaraderie among the ranks than he did among the officer corps. He had been put in charge of the Air Force boxing team, which brought him into regular contact with the other ranks for whom he felt greater empathy. Jerry had also been an avid horseman, so he frequently rode at the Recce riding stables, which made him a popular figure among the *Recce* Regiment. There he met the men who lived in the trenches of Ghana's military, hardworking and honest men wallowing in such lack, while the exact opposite was the reality next door. Thus it troubled him no end to know that corruption among his higher-ups was strangling every life out of the very base of the military.

I was not the least bit surprised at how the years were taking a toll on Jerry. Such was his nature. Jerry always had a genuine compassion for the underprivilaged and a natural impulse to protect and defend anyone he felt was exploited. At home, he spoke often and compassionately to me about the need to clear up the widespread corruption in high places.

"Nana, I'm disgusted by the abuse of power in the Armed Forces," he would say with frustration.

Both of us had been raised to believe that people in authority bore an even greater responsibility to display the highest standards of integrity, and yet everywhere we turned, there were numerous examples of people in authority illegally enriching themselves at the expense of the poor and helpless.

Given that the country was in such steep decline, I considered myself lucky to even have a job. Still, much like the rest of the country, Jerry and I were struggling. Even with two incomes, our only transportation was my small blue Fiat car, which my father had bought me the year I graduated from UST. Jerry and I shared the car for our daily commutes to work. But with prices soaring from the oil crisis of 1973, even that luxury became difficult and expensive to maintain, especially as petrol queues, three and four miles long, became a permanent feature all over Accra.

As the economy worsened, basic food items like margarine and bread became too expensive. Rice nearly disappeared. Then milk, sugar, matches, and sardines became rationed. And worst of all, the weight of political fear invaded and dominated every aspect of our lives. The Supreme Military Council (SMC) had induced so much fear into the society that even soldiers were afraid to openly discuss the glaring indiscretions and mischiefs of their Commander in Chief, General Kutu Acheampong, and his cohorts.

In early 1978, I was sitting in my office immersed in work when Jerry rushed in and blurted, "Nana, you have to stop work and go with me to this cocktail party."

"What! Now? I can't. I'm in the middle of work."

"Nana, please, you just have to ask permission and go with me. The Chairman and his wife are hosting it.

I did not think Jerry would be so unreasonable as to ask me to rush out in the middle of my workday so I reasoned it must be something important. He explained quickly. "Yesterday, all officers were called to Burma Hall and we were warned that each and every one of us must attend the reception accompanied by our wives."

During Acheampong's years in office, it had become a taboo for an officer not to attend a military function, but it was even worse if he attended the function without his wife.

Knowing this, I sighed in frustration. But I knew very well that seemingly ignoring another "invitation" from the General and his wife would be an offence, for which my husband would surely suffer the consequences. To avoid compromising Jerry's position, I agreed and asked my boss for permission to leave early.

We rushed to meet the three o'clock starting time. Jerry and I rushed home, and I quickly changed into an evening cocktail dress. We dashed out of our flat and arrived at the entrance of Burma Hall just before the doors opened, nearly breathless. Standing in the doorway with a pen and paper, a woman stood dutifully marking off the names of all officers and their wives who crossed the threshold. We entered slowly, and the woman in the doorway made eye contact and smiled scornfully. She sarcastically added, "Oh, so today you've decided to join us."

"Yes," I replied sternly.

"Today I was able to get off work early. But mind you, I am a working woman and in our household, I have the same amount of financial responsibilities as my husband." Leaving the exchange at that, I turned my gaze away and casually walked past her.

I took a seat in one of the chairs encircling the dance floor. Local highlife music filled the air. Along the back wall were tables displaying an assortment of luxury foods and assorted drinks that seemed to spread to no end. The vulgar display of wealth and abundance defied the realities of extreme poverty that were staring most Ghanaians in the face daily. It was incredible. Sitting there, I thought to myself, *how could these people live with themselves?*

A lady sitting nearby leaned over in my direction and asked, "Have you noticed that everybody is dancing around Mrs. Acheampong?"

"Yes," I replied. "Is that what usually happens?"

"If you don't join and dance around her, they'll target you and your husband," she said.

"Well, I've just come from work. So I am not getting up to dance around Mrs. Acheampong," I could not hold my words. I was disgusted at the sight of the greed and blatant recklessness around me.

Looking past my face at another woman, the lady leaned in again and asked, "You see that woman over there?"

"Yes," I replied.

"She just had a baby with the Chairman."

"What!" I exclaimed.

"*Ohh, yes,*" she said with conviction. "And not only that, she's a married woman ... one whose husband is a senior officer." It was as though the men who filled the administration and the military top ranks lived in a world of their own. Apparently, that was an open secret and I was one of the few women who was new to this club. For any Ghanaian doing their best to waddle through this economic chaos that had saddled the country, these stories were a bit more repulsive than soothing. I was appalled, but such stories had become the order of the day.

Stories about the chairman's womanising abounded in the political culture of the 1970s. Sadly, it got to a point where the single fastest way for a woman to gain any type of upward mobility was to catch the wandering eye of the General himself—or next best, one of his cronies. The Chairman scarcely worked hard to conceal his sexual exploits, nor did he hide the lavish gifts he granted them in return for such favours. A well-known womaniser, he was alleged to crown many of his female "conquests" generously with Golf automobile or with the favour of job security for the husbands of women that were married.

In the midst of the filth, dignity seemed to have taken a backseat to everything else. Although the SMC Chairman himself was a married man, he rationalised his philandering in a rather odd and childish manner, confidently saying "There was nothing wrong with having a backyard garden even if one has a farm." The General's compulsive pursuit of women became so rampant that it turned the presidential castle into a sort of brothel with a revolving door, spewing women in and out.

Power can become an aphrodisiac and at no time in Ghana's history was it more alluring than during the SMC's reign. In Accra, many women began using their gender — popularly termed "bottom power"— to gain personal and political favour from the Chairman or other men of high rank. Sadly, for women who were made to feel weak, vulnerable, and powerless in our society, 'bottom power' went a long way in creating a false sense of personal power, prestige, and financial security. This moral decline led many desperate Ghanaian women, married and unmarried, to discount their dignity to such a level in order to advance their business or gain easy access to scarce commodities.

Adding to this, a home-grown black-market system known as *kalabule* became the height of corruption. Characterised by cheating, smuggling, and racketeering, *kalabule* perpetuated "bottom power" and other crimes, while protecting the wealthy. In the name of exercising government control over the distribution of scarce commodities, SMC's regime instituted a system of paper 'chits' for the release of imported goods from state-owned factories and warehouses. Rationed out to the public as '*essential commodities*', imported goods such as milk, baby food, toilet rolls, sardines, St. Louis cube sugar, Exeter corned beef, Pepsodent toothpaste, Asepso soap, and Omo detergent were all allocated to designated supermarkets only. Any individual caught selling these items on the street would be subject to fines and imprisonment. But in spite of these 'controls,' the black market activity flourished.

The 'chit' system became the underpinning for deep-rooted, institutionalised corruption which permeated every level of society. It began with the government bureaucrat who issued the original chit and ended with the man or woman on the street who bought the actual goods at grossly inflated prices. *Kalabule* became the plague of this period, and the term came to be used for any kind of corruption or 'profiteering', including the selling of any goods above the official government-controlled prices, which were rarely ever recognised.

Ghana's misfortunes under NRC/SMC's regime had caused great distress to every man and woman who was not part of his administration. The repercussions of the strikes were widespread, and soon they came knocking at our door when we least expected it. Jerry and I were both asleep when someone started banging on our front door and woke us up in the middle of the night. In the doorway, a young woman was frantically wheezing and pleading for help as she struggled to breathe. She was our neighbour Elizabeth, who lived in the flat above ours.

I recognised her symptoms right away as an asthmatic attack and told Jerry that we have to rush her to a hospital. Jerry grabbed the car keys, and we hurried to the nearby Ridge Hospital. Getting to the hospital should have taken only a few minutes if it was not for the huge potholes that covered the once-paved roads. I sat in the front seat of the small Fiat car, my head turned the whole way and trying my best to keep her awake. I tried not to panic. We found our way to the entrance.

Jerry rushed Elizabeth into the building and yelled, "Emergency! Please! This girl needs help now. She can't breathe."

There were nurses in the room, and they met him. Their first words, "I'm sorry sir, but we have no doctor on duty."

"No doctor? What about medication? She needs something right now, please! She's asthmatic," Jerry pleaded.

"Sir, I am sorry. We have no doctor and no medication. There are shortages everywhere. You have to bring your own, and then we can administer it to the patient. Otherwise, you have to take her somewhere else."

I took off running through the hospital looking to find anyone or anything that could help. Jerry did not have the luxury of time to be dumbfounded. He held Elizabeth in his arms while pleading with the nurses to do anything they could, to find any medicine they had on hand. Anything. Elizabeth's condition was worsening by the minute. Unable to breathe, she was slowly losing consciousness.

Suddenly, she collapsed in Jerry's arms. The nurses stood by watching, while Jerry tried desperately to revive Elizabeth. From the glass window, I could see Jerry frantically trying mouth-to-mouth resuscitation to stimulate respiration in her body. It would be to no avail. Elizabeth died in Jerry's arms that night at Ridge Hospital.

Devastated by the loss, he voiced his anger at the staff. Jerry was infuriated by the inaction of the nurses and shocked by their indifference. We were both shaken by the death and took it very personally. We soon realized that the problem was not with the hospital, alone, nor was it an isolated event. The apathy and the lack of the most basic of healthcare services were symptomatic of a much larger problem happening in the country.

CHAPTER SEVENTEEN

ZANETOR
"Let the Darkness End": 1977 – 1979

On a hot day in the late months of 1977, I suffered *a severe asthma attack and slipped into a coma.* This was the first time I had been overtaken by such intense weakness and pain. I would never have thought what was to be a routine visit to the doctor that afternoon would become something much worse.

The previous time I was at the hospital, I had walked away with unexpected news, but nothing of grave concern. I had been at work in the afternoon when I started feeling sharp pains in my lower abdomen. I tried to ignore it, hoping it would subside, but every time I moved or even coughed, the pain got worse and, eventually, unbearable.

So after work, I finally decided to go straight to the Military Hospital to have it checked. In the consultation room, the doctor did a physical exam on my abdomen, applying gentle pressure on the painful area and then ran multiple tests, including blood and urine tests. Upon receiving the results, the doctor told me, "Nana, I have your results, and they reveal two different findings."

Two? I thought to myself. What does that mean? I was now truly petrified.

"Well, first of all," he said, "the pain in your abdomen seems to be your appendix. It looks like you may be suffering from appendicitis, which means your appendix is inflamed. The good news is we can operate right away to remove the inflamed appendix. The operation is a common procedure, so you don't have to worry, and it requires only a short recovery. But we want to do it before it gets worse."

"Okay Doctor. But you said there were *two* results?"

"Yes. The second result revealed that you… my dear… are pregnant," he smiled and then added, "Congratulations."

"Pregnant? I asked, in utter surprise. "Really?"

"Yes," he confirmed.

"How far?"

"Very early. From what I can tell, you're around eight weeks."

"Uhh, thank you," I replied, not knowing what else to say. At that moment, I was both astonished and elated, and then suddenly worried about the pregnancy, remembering I was to undergo an operation. The doctor wasted no time. He scheduled the operation, and I immediately had my appendix removed, thankfully with no complications, and the pregnancy stayed intact.

Incidentally, throughout this time, my parents did not know we were expecting a baby. I wanted to tell them but Jerry still insisted that we should not. We had been married for less than a year, and the pregnancy had happened much sooner than either of us had planned to start having children. Even so, I was excited at the thought of a baby in our home. Jerry's reaction was quite the opposite. He was definitely disturbed by the news, and my excitement did not help. I remember when I had first told him.

"Pregnant? How far?" he had asked

"It's still very early. The doctor said I'm only around eight weeks, so still in the first trimester."

"Do we have to start having babies now? What will your parents think?"

"My parents? What do you mean, 'what will *they* think?'" I asked. "It's not like we've had the baby out of wedlock."

"No, no. Nana, this is too embarrassing. It's too soon. At least we should let one year pass."

That's when I realized that Jerry was actually feeling embarrassed by the timing of the pregnancy because it was less than a year from our wedding day. He wanted to wait for the conventional one year or more before starting a family. We decided not to tell anyone, and I continued to work as usual.

Again, I tried to make the case, "It's not like we've become pregnant out of wedlock. This is not a scandal. So what's the problem?"

"No, no, no, we shouldn't tell them."

"Okay, fine."

So we left it at that but soon, I could tell that both of my parents saw the pregnancy growing. Their faces betrayed their thoughts, yet they did not ask me about it.

In the fourth month of pregnancy, my health took an unexpected turn. That was when the heat wave hit Ghana, and the weather turned extremely hot and humid. I started suffering from asthma attacks more frequently than normal. No one at work knew I was expecting a baby, so I asked for permission to leave work early because I was having trouble breathing due to my asthma. This time I went to see Dr. Addae, our old family friend, who my mother had originally wanted me to marry.

At this time he had his own clinic, and he knew my medical history with asthma. He took me in right away and treated me with medication and then sent me home to rest. But the next morning, I was back, suffering again from wheezing, shortness of breath, and difficulty breathing. So Dr. Addae gave me an intravenous injection (IV) and kept me there for a few hours to monitor me. Surprisingly, as he was treating me, he used this time as an opportunity to hash out old feelings concerning my choice to marry Jerry over him.

"Mmmm, you went to marry a junior officer. Now see how you are suffering? I could have taken better care of you."

In that moment of weakness, all I could do was ignore him and continue treatment until he sent me home. The symptoms recurred even more strongly the next day, and I returned to his clinic, this time barely able to walk. The weather was blistering hot, and I was struggling to breathe. He took my blood pressure and temperature and suggested that I be transferred to the Military Hospital for more advanced care. He wrote me a medical note and asked, "Who will take you to the hospital?"

"I will drive," I said.

"No! You can't drive in this condition. You can barely walk. Nana, did you drive here?"

"Yes."

"What? I am going to complain to your mother about this!" he raged. "What kind of a husband is that?" But I was too ill to put up an argument or defend Jerry.

Leaving everything, Dr. Addae opted to drive me to the hospital himself, where he put me in the care of his colleague, Dr. Sarkodie-Addo. His staff immediately provided me with a wheelchair, but I was so weak I struggled just to take steps to sit in the wheelchair. My blood pressure must have been dangerously low because I was faint and barely conscious. They moved me to a ward, and the last I remembered was the doctor giving me two IVs and urging me to rest. The next moments sank into a blur.

I was later told I had been unconscious and slipped into a coma for five days. Still, even in that delicate state, I remember several distinct things going on around me, like the sharp, piercing pain on my buttocks each time a nurse gave me an injection. I remember the muffled sounds of nurse's voices around my bed for what appeared to be hours of elapsed time, as they took turns repeating the same message to me: "Nana, open your eyes. Please open your eyes. We beg you, Nana open your eyes."

I recall one nurse I knew well from previous visits for my asthma, urging me to wake up in our local *Twi* language, "Nana, did you come here to give us trouble? Open your eyes and don't bring us trouble." I must have reacted, because I remember hearing her say, "Oh, look at her, she is smiling. Hey, if you do not open your eyes, I will give you another injection for you to cry again."

But the most memorable voice of all was Jerry's. Every morning I could hear him asking, "Is she awake? Has she opened her eyes?"

"No, sir," someone would answer.

On the third day of the coma, the doctors spoke to Jerry about the pregnancy. I remember hearing part of a discussion between a doctor and Jerry.

"… We cannot operate on her when she is in a coma."

I could faintly hear Jerry, "Can't you do a simple D and C?" He was referring to dilation and curettage surgical procedure that was often used on women in such situations to remove tissue from the inner parts of the uterus.

Replying in a low whisper, "We still need anesthesia, and she is not in good enough condition for that."

"She will not feel it if she's in a coma," Jerry chimed in quickly. I then heard footsteps fade out.

After losing our neighbour, Elizabeth, who had died so tragically in Jerry's arms after an asthma attack, I understood his anxieties about my health wholeheartedly.

On the morning of what was now the fifth day, Jerry told me a few years later of how he drove to the Holy Spirit Cathedral Church before coming to the hospital. The weather was extremely hot, and the blazing sun was beating down mercilessly. He later told me that he walked to the front pew of the church and knelt down and began to pray. As he prayed, he asked God to wake me up and to let it rain, so that the cool weather could help me recover. He said he prayed so intensely that he either fell asleep or went into a trance for short period. Either way, when he woke, he walked out of the church and into a downpour.

To his delight, rain was coming down so heavily that the moisture instantly *broke* the heatwave, giving way to beautiful airy winds and much cooler temperatures. It had to be a divine moment that brought much relief to all of us, and that was the morning I opened my eyes. The cool weather helped me to recover quickly. Before long, I regained my strength and left the hospital healthy, strong and about five months into the pregnancy.

I woke up at about 5 a.m. with a sharp, piercing pain. It had started in my back and had quickly spread to my abdomen. The labour pains kept increasing at short intervals.

"Jerry, wake up. I think it's time. I'm sure the baby is ready to come. I better go and have my bath."

"Ok, go to the bathroom. I'll go and get you hot water and a bucket."

As soon as I started with my bath, the pain increased in its intensity. I quickly realized that this was no time to have a bath. I poured the water over me and hurried to get dressed.

Jerry peeked in, "Have you finished so soon?"

"The pain is too much. There's no way I can bathe in this condition. I need to get to the hospital."

"Ok, I'm ready whenever you are."

Suddenly, we heard a big knock on the front door. Jerry answered while I was still in the bathroom getting dressed. I could not make out what was being said, but I heard an exchange between Jerry and another male.

Ah, who could be here at this time? It was around 5:15 a.m. The door shut and he came back to the bathroom to tell me that it was MI officers with orders that he must report immediately to the Military Intelligence headquarters.

"What? *Now?* Did you tell them that your wife is in labour?" I asked as shooting pain crumpled my face in waves.

"I've told them… and they said they are prepared to wait."

Jerry's mind was made up, "Look, I have nowhere to run. This is my country. I'm not going anywhere."

He tried to reassure me, "If they want to wait, let them wait. I will drop you at the hospital, and then I'll go to the Military Intelligence office."

My hospital supplies were already packed. So he helped me get dressed and then drove me to the hospital. We arrived around 5:45 a.m. and a midwife admitted me and got me a bed in the labour ward. I understood Jerry had to leave. He said, "Okay, Nana, I am going to report to the M.I. now. I shouldn't be long. I'll be back as soon as they are finished with me."

Before I could reply, a nursing sister responded. "Don't worry. I'm sure she won't have the baby before you return," she said confidently. "Usually when it's the first child, they really fuss and take their time," she added.

But she was wrong. Soon after Jerry left, I was fully dilated and I delivered the baby that morning.

My pregnancy could not have come at a worse time in Ghana's economic turmoil. It was at the height of the nation's economic decline, and it was not uncommon to find the halls of the Military Hospital plunged into darkness. The power outages were rampant. Partial lighting was provided by a generator and the flickering light of lanterns carried around by hospital staffers. The deprivation was everywhere. The hospital did not have any bedsheets or sanitary towels for the women and barely had any medicines. Other essential items like syringes and cotton wool were unavailable. In the darkness, the medical staff struggled to guide the women through labour, in the dim delivery rooms.

The sight of the struggling women was frightening. I knew that if I wanted any of those essential items, I had to bring my own. Fortunately, we could. Weeks before I had gone into labour, Jerry and I made the four-hour journey by road into neighbouring Togo to buy the list of hospital supplies my doctor had recommended. Without those, I would have been in the same situation as the other women whose lives hung in a balance just as dangerously as their unborn children's.

Even in the labour ward, I was forced to keep a close watch on my personal belongings and the hospital supplies I had to buy from the moment I arrived until the time we went home with the baby. Desperate nurses working in devastatingly poor conditions were known to sell patients their own stash of scarce medical supplies to supplement their incomes. Sadly, they made a lot of money from their vulnerable patients. Luckily, I had everything I needed.

It was saddening to face the fact that SMC's regime was so oblivious to the plight of Ghanaians whom they claimed to be serving. All the while, I could only think of the blinding fluorescence of the bright lights in every street corner and public facilities in Zurich, when I worked there under UTC. From Swiss banks to shopping centres to public universities, high-quality lighting and overflows of supplies filled every facility in abundance. I could only imagine the hospital delivery wards: the blankets, pink or blue, the menu of essential medications and painkillers, doctors in white coats with their sanitary gloves tending to patients under the calm white hospital light. I could only imagine it now, and ours seemed like it was a world away.

My little baby girl arrived on the first day of June 1978. After her birth, I was wheeled from the delivery room back to the labour ward in a state of extreme exhaustion. The nurses put the baby in a nursery to allow me to rest.

Jerry returned around 9 a.m., and it appeared as if I had not moved since he left.

"Nana," he called out.

I opened my eyes from a deep sleep and was surprised to see him back so soon. Usually, the M.I. would keep him for several hours for their interrogations.

"Have they released you already?" I asked.

"Oh, yes. They just asked me the usual questions," he said. "I'll give you details later." The M.I. had nothing on him. So, after interrogating him, like several times before, they had to let him go.

"When is the baby coming?" he asked eagerly.

"Oh, the baby has been born."

"Already?" he questioned, scanning my body, covered in blankets.

"A girl or a boy?"

"A girl. She's in the nursery." I was so exhausted, I drifted back to sleep. So, he hurried to the nursery.

Aba arrived later with Elizabeth. Aba had been around our home and been incredibly helpful to me throughout the pregnancy. She had been the one who washed my blood-stained nightgown after the delivery and my dirty clothes during my hospital stay.

She soon left the hospital to inform my mother at Tiny Tots Kindergarten. All Aba had to say was, "Maa, Nana has had the baby."

She recalled Maa did not even ask if I had a boy or a girl. She just started screaming in the class, "Oh children, Mrs. Agyeman is a grandmother, Mrs. Agyeman is a grandmother. Eh, all of you, Mrs. Agyeman is a grandmother." She knelt down and started praying. She still had not found out the sex of the baby. She was a grandmother, and that was all that mattered. That afternoon when Maa came to the hospital, she arrived thanking God and singing His praises out loud in the ward. I was so embarrassed that I asked her to please stop. Since the family was all arriving, the nurses brought the baby into my room.

Jerry's mother arrived. She embraced her son and was happy to see the new baby, but as usual, she had little to say to me. After observing the baby's features, she turned to ask my mother, "Ah, where could this baby's nose be from? Because in my family, we don't have such flat noses."

I was in disbelief that she could even start such an awkward conversation at this moment. I did not have the energy to entertain her off-handed comments.

Maa didn't hold back and immediately fired back, "Well this nose is certainly *not* an Agyeman nose because the Agyemans don't have such noses. So it didn't come from us. But Vic, I think if we look at you closely, this baby's nose is like yours."

"Oh no, no, no, no. You can't tell me that. This nose is not from my family. No! As for this nose, it doesn't come from us."

"You wait till this child grows a bit and you will see. This nose is definitely your nose," Maa said, knowing very well she was irritating Auntie Vic as payback for starting such a conversation. By this time, I was tired and annoyed with both of them. Jerry's mother suggested we name the little girl *Mawuena*, which meant 'God's gift,' and insisted on using that for the baby's first name. Oddly enough, this was the one thing that both our mothers agreed on, but neither Jerry nor I were happy with the name. Moreover, in the Ewe culture, it was the father who chose the name and not the grandmother. Jerry was not sure what name to give to his daughter.

It was not until our baby girl was three weeks old that Jerry said to me, "Nana, I want to call her 'Let the darkness end,' 'Let the night stop,' 'Let the misery end'… or something like that." He translated it from Ewe. That is when Jerry named his daughter Zanetor, to mean "Let the darkness end."

In early 1978, Jerry had begun to speak out. He became something of a 'loose cannon,' as they say, within the military, and his speeches seemed inflammatory. He was deeply frustrated by what had become the norm. At one forum for young officers and other ranks to express their anger and frustration, I learned Jerry had been the most outspoken. He demanded the immediate removal of Acheampong and pointed to other men like General Joshua Hamidu and Group Captain Okyne as the sort of clean and honest officers who could take over the country and rid it of corruption.

Jerry always had a great respect for the high moral integrity and code of honour of the military life, and yet he saw it daily being betrayed by the most senior officers in the forces. The military had become as susceptible to corruption as any other sector of society. With a consuming passion to right the injustices in society, he became involved in clandestine meetings to plot the overthrow of General Acheampong.

On Saturday evenings, he started meeting seriously with friends including Captain Mensah-Poku, Captain Boakye-Djan and Captain Ibrahim Rida at the military base at Burma Camp. Often they would end up at our home with the passionate exchanges.

By 1978, it was no secret that Military Intelligence had compiled a file on my husband, which had already been active for more than two years. As a consequence, Jerry was frequently taken in for questioning. They had concluded that "Rawlings' coup-making potential had been a cause of concern to certain senior officers for some time." During one interrogation, my husband was called before senior officers in the Air Force and warned to stop his clandestine activities.

About the same time, NUGS and the general student body had become the most vocal critics of the SMC government, and in May 1977, they held simultaneous demonstrations at all three universities. They demanded the immediate resignation of Acheampong. In the news, we heard of one student who was killed during violent clashes between the military and the students.

This sent shockwaves through the nation, and the universities were subsequently closed, then re-opened briefly until students went on strike, causing them to close again for a while. It was clear that the SMC was doomed. With a revolution in the air and several plots hatching among the military, it was obvious that some kind of violent revolt was likely to happen if the SMC was not removed.

Thus, it was no surprise when on July 5, 1978, senior officers of the Armed Forces intervened to overthrow Acheampong and his government. While isolating Acheampong from his bodyguard, a small group of senior officers forced him to sign his own resignation in a "palace coup." Lieutenant-General Fred Akuffo took over the chairmanship of the new SMC which came to be known as the SMC II, and also came with promises to reinstate civilian government and institute harsh punishment against the previous regime.

Over the next year, however, no significant changes occurred and the resentment of the lower ranks continued to simmer below the surface. Acheampong was never held to account, and no action was taken against him or any others of the former SMC. The new government merely retired Acheampong from the army and placed him in custody. To the watchful eye, it appeared that the relationship between the SMC I and the SMC II was a little too cosy, and the palace coup of July 5 had been merely an attempt by senior officers to stave off a mass revolt. Jerry complained bitterly and continued to demand that, "those who disgraced our military uniforms and brought this country to its knees must be called to account."

Towards the end of 1978, Akuffo's government, feeling threatened by my husband and the support he was mobilising against the military government, decided to act. Suddenly, Jerry was given orders to leave the country for northern Pakistan to attend a training course. At the time, the country was in a state of emergency and Zanetor was only six months old. Neither of us wanted him to be far from home.

Akuffo's government was desperate to buy time to diffuse the situation in the country, and this was an obvious attempt to remove a potential trouble-maker. With no choice, Jerry went as ordered. But soon after arriving at the Peshawar Training School, due to the extremely cold weather, he developed a shoulder problem that made it impossible for him to do his Instructor course as planned. It appeared there was no need for him to remain in Peshawar if he could not take the course. He requested to return home, pleading problems in the country and anxiety for his wife and young child.

By the time Jerry returned to Ghana in January of 1979, Akuffo had lifted the ban on party politics in preparation for general elections to hand the country over to a civilian government. But discontent had worsened, and lawlessness had become a way of life. The profiteering system was still as rife as ever and, in spite of clear evidence of corruption and abuse of power, Acheampong would not be put on public trial.

Under mounting pressure and criticism, the SMC II announced on May 1, 1979, that they had stripped Acheampong of his military rank, deprived him of his retirement benefits and banished him to his home village in the Ashanti Region under "house arrest."

Two days later, a committee investigating malpractices in the export of timber products revealed that Major-Generals E.K. Utuka and R.E.A. Kotei, both former members of the SMC, had been found guilty of embezzling huge sums of money from impounded timber in 1977. Instead of the Timber Marketing Board (TIMBOD) selling the lumber to earn foreign exchange for the country, the men accused "issued chits to their favourites" to take away large quantities of lumber. The nation lost precious foreign exchange, and as with Acheampong, no prosecution or legal action was taken against either of them. This is one of the revelations which had come to light.

There were numerous allegations. A committee set up to investigate loans contracted between June 1977 and July 1978 by the Ministry of Finance revealed improprieties; the leadership was alleged to have diverted millions of US dollars in government funds to buy houses abroad and to have distributed several millions of dollars among friends. The effect of inflation and *kalabule* were rife enough to send the nation crumbling. Mr. Acheampong's punishment was handed down: Not to hold any public office in Ghana.

Essentially, the drivers had changed, from General Acheampong to General Akuffo, but the train that seemed to be hauling away every state asset and entrenching the corrupt political culture was at full speed. Disillusioned, Ghanaians observed and questioned, "How is it possible that nobody was going to be held accountable for the past seven years and more of mismanagement and corruption which dragged this nation to the depths of economic despair?"

The situation had become so disheartening that I would not be the least surprised if Jerry was moved to act, but I had no idea how or when.

CHAPTER EIGHTEEN

Hope Rising
May 15, 1979

May 15. I woke up that morning around 6 a.m. to find that my husband had not made it home the night before. My first reaction was not panic, but rather a sneaky suspicion of his whereabouts. My mind raced. Wherever he was, he had used a friend's Datsun 140J car, which was left in our care temporarily.

I did not want to upset myself by jumping to conclusions. I resolved to focus my energies elsewhere and prepare for a busy day ahead. Normally, that would have included getting the baby ready to spend the day at the Tiny Tots kindergarten on Independence Avenue that my mother owned and operated, and getting myself ready for work.

This week was a bit different. I was attending classes as part of a four-week management course required for my position at UTC. So instead of going to the office, I was getting ready to attend another day of professional training at the Management and Productivity Development Institute (MDPI) of Ghana, in Accra. Suddenly, the phone rang:

"Nana, do you know where Jerry is?" The voice on the other end was panicky and breathless. It was my neighbour Miriam, calling me from her upstairs apartment.

"No," I replied, with deliberate calm. "I don't know," I added, believing that she knew the answer to her own question. Then I continued, "If you've seen him, you tell me." I was certain that for her to call me at this hour, Jerry must have contacted her for one reason or another. I brushed her question aside and said, "Look, Miriam, I don't want to be bothered. It's too early in the morning."

Though Miriam and I had been neighbours and friendly, the two of us had had our share of differences. One, in particular, surrounded an affair she was having with a married man, an aide to the Chairman of the SMC. The problem I had with her was more than the relationship, but rather the thievery and immorality of the people with whom she was mingling. While high-ranking military officials were stealing state funds to enjoy personal luxuries, their friends, girlfriends, and family members were enjoying the privileges of being part of the corrupt circle of civil servants. It was no secret between us that her friendships did not sit well with me. But on that day, I tried to be brief and get off the phone as quickly and courteously as I could.

"But," Miriam continued, "Nana, somebody just rung me from Burma Camp and told me that Jerry is going all around the camp shooting just everybody and anybody."

"What!" I exclaimed. "Shooting everybody? Impossible! I don't think Jerry would just go around shooting people. Maybe you just got the message wrong… or maybe someone's imagination is at work."

My mind suddenly rushed back to make sense of anything I could have overheard in any of Jerry's conversations with his friends. Nothing, in particular, stood out. If Miriam was not over exaggerating, Jerry could be in real danger.

"*Noo* Nana. I'm sure that is what I heard."

"Ok," I said in resignation. "Just wait. I'm coming up…"

"No, no. It's okay. You let me come down and I'll tell you the rest."

In a state of confusion, I hung up the phone trying to make sense of Miriam's remarks. Then it occurred to me—all of Jerry's assertions about trying to force a confrontation with the military hierarchy. *Had he gone ahead?*

My mind began racing with questions. *What was really going on? Is he all right? Who was shooting who? Was Jerry involved? If so, in what way?*

Within minutes, Miriam appeared at my door, still in her housecoat with a cup of coffee in hand. No sooner had I opened the door than she launched into a hasty report of what she had heard. "This is what is happening..." she started with boundless energy and continued in a dizzying circle of rants and ramblings, none of which seemed to make sense. Enjoying the position of being the exclusive reporter of breaking news, especially concerning my husband, Miriam followed her report with a tirade of criticisms and accusatory questions directed at me.

"Nana, what is all this? I mean, there are other people who are trying to run the country. And how can he think he is the only one who can run this country? Any day now, we are going to have elections. Why should he come and disturb our elections?"

I could not distinguish what was fact from what was fiction, so I just stood there, quietly mulling it all over and when I had heard enough I cut in.

"Miriam, who told you all this?"

"Oh... well... ," she said hesitating as if to ponder whether she should reveal her source. "Um... well, you know... I got a call... and it was Felix and he told me." That alone explained a lot. Felix, who was Miriam's boyfriend, was in the military government. "Anyway," she continued, "he's going to call me back in ten minutes to let me know exactly what is happening."

For the moment, both Miriam and I knew that she was my only source of information, so I had no choice but to follow her upstairs. But first I went to check on the baby. Zanetor was then eleven months and was sound asleep. In helpless desperation, I made up my mind that it would still be another hour before she would wake and I knew I'd be back long before then. So I decided to leave her alone to sleep and made a quick dash for Miriam's place.

Miriam's flat was a bed-sitter, a modest one-room apartment that serves as a living room and bedroom with a little kitchen area. Just as she offered me coffee, her phone rang. She flashed a serious glance in my direction and then picked up the receiver. Before she spoke, she stretched the receiver broadly above her head to untangle the long and twisted cord away from the base. Then, putting the receiver to her ear, she fixed her eyes to the ground and spoke in low tones, "Hello... yes... a-*haaan*, ok... yes." She continued on this way, her eyes staring downward, avoiding my gaze. But I stared back at her expectantly, trying to surmise from her face what was going on. Yet the more my eyes begged for information, the more she turned away and eventually slipped into the kitchen and out of my view as if to avoid me altogether. I strained my ears to listen harder.

I fidgeted but waited patiently. It was now about 6:30 a.m. Within a couple of minutes, she returned to the room, the phone receiver back on base. "Oh, it's okay," she started, her face devoid of expression. "They have been able to overcome and overpower him. And... you know, they're asking him questions—about why he did that," she said calmly as if it was all over.

"They overpowered him? What do you mean?" I said, perplexed.

"Because of the killing and all I was telling you about," she said nonchalantly.

I was incredibly nervous, confused and growing more frustrated at the disjointed pieces of information. Nothing she said made sense to me. So I remained quiet, hoping to hear something more substantial, something concrete. But the more she talked, the worse I felt. My head was spinning. I stood there in deep contemplation. Feeling helpless, I began to think, well, she must know what she's talking about.

Then, within a couple of minutes of hanging up the phone, Miriam's doorbell rang. She opened the door, and there were three men standing in the doorway. Their sudden appearance sent me tumbling into terrifying paranoia. I recognised one of them as Miriam's boyfriend. At that moment, in my mind, there was not the slightest trace of uncertainty that I had been deliberately set up.

The men began fraternising superficially. I sat there, my defences up, feeling trapped, with a feigned smile pasted on my face. Without delay, questions started firing at me from each direction.

"Did you know your husband was going to do something like this?"

"No," I said.

"Do you know where your husband kept the money that was given to him?"

"Money? What money?" I questioned.

"Hasn't he been spending money recently... ?"

"Well, if he has, I haven't seen it," I said, trying not to sound too defensive.

"Did your husband give you any reasons why he would want to take arms against the government?" one of the men asked.

Here I was, caught in an encounter with men whom I suspect were Military Intelligence while my neighbour, and supposed friend, stood by idly. In the process, however, I was quick to realise that the men took me to be simple-minded. So I played along, trying not to show anxiety, but knowing perfectly well I was stepping around a landmine.

"Well," one of them continued, "we are just wondering if anybody gave him any money to do this coup... you know... to do what he did?" the man asked, searching my face as if to imply I was hiding information.

"Look, if he has any money, he hasn't given anything to me."

"What about a speech?" one of them asked.

"I haven't seen any speech." Cutting the exchange short, I asked abruptly, "Why are you questioning me?"

Stiffening his posture, his eyes locked with mine, the same man answered, "We're from Military Intelligence." The silence stretched between us and I began to feel nauseous. What had I done? Was following Miriam a big mistake? Had I said anything wrong? His words confirmed my suspicions, and I knew for sure that my friend had betrayed me for her own personal gain.

Even at that heavy moment, I maintained my composure. I stood, looked in her direction and calmly said, "I have to go, the baby may be up now." Then I excused myself and walked straight for the door. Despite my outwardly confident, unfaltering delivery, my mouth was now dry, my heart, heavy and pounding.

I returned to my apartment, and Zanetor had just woken up. As I tended to her, I realised that I was too nervous and too shaken to go anywhere, so instead of rushing out to the management course at the Management Development and Productivity Institute (MDPI), I decided to stay home.

I was now committed to finding out exactly where Jerry was.

In Accra, meanwhile, much like any other morning, people had made their way to work by 'tro-tro' public transports, by taxi, by private car or simply by walking. Most people would often be unaware of any such event taking place before sunrise, especially in the early hours of that morning. I imagined the women of Makola market would be busy setting up their stalls, while the men and women who filled the government ministries would be starting what seemed like a routine day at the office. But soon as the news filtered through the city, the normal scenes of cheerful morning bustle were abruptly thrown into a tailspin of chaos.

It started with the few people who heard the sound of gunfire from the direction of Burma Camp on the north-east side of the city. Within minutes, the rumour spread the news to Accra's city centre, and not surprisingly, the cause of gunfire was embellished with the passing of every kilometre. It would not be farfetched to hear people jumping to their own conclusions or making incredibly clever inferences. "The army and police are fighting," "The students are fighting the police," or that "Soldiers are marching into town, shooting everyone in sight." Whatever random stories flew into the air, stuck. Most people would normally count on second-hand information and would not have any way to verify the facts quickly. Panic reigned.

Nobody waited to confirm the rumours. Just as quickly as the stories swirled, we heard that traders abandoned their wares in a desperate attempt to seek dear life. In a mad scramble, traffic gridlocked streets and major roads into the capital city jammed as drivers tried to manoeuvre their cars off the streets into hiding. Some passengers got out of the cars and took off running. The pandemonium had plunged Accra into an ugly spectacle of terror. Everywhere people fled in the direction of Kaneshie and McCarthy Hill, away from the city centre and away from Burma Camp - the military barracks.

By around 1:30 p.m., my mother came by. She looked exhausted.

"Maa, what happened? I asked her.

Winded, she took a moment to catch her breath and said, "Brigadier Ashley-Larsen rung me this morning and said, 'Listen, your son-in-law has been arrested.'" Between breaths, Maa continued, "The moment I heard the news, I got in my car and drove over to the State House to find Jerry's mum. She knew nothing. When I informed her that there's been an uprising and that Jerry may have led it, the woman nearly collapsed in my arms. I told her to pull herself together so we could go and find out more."

The two of them had set out in Maa's car to go and look for Brigadier Ashley-Larsen, who had previously served as Commander of the Air Force, and was a close family friend. Their hope was that a person who had been a senior official could tell them more. Then Maa said, "But while we were on our way, and both in a panic, I ran my car straight into a gutter..."

Uncontrollably, I burst into a fit of laughter—a reaction that even took me by surprise.

"Don't laugh!" Maa said sharply, looking offended. "This is a very serious matter. Do you know how long it took us to get help? A good thirty minutes went by before we could get someone to pull my car out of the gutter."

Yet the more details she gave, the more hysterical I became.

For a moment, it felt so good to break the tension with laughter—a deep hearty laugh, even at the expense of our poor and panicked mothers. After their ordeal, Maa had taken Auntie Vic back to the State House before coming to check on me. After making sure the baby and I were okay, she rushed out to go back to the children at Tiny Tots kindergarten.

Ironically, our own mothers were in search of answers from the very people who were the symptoms, if not the root cause, of our nation's problems—the senior officials of a corrupt military government. They meant well, but the overriding truth had become that the generation before us held on to very conservative ideals, which included an unquestioning allegiance to, and reverence for authority. The economic and political crisis had found fertile grounds to sprout for years because of a society's inherent trait which made them less inclined to embrace any revolution as a means of ending corruption in our society.

Our mothers, like many Ghanaians, saw the filth and hated it, lived in the crumbling economy and were shaken by it, yet only hoped that someone or something would someday change it all for the better.

Soon after Maa left, Aba and Elizabeth arrived at my place. I was so happy to see them. "Aba, you are back in Ghana. When did you arrive?"

Aba was supposed to return to Ghana the night before on May 14, so I was expecting to see her that day or sometime soon.

"Last night." Aba could not spare a moment for small talk, "Nana, what is happening?" Apparently, they had been trying to make their way to my house since the morning, and it was as she watched the mayhem unfold through the windows of the taxi car that she realised something unusual was happening in town. On the main roads, all the cars speedily made U-turns with headlights on and left both of them wondering, *why are all the people turning around?*

"Hmm, I'm still not sure," I said anxiously. "Last night, Jerry left the house with your car to go and drop off some friends, and that was it. He never returned… and I haven't seen or heard from him since."

Before they arrived, both women had started making phone calls to different sources to find out more or if anyone knew what was indeed happening in Accra. One of the people Aba had called was her gentleman friend in the SMC government. Apparently, the only response she got was, "Oh, it is your friend causing trouble."

"Which friend?" Aba had asked.

The person had confirmed it was Jerry. I did not know what to say and was certainly unsure of what to do. All I could do was to wait.

I offered them something to drink. They, in hushed low whispers, advised that I look around the flat to gather anything I wanted to hold on to. She reasoned, "Nana, it's only a matter of time before the M.I. arrives." So with feverish haste, we searched around the flat for anything that could remotely or even inadvertently incriminate Jerry. We found nothing.

I had to take anything worth holding on to, as any military raid could ransack our whole house or valuable items could be easily stolen. I collected our passports and other important documents in addition to Jerry's handgun, which was officially registered in his name and assigned to him by the military, and we put these items in the boot of their car for safekeeping.

We went back up and sat around waiting. Then spontaneously, we thought of something that might be clever and hopefully plunge us into the middle of the story to better uncover the truth of the events no one seemed to have all the details on. The three of us deliberately started insulting the government and its security forces out loud. We knew very well they could be lurking around the building or even hiding under the windows listening to what we were saying.

Sure enough, in no time, Military Intelligence officers showed up at my front door.

"Open up! Fists banged at the front door. "It's M.I. We're here to search your house."

I felt a tightening in the pit of my stomach as if someone had suddenly taken hold of my gut and twisted it into a knot.

For a second, I scrambled, pacing up and down, trying to collect my thoughts. The knocking persisted and steadily grew louder. "Open up!" a voice bellowed near the window. "We know you're in there." I tip-toed slowly and opened the door. Two large men in army uniforms towered over me and stared sternly at me.

From behind, one of my friends gathered up the nerve to yell, "On what basis and authority are you entering this flat?"

"Military Intelligence," the officer spat out. "We're here to search the home of Flight-Lieutenant Jerry John Rawlings."

I gathered my wits and blocked the doorway. "Where's your warrant?" I challenged the first officer, looking him square in the eye.

In a look of disbelief, the officer's eyes grew big and his tone more menacing. "Don't you know that we can force our way in here?" he said gritting his teeth in anger.

"Of course you can," I replied with a posture that in my mind was supposed to exude confidence, "but that wouldn't be legal, now would it?"

Staring each other down, he glared at me, and I defiantly glared back, for what seemed like an eternity. Then to my astonishment, he suddenly loosened his posture, still holding intense eye contact, but backing away. "Rest assured, we'll back with a warrant!" he warned fiercely, at which point both men turned and walked briskly away.

I stood in the doorway, almost frozen with fear, and in total disbelief. I could not even comprehend having just turned Military Intelligence away from my door. I tried my best to hide my terror, but on the inside, the confrontation unnerved me.

The two women drove the car away and promised to secure the passports and personal items we left in it. I refused to leave our home empty, knowing the M.I. might soon return. So I sat there alone with Zanetor, pondering my actions with the M.I. and wondering how I was able to muster the courage to speak up, with a presence of mind, in spite of fear. The two women had been incredibly reassuring at the moment where I could have caved into my own trepidation. I stood at the edge of my own courage, and the reality of what my life had become begun to slowly sink in.

In a strange way, the only comfort that I seemed to find was the fact that perhaps the M.I. holding Jerry would be like any other time when they questioned him for hours and let him leave. The woman I had become had been refined through the years of watching the world spin around me, seeing people rip Ghana our own beloved country into shreds with greed, and at every turn having to make sense of it. I sat in the house alone, with little Zanetor. If her little eyes saw anything at all, maybe someday she would remember her mother standing in a moment when she could have fallen apart, and let that guide her own.

Perhaps any bravery left in my veins in that afternoon had been infused by what I knew of some of the women in my family who held their ground in the face of danger to protect their families. It was always reassuring to recall how my grandaunt Afua had faced a chorus of hecklers back in 1935 and had to stand tall. Her fight had been after the British governor issued an order of deportation, banishing her brother (my grandfather), from legally crossing beyond a 40-kilometre radius into Asante. Boldly facing her tormentors, my grandaunt stood defiantly on the porch of my grandfather's house determined to protect everything her brother had worked so hard for—his family, his properties and his thriving cocoa business.

More than four decades later, on the steps of my own home, the M.I. had become the same for me as those hecklers did for my late grandaunt. In that moment of confrontation, Afua Konadu's voice would be echoing quietly in my ear: "Stand your ground Konadu! Stand up to the indignity. The eyes of the entire nation are on you. Don't give an inch. Fight 'til the end."

An hour passed.

The Military Intelligence returned with a warrant and excitedly searched every corner of our home. They flipped through pages of books, and searched through drawers, between mattresses, inside sofa cushions, and underneath rugs. They found nothing. There was nothing to find. They left the house in a mess and clearly frustrated, yet again, they threatened to return.

I soon found out that Jerry was behind bars.

Later that afternoon, at 5:09 p.m., a commentator on the British Broadcasting Corporation program *Focus on Africa,* reported:

"… How serious this uprising was is far from clear… What the motive would be is also less than clear. Ghana is of course scheduled to return to civil rule at the beginning of July, and it could be that some soldiers of the armed forces would like to stop that from happening. It is known that a number of army officers are worried that any future civilian government might vigorously investigate the military for corruption and malpractice during their seven years of administration."

The next morning, Wednesday, May 16, I caught a glimpse of the morning paper's bold lettered headlines:

UPRISING QUELLED: WHY THIS DISTURBANCE?

Under the heading, an editorial comment in the *Daily Graphic* said in part:

"… The shock is deepened further that yesterday, a three-man delegation… was scheduled to present the final draft of the Constitution to the Supreme Military Council at the Castle; a ceremony symbolizing the meticulously planned coup and the steady steps being taken towards the June 18 election day…

"The question then arises: what had the adventurers hoped to achieve at this period when the majority of Ghanaians have all turned their minds to June 18 and after?

"Were they propelled on by mere love of power? Do they have

genuine grievances which they hoped can be redressed only through staging a coup? Couldn't they have directed such a grievance, if any, through the appropriate channels?"

The same day, a popular radio program *Voice of America* reported the incident for the first time on its French Service at 7 a.m.:

"... *This is the first attempted coup since General Akuffo took office in July last year. Elections are to be held in Ghana next month for a new civilian government.*"

That afternoon, the military authorities in Burma Camp named the leader of the uprising as Flight Lieutenant J.J. Rawlings of Air Force Station, Accra. From America to Europe, headlines buzzed of the uprising, but neither the perpetrators nor their motivation was yet known or understood by the general public.

I would later come to find out that Jerry had led a small group of junior officers in an attempt to force an end to the plundering of the state by the military hierarchy. His aim was to get the Armed Forces to use their final weeks in power to investigate and hold accountable those responsible for corruption and malpractice in their administration. But during the course of the uprising, which the military called an abortive *coup*, gunshots had been exchanged, and unfortunately, an Air Force officer had been killed. Jerry agreed to disarm his men and surrender. At this point, the Ghanaian public had no information as to the possible motivation of the uprising and Jerry himself was little known outside the military establishment.

Charged with mutiny and treason, both crimes punishable by death, Jerry and the other men were immediately imprisoned at the Military Intelligence Special Branch Annex. The uprising shook the Armed Forces and infuriated the senior ranks of the military. For their actions, my husband and the six junior officers would all to be subject to a public trial by Military Tribunal.

I was broken. My mind was made up, knowing very well that I did not have the luxury to fall apart. I was a thirty-year-old mother of a little girl, my husband's life dangled in a balance, and any hope I had for a better country was at the mercy of a government whose integrity withered long ago.

CHAPTER NINETEEN

A WORLD APART
Truth and Valour on Trial

Perhaps the strangest twist to this turmoil was the fact that, iron-ically, during Acheampong's regime, General Akuffo had tried to use Jerry to get rid of Acheampong in his own plot, so that he (General Akuffo) could take over as head of state. The modality of this plot and its latent consequences were not spelled out clearly to Jerry, except that he was to use a fighter plane and drop a bomb on the Chairman's house, and then leave the country. The plot seemed fundamentally flawed in that it required Jerry to flee from Ghana instead of being in the country to explain himself. *"Why do I have to run,"* he must have thought to himself. Jerry could not fathom the vision behind this plan, and refused to take part. That plot never materialised.

Now, after the May 15 chaos, General Akuffo and the other leaders of the military regime resolved that the best way to teach my husband a lesson was by arraigning him and his six co-conspirators before a public court-martial. During Acheampong's time, there had been a long tradi-tion of putting attempted coup-makers on public trial.

With the general election barely a month away, Akuffo strongly be-lieved that he had the support of the civilian population and that his regime's remaining weeks in office were very secure. So that weekend, a highly confident General Akuffo left the country for Senegal on his final diplomatic mission abroad. In an unusual turn, the head of the SMC was absent from the country when my husband and his co-conspirators were first brought before the Military Tribunal in Burma Camp on Monday, May 28, 1979.

"Plead that Jerry's insane," were the first words of advice I received after Jerry's arrest from one of his closest friends. This was a man who had served with Jerry in the Air Force, and one who was not oblivious to the prevailing sentiments around the country.

"What? No!" I said emphatically, "I can't plead that he's insane."

He tried to convince me to change my mind.

"That's the only way he'll get off," he said striving to be the voice of reason. "If you can get a doctor to certify that he's insane, they will have to let him go," he said referring to the military government.

"No! I'm not going to do that. If I do that, it's going to follow me for the rest of my life."

"Listen, Nana, that is his best bet. Otherwise, he's definitely going to be executed," he said bluntly.

"No, no. I can't do that," I told him firmly, standing my ground. I knew the man I had chosen to spend my life with, and the passion that drove him every moment. He would rather I never show a moment of weakness for anyone to exploit. "It's better for him to die in dignity, than for him to be imprisoned, and labelled insane, and have to live out his sentence in 'indignity'. He put his life on the line for what he believed in, and I know he would not be happy for me to plead insanity or claim he has a mental problem just to save him now."

All this was happening quickly, yet very slowly. I was confused and tried my hardest to articulate my thoughts in my own mind.

Leading up to the trial, getting through the night became increasingly difficult for me. The first two days went by torturously slowly. With Jerry in the custody of the very regime he sought to overthrow, I knew the chances of him getting out alive were slim to none. That thought startled me to the bone every time it came to me. His predicament left wide open the most likely possibility—that he would suffer death by firing squad—if not for anything else, to remind others of the grave consequences of attempting an uprising.

The shock of what seemed inevitable weighed heavy on me. In spite of this, my immediate concern was that he be given a fair trial. Without one, his intentions would go unknown and travel silently with him to his death. The least I could do was to prevent that from happening. It would be difficult, but not impossible.

Shades of denial set in. I had to find some courage to believe that there would be enough honest people in the country to want to unwrap the truth, no matter how uncomfortable it might seem. In times of hardship, there had been many women who were forced to rise to unpredicted moments of leadership to preserve their families, save their communities, lead nations, and at one extreme, even declare war. So in my own time of adversity, it was simple. I did not want the reality of the day to make me crumble. I had to be worthy of them.

So I made it my mission to get my husband the best defence team I could find—who would both defend his actions in court and bring his motives into the open. It would be a tall order. Unfortunately, from the time my husband was arrested until the opening day of the trial—a two week period—I had been denied access to him. Despite several attempts, I was blocked from talking to, or seeing, Jerry until the opening day of his court-martial, on May 28, 1979.

Every minute seemed a bit more overwhelming than the one before. In this desperate time of need, I reached out to a number of people, many of whom had availed themselves unconditionally to us in the past. Some graciously embraced me and helped wherever they could. Sadly, many of the people I had once thought to be our friends now sought to distance themselves as far as they could. To them, my husband was a moving target, his life at stake, and perhaps the lives of those close to him.

Nothing struck me harder than my running into one of Jerry's close military friends, who had suddenly disappeared. During the week of May 15, I spotted him in town while both of us were driving on the Ring Road in Accra. Eager to speak to him, I sped up to his car and flagged him down until he saw me, and then signalled for him to pull over.

To my surprise, he made no attempt to slow down and, instead, began to speed up. I was baffled. *What is he running from?* My first impulse was to chase him down. As I overtook his car, I turned my car in front of his and stepped on my brakes, blocking his car with mine, and he was forced to stop. As he stepped out of his car, I jumped out of mine and charged toward him.

"Why are you running away?" I demanded.

"Look, these are dangerous times..." he started, looking around with fear in his eyes.

"I just wanted to talk to you about something..."

"No, no, no...," he insisted, cutting me off. "Not here. I'll come to the house. I'll come to the house this evening."

"Are you sure you'll come to the house?" I asked, doubting his every word.

"I promise you. I'll come to the house this evening."

And that was it. I never heard from him again until after June 4.

I vividly recall telling this incident to one of our lawyers, "Honestly, this guy was running away from me," I said. "Someone I thought we were close to. I was just trying to talk to him and he was running for his dear life. Meanwhile Jerry, supposedly his good friend, was locked behind bars."

Unfazed by the story, the lawyer responded calmly, "Mrs. Rawlings, you have to know, in times like this, that's how people behave." He was right. While my mind raced every minute, I only hoped that the men and women who knew the truth about my husband's life would remain the ones I could lean on. People I called on either withdrew, went silent or tried taking advantage of me, knowing I was alone and in a vulnerable state.

My frustration mounted. But before my thoughts sunk me further into self-pity, I forced myself to bring them to a halt. I channelled all my pent-up energies into acquiring the legal services of a widely-respected defence team, led by Lawyer Adumoah Bossman, who was the President of the Council of the Bar Association, and another lawyer, Tsatsu Tsikata.

On the first day of the trial, I arrived in Burma Hall dressed casually in jean overall trousers and accompanied by a group of women friends. We entered a hall packed with journalists, soldiers, some officers and airmen from the lower ranks. At the time, not many people knew who I was, and I planned to take full advantage of the anonymity. On the other hand, quite to our amusement, many soldiers quickly assumed that Aba, because of her fair complexion, must be Jerry's wife because the two of them had that in common. It did not help that between the two of us, her nerves had her crying a pool of tears on the opening day of the trial.

To avoid the television camera, I made a discreet entrance, making every attempt to remain anonymous. But before I could sit and blend among the crowd and friends, some of Jerry's fellow air force officers recognised me. Out of a sense of duty to my husband, they immediately took it upon themselves to seat me in the second row, and I could not refuse their kindness. Still, the exposure from sitting up front initially made me feel uncomfortable. This was especially true as I sat waiting to see my husband for the first time since he had been arrested and incarcerated.

Even before the Judge and members of the General Court Martial entered the hall, I could sense the tension in the warm, humid air of the courtroom. It was written on the faces of anxious soldiers and civilians alike, all of whom stood by impatiently waiting. Every available space in the courtroom was occupied. There were almost as many people standing as sitting. Those who came to this public tribunal, which was to be a showpiece for anyone who attempted a coup d'état, came to catch a glimpse of this courageous man. It had never been easy for soldiers to overthrow a military regime. The nearest in Ghana's history was the palace coup the year before.

Sitting among the thick crowd, pictures of my husband's sentiments, actions and words raced through my mind like a screenplay. I remembered how before we were married, Jerry would jokingly tell me that he did not think I would enjoy being his wife because he was going to be involved in a struggle all his life to helping the poor whom he saw as being unjustifiably exploited. It was a conviction that seemed to have been etched in his veins since his childhood. I once replied, "Then I will struggle with you."

Soon after marriage, we had settled into a quiet life. But it was evident from the moment I married Jerry, that I indeed married the struggle. Jerry has always embodied the "human" struggle. It had been his nature to share the agony of a weaker person. I had known him long enough to know that he had never been the kind of person to calculate what he could gain out of a process, but rather what he could do to change the plight of those he truly believed were suffering. He was refreshingly unpretentious. There had to be a few people in every society who held on to their convictions and lived every word they uttered, without any long-winded political ideologies, and Jerry was easily one of such. These thoughts brought a little comfort, even though I knew my husband could sacrifice himself to bring reprieve to his country if he deemed that to be his last resort.

The pressmen were ready. The television and news cameras had been set. Then the court was ordered to rise. All eyes were fixed on the main entrance to the hall. Justice Wiredu, the trial judge for the government, entered first followed closely by members of the General Court Martial. The prosecution team then followed. And, finally, the accused persons were marched in, led by my husband, Flight Lt. J.J. Rawlings. Jerry wore his Air Force uniform and dark glasses. He held something in his hand that looked like a scroll sheet. My heart raced, over and again.

Jerry was identified as the first accused and the principal architect of the mutiny. From the corner of my eye, I could scan parts of the room and see the curiosity among the crowd running high. For the hundreds of civilians present, Flight Lt. J.J. Rawlings was a new face. In my heart, I was simply hoping and praying that his voice would be heard and his motives revealed.

The first day's hearing was taken up by the opening address from the Director of Public Prosecutions, Mr. G.E.K. Aikins, who read out a statement by my husband explaining his reasons for taking action.

"Mr. President, the principal architect and ringleader in the carrying of the mutiny is the first accused, Flight Lieutenant Jerry John Rawlings of the Ghana Air Force Station, Accra. He is a young man, aged about 31 years.

While Jerry was deprived of a public forum on May 15, due to the failed uprising, my husband now heard the Public Prosecutor doing the job for him by publicly quoting him verbatim. Addressing the Court Martial, he read:

"Mr. President, the first accused had for a long time felt disillusioned about the injustices in our society, more particularly under the Acheampong regime; and so when in July 1978 the SMC was reconstituted with the removal of Mr. Acheampong as Head of State, Jerry John Rawlings thought things were going to be improved. When he realized that there were no improvements in the general conditions of life he was struck with dismay and lamented over what he termed 'the tarnished image of the Armed Forces'. He regretted that at a time when the Military Government is due to hand over to a civil government, the Military Government had done practically nothing to improve the image of the Armed Forces."

The crowd in the court broke out in applause. The general acclaim seemed to be that J.J. Rawlings had expressed the true feelings of the junior ranks in the armed forces. For a moment, the President of the

Court Martial was unsure whether it was safe for the proceedings to continue. As the trial progressed, all eyes, followed by cameras, shifted from the Prosecutor to Jerry, but I was so filled with anxiety that I was afraid to even look at him. He sat with his legs crossed, looking serious, but calm.

My hands endlessly fidgeted in my lap. I sat upright trying to look composed, but inside I was trembling, my stomach was in knots and my mind was racing. I had never lived through a moment of this magnitude in my life.

As Mr. Aikins continued, he explained to the court that Jerry's principal motivation was a desire to restore the image of the Armed Forces by getting them to use their final weeks in power to clear up the "widespread corruption in high places" and to investigate the "nefarious activities" of those Syrian and Lebanese businessmen who controlled most of the country's wholesale and import trade and who had been "growing fat" at the expense of the starving masses. None of these opinions had come as a surprise to any ordinary Ghanaian, especially the millions of people who were not beneficiaries of a government that seemed to take pride in enriching itself.

The murmurs of approval grew louder among the crowd, and it was clear that Jerry was winning great sympathy. But there was much more than sympathy needed to vindicate my husband. As the Prosecutor read his statement, Jerry listened, unmoved, nodding his head once in a while.

The Public Prosecutor then went on to explain that in the course of some heated argument with officers who were taken hostage in the early hours of May 15, Jerry had said that if the military did not act immediately to 'cleanse the system' then the only solution that remained would be to "go the Ethiopian way". Hearing this, the court erupted into wild cheering, particularly from the long-oppressed rank and file. The 'Ethiopian way' had been a clear reference to the Ethiopian Head of State's summary execution of hundreds of perceived opponents of the Ethiopian "revolution" in 1977.

The floor was throbbing with excitement. It got so loud that the President of the Court warned that he would not hesitate to stop proceedings. The court was adjourned for two days, but the die had been cast. The press gave prominence to his statement, and this drew enormous support from the public. From the moment Jerry's statement was read explaining the social injustices that had prompted him to act, his case drew such unexpected excitement and attention from both the general public and the international media, alike, that I was forced to arrive at Burma Hall earlier each day, to secure a front seat.

After the closing of the first day of the trial, I was finally given access to visit Jerry privately. A military escort led me into a narrow passage at the rear of the courtroom in Burma Hall and through a side doorway. A moment later, a small, dimly lit, bare-walled room stretched before us. Feeble sunlight filtered through the room's window and two low, square tables sat near the centre, not beside each other but at right angles.

On guard in the holding room was a young officer whom I immediately recognised as one of Jerry's guys. On each side of the young officer's cheeks were distinctive tribal marks that were easily recognisable. "Good afternoon, Madam," he greeted me quietly and respectfully as I entered the room.

"Good afternoon," I replied, as I waited near the doorway for whatever protocols I would be subjected to before I could talk to Jerry. It had been thirteen days, so I was anxious.

"No worries, Madam," the soldier assured me, waving me in. "Come in. You are welcome," he said noticing my apprehension. After what I had been through over the last week, his moment of kindness was a welcoming gesture. I immediately felt at ease. The young officer showed none of the belligerence and arrogance I had come to associate with officers of the day.

My eyes immediately shifted to the image of Jerry sitting behind one of the tables. I inched slowly toward him, trying hard to contain my excitement. As I walked in his direction, he stood, looking jovial and softly called my name. "Nana, come," he said with open arms, gesturing for a hug. I could sense the fatigue in his voice and his excitement from his touch.

In the front pocket of my overalls was a note I had handwritten especially for him. It must have been some loving words of support from a petrified young wife to help keep her husband's spirits and hopes up. But that was the letter that would nearly cost me my life.

Though we were not allowed to exchange items during our meeting, I honestly felt that because the letter was of a personal nature, from a worried wife to her jailed husband, it would be harmless to pass it on during our meeting. So when I embraced Jerry I quickly whispered and signalled for him to grab the note from my front pocket. He immediately did, and we embraced until he transferred it into his hip pocket. Feeling triumphant, the two of us enjoyed a satisfying giggle together.

I was happy to see him and to feel his familiar embrace once again and I could see the joy in his eyes as he stared back in my direction. Even in these uncertain times, as we sat there together that afternoon, it felt like we were in our own world.

We did not get much time during this meeting but the time we had was uplifting. I quickly filled him in on Zanetor and my well-being. He filled me in on his. "Nana," he whispered, "these people are not really watching me that well. I could run off if I want." Before he could finish his thoughts I jumped in, "No!" I pleaded with him, "Don't do such a thing. That is probably what they want you to do so they can kill you."

Jerry assured me that he was only saying that in jest, and he agreed with me. Not much else needed to be said.

After the visit and a hopeful first day in court, I felt for the first time since his arrest that there might be a glimmer of light at the end of this very dark tunnel.

I returned home in good spirits. After seeing my husband, I could not help but smile and be hopeful. I was reflecting on the day's events when I heard a knock at my front door. As I unlatched the door, it swung wide open with tremendous force from the other side. Forcing himself in was the young officer with the tribal marks on his face who stood guard during my visit with Jerry in Burma Hall. The young officer savagely grabbed me by the neck with one hand and placed a gun next to my left temple with the other. "Do you know what you did today was very bad?" he hissed with fire in his eyes. Fear gripped me, and I was mute.

He cocked the gun to my ear. He forcefully said, "Don't ever pass papers to him again." I had been a bit naïve or perhaps even careless, but I had never assumed any consequence from giving a loving note to my husband a second thought. The man continued, even more aggressively "Do you understand me? I will blow your head off!"

I stood still, trembling with fear, and said nothing. He released his hand from around my neck, put back his gun and stormed out the front door.

I was so shaken up by this encounter I could not sleep after that. It turns out the young officer was a member of the Military Intelligence. It was terrifying to fathom the reality that whatever charge my husband faced, I was connected to him in every way, and my life was very well in danger too.

On Wednesday, May 30, the Court Martial resumed. I arrived early to a shocking, but significant difference. On the walls of Burma Camp, leading to Burma Hall, posters appeared calling for the halting of the trial and the immediate release of Rawlings and his men. Some threatened death for the officers of the court while others openly called for nothing less than outright revolution. Some of the blunt messages had been written in chalk:

"STOP THE TRIAL OR ELSE…"

"IF YOU WANT TO DIE, CONTINUE THIS TRIAL"

"REVOLUTION OR DEATH"

"THE STRUGGLE WILL CONTINUE"

I was dumbfounded. But in no time, the military authorities tore all of them down, just in time for the Court to be seated. The front page banner headlines in the daily newspapers spoke of Jerry fighting against injustices. This perhaps explained the huge uncontrollable crowd that milled in the hall this time. Many people had caught wind of the significance of Jerry's trial, and many more men and women were willing to let their presence be part of the massive popular support that the trial had quickly garnered.

During the course of evidence presented that day it was revealed that, at the time of his surrender on May 15, Jerry had called for the release of the men under his command on the grounds that they were only acting on his expressed orders as an officer. The Flight Lieutenant J.J. Rawlings who most Ghanaians knew very little about was accepting full responsibility for the events of May 15. The court was once again disrupted by wild cheering from the ranks.

Then the first witness, Flight Lieutenant J.B. Atiemo, one of ten Air Force and Army officers held hostage during the events on May 15, confirmed that the first accused (Jerry) had declared that he was prepared to die on behalf of the rest of the accused.

The applause grew wilder despite warnings by the Court President. That avowal made its way into the next morning's newspaper, as the banner headline of the *Daily Graphic* read:

"LEAVE MY MEN ALONE!… I'm Responsible for Everything."

The fire caught on. Even those who did not know Jerry before these events saw someone who personified the challenge that had engulfed the country. This was the first time that an officer leading a failed coup had actually accepted responsibility for his actions and, in so doing, had sought to exonerate his men. His voice had been heard! I could sense a shift in the air, but just when I began to bask in any optimism, the reality came to me again that it was my husband's life at stake. People in Ghana seemed overwhelmed and in the eyes of many, Jerry had become a hero. The trial in Burma Camp had inadvertently lit the fire for the People's Revolution.

The third appearance at the special court was on Thursday, May 31. The defence counsel cross-examined the first prosecution witness amidst shouting and clapping in support of the stand taken by Flt. Lt. Rawlings. Before the Court President adjourned till Monday, June 4, he gave what he called a final warning to the public gallery "to desist from any further shouting and clapping." He added that he would not hesitate "to stop the public from listening to the rest of the proceedings." As Jerry and his men were being marched away, the public waved at them, some with raised fists, as a symbol of solidarity and support. Ghanaians had found an opening to rewrite their country's history and people were determined not to sit back to let this moment pass.

It was much later that I learned how after Jerry's arrest following the May 15 mutiny, a Section Commander had assigned and ordered seven soldiers to keep him under close arrest at the Special Branch annex where he was locked up.

Interestingly, while he was in custody, he used the opportunity to explain the details of his motives to the guards on duty who were under strict orders to watch him. Jerry had plenty of time to share his vantage point with the men who perhaps shared the same anger and resentment. The conversations drew interest from the guards, and they turned to like him. Apparently, he would share cigarettes with some, and it did not take much for his message to resonate with them all. Once they could identify with his motives, he fired their principles.

Perhaps, as many came to suggest, Akuffo's biggest mistake had been to put my husband and his men on public trial. The hardships had seeped into every corner of the country, just as clearly as the masses saw military governance that had spent much of the last decade enriching themselves and basking in their lavish lifestyles. Ghanaians had been witnesses to an administration with short-sighted agendas that had degenerated into sleaze and apathy. "They thought they were trying me alone," Jerry would later say. "Little did they know that they were trying the conscience of the Armed Forces, and indeed of the people."

The trial became a true test of my husband's character. His life was on the line. It was well known that he would likely suffer execution by firing squad, but more important to him was his integrity. It did not lessen the anguish I had to live with if everything I had hoped for and dreamt of suddenly vanished into thin air.

It was at this point that the name Rawlings struck a popular chord among the masses of suffering Ghanaians and the long-oppressed rank and file. The grassroots of our country had been left without a leader. In their eyes, regardless of the outcome, a real leader had emerged. I could only pray this would not be the end.

CHAPTER TWENTY

JOLT

June 4 – A Nation Beyond the Limelight

On June 4, 1979, the ongoing trial came to a screeching halt when a group of junior military men broke into Jerry's cell at the Special Branch headquarters where he had been locked behind bars. It all began in the pre-dawn hours that Monday.

The tension at Burma Camp had become so high that a reported disturbance involving gunfire between soldiers broke out around 2:30 a.m. In response to the outburst, the Special Branch guard in charge of the key to Jerry's cell disappeared. Apparently, they ordered the other guards to keep a close watch and refrain from relaying any information of what had happened to anyone, especially in case they were called as witnesses at the hearing. Moments later, the whole place erupted.

The first Jerry knew of anything had been around 4:00 a.m. when a handful of soldiers barged into the Special Branch annex where he was being held. They took an iron bar to smash the lock on his cell door. After repeated attempts, one impatient soldier suggested firing into the lock with his handgun without giving much thought to the fact that the bullet could ricochet and harm either Jerry or any of the other men. Jerry stopped him.

The lock finally gave way, and the cell door opened. The soldiers dragged Jerry out and some proposed shooting the guards on duty who had been holding him. Jerry had immediately charged the soldiers to desist from any such violence, to leave them alone, as they were only doing their job. This was unfolding at a time when no one seemed to know which military officer was sympathetic to the government's agenda, and which of them was frustrated enough to identify with the men who were determined to change the downhill path our country was rushing fast on.

I learned the details of these tense moments from the soldiers who had been there. Sergeant Akoto, Corporal Issaka, Lance Corporal Tasiri and others vividly recalled those challenging hours. The soldiers then ran with Jerry, straight to Broadcasting House, which had already been seized by their men, soldiers of the Fifth Battalion. This is where Jerry made his first public broadcast to the nation:

"This is Flight Lieutenant Rawlings. The ranks have just got me out of my prison cell. In other words, the ranks have just taken over the destiny of this country. Fellow officers, if we are to avoid any bloodshed, I plead with you not to attempt to stand in their way because they are full of malice, hatred—hatred we have forced into them through all these years of suppression. They are ready to get it out – the venom we have created.

So, for heaven's sake do not stand in their way. They are not fools. If you have any reason to fear them, you may run. If you have no reason to feel guilty, do not move... We can't restrain them."

There would be no turning back. He then requested that all units send representatives to the new Revolutionary Council that was to replace the Supreme Military Council (SMC) which is, as he stated, *"no more."*

For everyone listening to the news, no one could be sure what the next minute held in store. Would the military government go away quickly or fight through the mayhem led by a man they had considered dangerous, yet uncompromising? Jerry then gave a reassuring message to the civilian population, and one that was key: *"The Ghana Armed Forces will be handing over to the civilians in due time. Elections will take place."*

Jerry continued to articulate what he was sure had become the feelings of frustration of the long-oppressed rank and file soldiers: *"But before the elections go on, justice, which has been denied to the Ghanaian worker, will have to take place, I promise you... Some of us have suffered for far too long."*

No society or government would be perfect, yet Jerry had forged his own resolve out of the belief that it was the duty of the leaders to do all they could to strive towards that perfection. There were bound to be days that they would falter, as all humans do, but their overriding ambition ought to be a service to the people, irrespective of their status, their value or their culture. This was what all Ghanaians had hoped for.

For a country that had wiggled its way out of colonial rule just some two short decades prior, men and women wanted a chance to carve their own destiny in a society that would be fair, rather than one saddled with dishonesty and a country where the thought of a future made us cringe.

My most vivid memory of that hot and rainy Monday morning was hearing the tremor in Jerry's voice while I was listening to the broadcast in my mother's house. My heart pounded, still. Jerry sounded unrehearsed, yet confident.

In the same breath, while he spoke, opposing forces moved in, and armed men mobilised around Broadcasting House, awaiting Jerry's exit. We had no way of knowing that as the soldiers of the Fifth Battalion escorted Jerry back to Burma Camp, they came under intense fire from soldiers of the Recce Regiment. It was clear to them that the commanding officer had ordered the assault on Jerry and the others. As I was later informed, the result was a gun battle that would continue throughout the morning between members of the Recce Regiment on one side and the soldiers of the Fifth Battalion and Air Force on the other.

In the meantime, at my mother's house, we did not know what was going on. All we could hear were the rounds of gunfire coming from the direction of Burma Camp and Police Headquarters, a clear indication they were still facing resistance. I knew my husband could be caught in the middle of all the mayhem, and every hope he had to affect the lives of the people in the country for which he was willing to sacrifice his own life, would be no more. It was agonising for me to hear one gunshot after another.

I sat in Maa's living room, engulfed in worry. I could not help it. The consoling words of one woman bolted me from reverie to reality: "Nana, think of the baby." I had done all I could to remain calm, and every emotion left in me seemed to swing from one extreme to the other. Each time I glanced over at my daughter, who clung innocently to my mother, a slew of thoughts rushed through my mind. She had just turned one three days earlier on June 1, and now Zanetor was the only bond I had with Jerry, and that brought a little calm even if only for a moment.

I did not want to even conceive of the thought that perhaps I would not see my husband again. Whatever it took, the hope nudged me that he would survive. I could not imagine having to explain to a little girl, someday, that her father had been an architect of a courageous under-taking for our country, but had not made it out alive. How could I ever explain that to her? I wanted my husband home.

I was living through a nightmare, my eyes wide open and my heart shredding into little pieces with every second. I had always believed that it would take citizens that cared enough to sacrifice their own lives to pull our country together from the rot that had found its way to the very top. I just could never have imagined the anguish I would go through as the unrestrained moments unfolded. As I sat there, crippled by fear, I wondered how I would ever look into her eyes and explain the outcome of this fateful day, if my worst fear came true.

Just over an hour after Jerry's broadcast, the Army Commander, Major-General Odartey-Wellington regained control of Broadcasting House and announced on the radio that the coup had been foiled. He called on all ranks to return to their barracks. In disbelief, I sat there struggling to control my emotions. Then letting out a deep sigh

I murmured in deep resignation, "Well, I guess that's it," and felt the sudden need for seclusion. I got up and went to lie down in Maa's guestroom. I could not muster the courage to speak to anyone. With a heavy heart, I lay still. I was numb.

Meanwhile, at Burma Camp, the continued exchange of fire between both sides required Major-General Odartey-Wellington to return to the GBC studio about a half an hour later with an appeal to all members of the Ghana Armed Forces to stop firing, adding:

"I also urge Flight Lieutenant J.J. Rawlings and any following he has with him to meet me at headquarters."

Soon afterwards, I heard the sound of a jet engine coming from outside. I sprang to my feet and headed for the front door as if I could see the people in the aircraft. Looking up, I spotted an Air Force aircraft in the air, and all I could mumble to myself was, *please Lord, let that be him, but don't let him land in Ghana!*

In spite of the Army Commander's repeated pleas, the fighting intensified. Major-General Odartey-Wellington left the Broadcasting House and came under attack, and was chased to the Nima Police Station where he was killed. Following his death, what had been a resistance to the revolution began to fall apart.

Just after 3 p.m., the Chief of the Defence Staff, Major-General Joshua Hamidu's words captured everyone's attention in a radio address. He wanted to clear up any doubts for the public once and for all. Surely, it would take much more than a public radio address to calm the fears of men and women who woke up one unsuspecting Monday morning to a rain of gunshots. It was time to relinquish the convention that we had to sit by idly while a group of men and women pulled apart every hope we had as a nation. Identifying himself firmly with the uprising, Hamidu announced that the revolutionary forces had prevailed.

He continued, "I am happy to announce the hypocrisy of the Acheampong and Akuffo regimes... has been brought to an end." I could sigh in relief. Hamidu requested all former SMC members and leading functionaries should report to the police headquarters "for their own safety." He then emphasised Jerry's initial assurance that elections would go ahead as planned, and explained that the current revolution had been in our "national interest," adding, "We have suffered for far too long... May God bless this nation."

During the broadcast of that day, Jerry apparently made an appeal to the officers that he knew would be needed to establish control over the forces that had now been unleashed. Pulling from a list of people he knew and trusted, Jerry read out a list of specific junior officers and ranks who were to report to Burma Camp immediately. He also called on a number of prominent civilians and church leaders from whom he hoped to gain advice.

Ghana was stuck at the tipping point of walking into our destiny, the same one that Dr. Nkrumah and his colleagues once boldly declared. It now sat on our shoulders to march it forward. What I never knew until much later was that after some initial direct involvement in the fighting on the ground, Jerry had taken up an aircraft. While he was in the air, it was difficult to monitor events at the barracks or in the country. When it was time to refuel the aircraft, he tried to land, only to find that the landing gear on the fighter jet had jammed.

The tires were stuck. He did his best to manoeuvre the aircraft into a belly landing, which, if done improperly, could have exploded the plane upon landing. What saved him had been his piloting skills, which enabled him to successfully "belly land" the damaged plane and step out of it safely. Jerry had to be fiercely determined to end the day seizing any moment and every opportunity.

I think it was Flying Officer Fordjuor who told of how during that rainy morning, they decided to drop Jerry in a wooded part beyond the Achimota Forests area. The plan was to leave him there until the unrests had calmed down, then they would return to get him. Jerry was suddenly cut off from the events that were unfolding rapidly. But like any soldier, one thing his instincts would not easily allow him to do is to sit back and wait to be rescued when he was convinced that he could set out and take his chances. Furthermore, he could not risk staying in the same place just in case the other forces had taken over, and can track his position.

For hours thereafter, Jerry was on the ground near Legon, separated from the fighting. He soon learned of General Hamidu's broadcast. It was the first he had heard of the government throwing in the towel and giving up.

As nightfall came, he decided it was too dangerous to move through the city during the curfew. During the hours between dusk until dawn, he stayed out in the bush and spent the night in the servant's quarters of a nearby house. The following morning, he set out again and made his way back to the Air Force Station.

I was worried and terrified at every passing second. For me, the importance of this day was that Jerry's radio broadcast succeeded in raising the political consciousness of the ordinary Ghanaian and hopefully set us on a path to restoring a strong sense of hope for our future. No one knew at the time where this would lead, but it had pulled back the curtain of ambivalence and terror. This was vital and necessary.

The soldiers who broke into Jerry's cell did so because they wanted to build on the goodwill and the overwhelming popularity that Jerry had garnered during the public trial. It had seemed to them that this was their best chance to shape their own future and that of their children. His courage and independence of character apparently sparked a climate of resistance and restored a strong sense of national pride. Faced with his greatest test ever, in the midst of an explosive situation, Jerry was able to identify with the plight of the ordinary Ghanaian while conveying the aspirations of the rank and file. The jailbreak ignited a popular uprising whose flame he had fired.

On June 4, 1979, my husband went from facing the death penalty in a monumental public trial, to being hoisted onto Ghana's political stage as the country's youngest head of state. I could not believe it. With widespread support from both the military and civilians, the ranks ultimately decided that my husband, Flt. Lt. Jerry John Rawlings, would become the undisputed leader and chairman of the newly-established Armed Forces Revolutionary Council (AFRC) that was to rule the country.

This moment had not come with a dress rehearsal. He was on a national stage, his every decision and indecision affecting millions of people. One thing that gave me a sense of calm was the fact that I knew a man who truly cared for the people and was desperate to reassure every one that they had a stake in the future of their own country. Like night instantly turned to day, it was a turnaround so sudden that it felt surreal. Only one day before, Jerry was on trial for his life for a charge punishable by death. Twenty-four hours later, his life's trajectory had shifted forever.

Without delay, he began a revolution aimed at uprooting from both the military and society at large, the marks of corruption, social injustice, and other abuses. It would be a daunting task, and he would need everyone striving for the same ideal to make it possible. Much like the rest of the country, I was relieved that someone was finally strong enough to risk his life for truth, social justice and the greater good of the nation. But I also knew immediately that my life would never be the same again. I did not have a choice.

Following June 4, I was deeply moved by the outpouring of emotion and the spontaneous demonstrations of support that took place throughout the city. Nobody seemed to organise the people, yet scores of desperate masses poured into the streets with placards hailing Jerry and urging him on. As if to say Jerry had sacrificed his own life for his people, people held signs and chanted a host of declarations. I was overwhelmed by the warmth and excitement in the crowds. I was also amazed that the people's affection for Chairman Rawlings could elicit such an emotional response.

One reality that seemed to fall through the cracks of history was that the actions that took place on the morning of June 4 had not been the makings of a coup d'état. It was supposed to be an 'uprising' by the rank and file military officers which turned into a historical revolution in the country. It had become a watershed moment in our political history.

What made it different from any other in the country's young history had been that it was orchestrated entirely by the ordinary rank and file. This was a first. And this was captured in Jerry's statement when he announced by radio that "the ranks have just taken over the destiny of this country." It was ordinary soldiers expressing their disgust with the decay in the Ghana Armed Forces and the total degeneration of society at large.

Behind the scenes, the agenda of the newly established AFRC was initially championed by a "radicalised" group of junior ranks—namely, sergeants, corporals, lance corporals, and even privates. They ostensibly demanded answers from those at the top as to why they led the nation into a state of political and economic ruins. Expressing outrage at the current state of affairs, the rank and file made clear that those responsible would be made to pay with their lives.

During the first few weeks of the AFRC, the few officers led by Jerry were forced to submit to the demands of the ranks, just to stay alive. At the helm of the country's leadership, this meant walking the fine line of trying to cooperate with the resentful soldiers in the messy administration that was far from taking shape. From the little I knew, it was not hard to imagine my husband and his men stuck between a proverbial rock and hard place.

In the climate of a revolution, the business of governance had to proceed in some sort of normalcy, while maintaining calm. The challenging task would become maintaining some level of control in the highly volatile situation in which they found themselves.

By 1979, it had been ten years, two military coups d'état and two military regimes since the country had held democratic elections. Thus, I knew that Jerry's promise of elections during the June 4 broadcast would resonate to the core of the masses. But how this was to be guaranteed was far from certain at the time. I remained nervously optimistic like most Ghanaians. We wanted desperately for our country to be back on its feet once again.

The remaining days of June 1979 came along with the most unnerving of hurdles; the most immediate crisis facing my husband was controlling the vengeful behaviour of the soldiers. They were determined to be rancorous and wild.

As Chairman of the new AFRC government, his first order of business had to be channelling the intense passions that June 4 had unleashed and direct flaring tempers in positive ways for the country. He believed that resorting to destructive acts of vengeance would be counterproductive and reckless. If not handled well, Chairman Rawlings was well aware how easily Ghana could slip into a state of anarchy followed by a fully-fledged bloodbath.

Already, on the streets of Accra, groups of armed soldiers were reportedly ransacking shops that sold expensive imported luxury items. Such businesses were easy targets for the rage, frustrations, and bitterness of angry soldiers who regarded their looting as the justifiable "redistribution of wealth." Particularly singled out were some Lebanese businessmen – they were subjected to personal assaults and vengeful acts of harassment. In the eyes of hungry Ghanaians, they represented a sinister force that was a willing participant in the mass destruction of Ghana and the suffering over the last several years. The general sentiment for some of these businessmen had been that they had enriched themselves illegally, and thus they were quickly identified as *part of the problem*.

The rioters' actions were extreme, rash and harsh, but the soldiers' discontent was understandable. The brutal suppression and corruption over the last few years had emasculated and degraded the junior ranks, stripping them of their dignity by depriving them of basic military supplies and the means to provide for their families and loved ones. By repeatedly denying them the right to earn a living in a way that gave them dignity, the senior officers had carelessly turned much of the military forces into a bitter and angry lot.

What troubled me the most, however, was the indiscriminate harassment of innocent civilians, many of whom had suffered just as much, if not more, than the soldiers, themselves. In the mayhem, thugs had taken the opportunity to wreak havoc. The culprits were radicalised factions of uncontrollable soldiers.

Throughout Accra, improvised roadblocks were set up and innocent civilians who stopped there were often harassed by merciless soldiers brandishing rifles. At the same time, other soldiers were busily arresting all the senior officers they could lay their hands on, subjecting them to rituals of public humiliation, including shaving their heads bald. Calling for blood, soldiers, the public, and students, alike, wanted nothing less than to slaughter all senior officers and Military Intelligence men who had been humiliating them for the past eight years.

For military personnel who had harboured such strong ill will against the government, turning into mobs overnight, and arbitrarily terrorising and humiliating the mass public seemed so terribly self-defeating. This was happening so hurriedly.

My husband had been only partly apprised of the full extent of the malaise in the country. It took everything for him to try to calm the lower ranks and the radical group who would stop at nothing. One of the gloomy aftermaths of a golden opportunity for a country to stand together happened when eight senior officers were publicly executed to the cheers of the Ghanaian public who clapped and jeered shouting, "Let the blood flow."

It was eerily frightening to see groups of young men and women walking the streets of Accra, angrily chanting what was obviously their pent-up anger. They were hurrying towards the Teshie military shooting range where supposedly many had heard the news on the radio of an execution to take place. It was an incredibly terrifying day. I made my way to my mother's house, who was equally alarmed and found every opportunity to ask the people parading the streets what they knew. I was frightened.

In a charged political climate, the leaders scrambled to maintain law and order and spent much of every waking moment steering the country towards peaceful elections, but their most dangerous challenger had become the military men who were now armed and bent on revenge. For good reason, my husband's attention was fixed on leading the revolutionary struggle as Commander-in-Chief, and he threw himself into his new role with intense commitment. Overnight, Jerry had become a politician and a symbol of the collective hopes of the entire nation. Yet, the more political he became, the more isolated I began to feel.

And it was lonely.

CHAPTER TWENTY ONE

TIME FADES AGAIN
The Aftermath of June 4

What I did not anticipate was the overwhelming feeling of loneliness that seemed to have pervaded my life in the immediate aftermath of June 4. The whirlwind of events had been remarkably significant, yet I spent much of the weeks and months after that changing tide in uncertainty. Suddenly I was alone, and almost a single mother without a companion and my best friend. Jerry was no longer around the house building cabinets, chairs or wooden tables or engaged in home repairs. The country needed him, and I was coming to terms with the fact that I had already lost my husband to his calling.

With Jerry around, the house was always bustling, sometimes with his friends coming in and out, for a meal or a cup of coffee or whatever we could spare. Through the haze of the revolution, it was difficult to see my family as they once had been. Jerry was not home each day giving Zanetor her morning baths, which he loved to do.

Nothing had prepared me for the sudden sense of obligation I now felt to protect the life of our only child and infant daughter, who was now barely a year old. Motherhood had become a trade I could not help but learn as I went along, but when the patterns of daily life are jarringly disrupted by events outside of our control, it leaves fate hanging loosely in the balance.

My father was hopeful. He was not the one to panic when everything seems to untangle around him, and he urged that I do the same. My only option was to keep a straight head, knowing that anything I said or did in these moments could have grave ramifications. My mother, on the contrary, could not help but fret, but for good reason.

It was at the height of the chaos that my mother decided that I should take some food to Jerry at the Burma Camp. I was not too sure where he would be, but I imagined that the Air Force Station would be a good start. She was convinced that he had not eaten, so she cooked fufu and soup, jollof, yam and plantain. I never took the time to wonder if my mother was indeed wondering if Jerry and his inner circle had anything to eat, or if she was overwhelmed by stress. Cooking was a way of deflecting the emotion without making it too obvious.

In the process of trying to deliver the food to my husband at Burma Camp, I was arrested and locked up in the Air Force Station guard room. "Why, what have I done?" I demanded. "The Chairman is my husband, and I'm just trying to see him." Dismissing my claim with the wave of his hand, the soldier shouted, "*Ohhhh... you women are all the same...* trying to disrupt us with your 'Bottom power'! And this time we do not want women to come and corrupt our new leaders." This happened twice, at two different locations, the other time being at the Arakan Barracks, Fifth Battalion.

It was useless to try to reason with the soldiers that closely guarded the AFRC. They obviously had no idea of who I was, and they were not interested in anything that supposedly was against the strict orders they had been given. In essence, they were placing all the negative behaviours of the male-dominated leadership on women who had been girlfriends to the leaders of the NRC, SMC I and SMC II, as if they had been the architects of our country's economic and social decline.

A few days later, I felt anxiety set in, compounding the ordeal tenfold. Then I fell ill. A friend recommended a doctor for me to see immediately in Tema, a port city outside Accra. I packed enough clothes for myself and my little baby as we were not sure when we would be back, or what we would find upon our return. There was no way to reach my husband on the phone, and suddenly he was so understandably immersed into governance that he could not find a breathing moment to see his own family.

At the time, the only news that I had been a part of the story was a BBC interview that was replayed on GBC radio. Jerry mentioned his wife and child, and as volatile and dangerous as the situation had become, perhaps it was fortunate to have been just one of the many faces in Accra. For the next three months, Jerry acted as Head of State with his own administration, before handing over power, as promised, to a newly-elected civilian government on September 24, 1979.

Ghana had to be courageous and optimistic. Whether my husband accepted the charge or not, he had now become the person with the arduous task of modelling these traits, and on whom the eyes of the world would be fixed. Even though he was an extraordinary gifted man, he had to remain unpretentious and humble, if he was going to have any success calming the military vigilantes and restore civil society. In a matter of months, many had watched Jerry's life with an eye-opening wonder and seen every bright light reveal parts of his character.

My prayer was that my husband's sacrifice and vision will not be overlooked like drops in an ocean, and be heard of no more. The tragedy would be that our country may have become numb by a world filled with indifference, one that had been created by the governments we had now inherited. It would hurt to live with the truth that we, as a people, wouldn't have the resilience to look ahead and dream of a future even though the journey was bound to be fraught with its own difficulties.

In my own world, however, it still felt like the sun had ceased to shine on my life and suddenly everything around me felt empty. It was not. The rush of emotions I felt just thinking about the poverty that many would hope to rise from made me wonder if there was anything more I could do.

With my career ambition drifted into an unexpected place, but thrust into an unprecedented spotlight, I had to quickly embrace the new order. Even with my own privacy and that of my little baby stripped away, it was a chance to help my husband forge ahead, and most importantly, to never lose sight of the plight of the ordinary man that nudged him to fight.

At the inauguration of President Hilla Limann, a former school-teacher and diplomat, Chairman Rawlings said: "If people in power use their offices to pursue self-interest, they will be resisted and unseated, no matter how unshakeable their oppression may seem to be." In that same speech, delivered before the country's new 140-member Parliament in a packed auditorium, Chairman Rawlings looked squarely at President Limann and said: "We have every confidence that we shall never regret our decision to go back to the barracks."

As part of the inauguration festivities, a parade was held at the Black Star Square in Accra. Jerry joined the military troops, and I found my way up the steps to the public section. I was pregnant with a second baby, but I was no different from the host of women who were in the crowd on both sides of the political dialogue.

I stood quietly as I listened to two women loudly yell their sentiments. They did not know who I was and perhaps did not care who stood next to them. The next thing I heard was, "Now we have our president, the Ashantis can go away, we will not sell groundnuts anymore." Then they went on hurling insults at my husband and the military soldiers in the distance. They knew absolutely nothing about them, but that did not stop them from voicing their opinions, loudly.

It was rather sad to hear their points of view because they missed the significance and magnitude of the moment that was unfolding before our very eyes. I did not have a reason to be angry. It affirmed for me that not everyone would be hailing Jerry in admiration and that some would hate him and there was absolutely nothing I could do about it. It surprised me a great deal. I walked away from the section to a place that seemed a bit less dramatic and offensive.

After he stepped down, my husband reiterated several times that he, - just like any other well-meaning Ghanaian – would closely monitor the political and economic performance of the country's new leaders. The stress or accomplishments seemed not to turn his head. When the seasons had been their harshest, I had seen him crawl his way past what often seemed insurmountable. He had been the same, striving to rise above the madness of the moment and surprisingly unwavering in his belief and person. Jerry had been loyal to his faith, and the blisters of the struggle had not taken a toll on him and changed him into something he was not.

I was looking for a moment to catch my breath. My thoughts seemed to crumble and fall apart. Like a person feeling pushed into a corner, and needing faith to ride on a wave because they are terrified and unsure of the next moment, I had to remain calm.

My husband's drive had taken me to a far-flung place, but nothing in me said I was not equipped or I could not stand on my own. The journey ahead would be much different than I envisioned, but when I had the chance to look back at the moments that led me there, there would not be anything overwhelming about the next step.

Jerry was fighting for what he believed in. Ghanaians urged him on to fight for what we stood for. But soon memories would fade, and people would forget why men and women had to put their lives on the line on June 4. When time fades, the unfortunate lives we lost would become a distant memory rather than a solemn reminder of our duty in service to our motherland. The priceless urgency of that revolt would someday diminish when the very people who clapped and cheered with such unbridled joy soon forgot why they had to clap and cheer. I would have to remind him.

Under the new civilian rule of President Hilla Limann, our family was hounded by Military Intelligence and Special Branch agents who scrutinised our every move. The politicians of the Third Republic viewed my husband and anybody associated with him as a threat to the future of their administration.

Rather than seek to prove their worth as a selfless government, President Limann's government, drawn from the People's National Party (PNP), focused much of its energy on trying to undo and undermine the actions and achievements of the short revolution. It was determined to reverse court decisions made in the Special Courts of the AFRC. It also did all they could to defame Chairman Rawlings and his administration, but most importantly, remove them from having direct contact with the armed forces.

Within a few months, President Limann retired Jerry from the Air Force. But that did not stop my husband.

Over the next two years, we were perpetually watched and followed. The police kept 24-hour surveillance on my family. Anybody who attempted to visit us at home was harassed or warned off by Military Intelligence, and soon the people who had been our friends had to stay away for their own safety. Informants, whom people had begun calling Limann's vigilantes, mushroomed all around the country. And our home was no different. Even our house help was set up as an informant by members of President Limann's government to gather information on us.

While driving in town with Zanetor, I was often tailed by unmarked cars of heavily armed men and a motorcyclist, so I occasionally would intentionally drive in long and circuitous routes in attempts to lose them. The more I did this, the more they drove so close to the back of my bumper that they often hit my car while I was pregnant with our second child. In their minds, they were following orders, doing whatever it took to make sure they knew everything about our every waking moment.

Within months of the handover to President Limann, I was "politically" laid off after seven years with Union Trading Company (UTC).

I had been on leave from work at the time when the crisis took centre stage in Ghana. One morning as I arrived at the office, I was called into the CEO's office. "Good morning Mrs. Rawlings."

"Good morning Sir," I said smiling, completely unaware of what was coming.

"Mrs. Rawlings, I'm very sorry… unfortunately, we have to let you go," were the abrupt words of my Swiss boss.

"*Let me go*? Why?" I questioned, dumbfounded at the news received while painfully pregnant.

He could not disguise the reasoning. "Because under this new government, our affiliation with you is already costing us heavily in the loss of important business. We are here to do business, trading business… and if, because of you, we are being denied an import license to import the items that we need for the shops, then you have to leave. We simply cannot afford to continue operating that way," he said. His eyes turned downward. "I'm sorry."

I was devastated. From this point forward, I began to release any fixed ideas I had of career, marriage, motherhood or raising a family and accepted the possibility of a rather unconventional existence. Perhaps my life's work was to be much different from what I had scripted in my mind from the very day I left university and landed a job with UTC.

In early 1980, it felt like I had reached my lowest point. I was jobless, a lone parent, and suddenly without income. The sudden insecurity had not been by my doing but brought on by our circumstances. Yet, the worst part was feeling out of control. While I was proud of my husband's courageous stance, I harboured personal feelings of failure, loneliness and perhaps resentment.

Suddenly, it felt like everything I had worked for up to that point—my career, my degree, my credibility—was gone.

Although public life was not what I had envisioned for myself, I was prepared to embrace the struggle for social justice. I could not have imagined that a journey into political life would become a powerful pull and personal calling for me. I had seen the country through different lenses, and each of them seemed to bring on an even greater sense of urgency to me. The revolution was just beginning.

While the masses of oppressed and impoverished Ghanaians were now being mobilised for change, it was obvious also that sizeable gender gaps remained. Women-headed homes represented the vast majority of poor households. In spite of the fact that women seemed to bear almost all responsibility for meeting basic family needs, they were often systematically denied the resources needed to fulfil this responsibility. That reality had its roots in generations before our own when mothers and daughters had to assume their roles of relative insignificance in society. Quietly, they did their best to encourage their men and keep their families together. Somehow, the women had come to understand the tremendous roles they played even though their voices were muted in a male dominant culture.

What quickly became striking to me was that so long as women were subjugated to the periphery of the national economy, our revolution was incomplete. No economy can turn around and grow by excluding any part of its people. In a society where women remained the most vulnerable to abuse, domestic violence and poverty, protection was essential. But this was a task too large and too important to be left alone to the government.

As I crossed the paths of many women and heard their stories, I was living through the challenges of having to rediscover my own voice, and fortunately, I could relate to every one of their hopes and even their fears. It is good to be reminded of the responsibility to bring about social and economic change for ourselves.

I could not stop reaching. There were many days when I hoped the clouds would disappear so that I could see a picture of what the next chapter of my life would become. Nothing in these moments had been as I had planned. Somehow I hoped my childhood had prepared me for the life ahead. I hoped every one of my father's embraces and reassuring words would come back to comfort and counsel me. My family's heritage had carried a weight of its own, and I knew I was fortunate to have rested on the shoulders of these courageous men and magnificent women to now make my little contribution. That was all I had, and I did not have the luxury of falling apart.

I could not let the challenge of being a young mother and wife in such tense moments overwhelm me. It was nerve-wracking and often crushing. Yet there had been many women who had been unfailingly remarkable examples for me.

There had been the women like Asantehemaa Nana Konadu Yiadom II in whose unflinching and caring hands the Ashanti Kingdom found its security when no one knew what would become of an empire in the absence of their king. In 1896, she understood the extent of her task, but she also had to embrace the chance to be a guiding hand to her people, just as she had done over and again for her own children. In their own lives, these women had to wipe their tears quickly, because their sons who would be leaders of their nation were inspired by their bravery to forge their own. This was what it took to be a woman, one whom her people could depend on to hold on to their dignity.

Yaa Asanteawaa's story in Ashanti history had not ended with her gutsy stance against imperial oppression. It was her audacious stand that my own mother reminded me of as a little girl, so that I would not lose sight of the fact that irrespective of how society or our tradition seems to have shaped our voices, there was still the greatest part of ourselves that the world around us needed us to bring to the fore. Our hands were to be incredibly powerful, the air around our every step had to be ever so gracious, and our resolve to be forever resolute.

In the quiet moments when I wondered what would become of the future ahead for my family, my mind would race back to Maame Afua Konadu's long chats under the open skies, even when my young mind occasionally drifted out of the moments. Something about what she said stayed with me. The honesty in her eyes was refreshing. Even in her final days, nothing seemed more pressing to my grandaunt than my finding an inner resolve to fight through everything till the end, just as in the name we share, *ko-na-du.*

Now I knew why Dr. Kwegir Aggrey became famous for his words, "If you educate a man, you educate an individual. If you educate a woman, you educate a nation." I had come to understand why his shadow loomed large over Achimota School and his persona seemed so monumental. It was ripples of this belief that were to transform a nation. The women were to be inspired to rise. It was a beautiful reminder that thoughts could be contagious and powerful, and able to urge every person on to reach his or her potential.

Madam Agbotui's heart had carried her son Jerry. Every waking moment seemed to have been consumed with a mother's grit to see her child's dream beyond where she could herself not even imagine. Her own faith encouraged her confidence, and she hoped someday for a man whose story would make her proud, and whose pursuit would make it a bit easier to numb the pain of any disappointment, just like my own mother, Maa. Madam Agbotui and Maa had an extraordinary duty of empowering themselves in order to lift up their own sons and daughters and their communities. It was a quiet strength that built their own devotion and carried their imperfections and hopes with pride.

My father said our names ought to be the weight or anchor that kept us striving and believing in something much more significant than ourselves. My own sisters, each stepped out into life with a picture of the world they wanted to see in their own hands. Then we were reminded at every turn that God had given us all every ability we needed to fight the rest of the way. Someday we were to grow into women who would have to remember what was tucked deep into our minds, that nothing, even for a moment, was inconsequential.

The traces of nurturing in motherhood were evident in past generations when the women were relegated to the roles of homemakers and housewives. Some had no leading part to play even in their own homes, let alone outside the confines of the home. Yet they bore the most crucial task of nurturing the hearts and minds of young men who would become leaders of the nation, largely because they spent the most time with their sons and daughters.

The society was at a juncture in its history where it had not found it important enough to allow women and girls to search for their own destiny, and now it had become an urgent cry of every heart to pull every girl along, and anyone who would be bold enough to dream, no matter where they had come from.

So too were the women in the Makola market who showed up every dawn with a new hope that the day would bring a sale, no matter how the day before had turned out. They did not have any choice but to stand through the sun and the rain to earn a cedi. The woman who sold the hot rice and stew that I could not wait for a chance to eat walked the same trail too. Market women surrounded her as far as the eyes could see.

Many more even spent their nights on long benches with the mosquitoes that swarmed around the stalls. Somehow, underneath the scarves and the worn out clothes which they used to whip away the flies in the day, was an incredible drive to change the lives of their sons and daughters. Long ago, they had gone to pick firewood, and gave the place its Ga name *"ma ko la"*, and now it was this fire that burned in their hearts to change their future.

It was this resolve that woke the women up every morning to the city's streets before sunrise to sell their yams and tomatoes and garden eggs that could rot under the hot sun at day's end. They had a little faith, and that gave them the energy to sell whether anyone bought the day before or not. Their sons and daughters waited for them to provide a meal, and their men too, would be inspired by their fortitude and courage.

I remembered the women, young and old, who I saw walking along the quiet streets in the small towns I drove past. Somehow they found a reason to plough through the heat and the dust and make their lives beautiful and meaningful. But for these women, the sweat running down the sides of their faces held their story. Their little children tucked in their cloths tightly on their backs had to grow in a Ghana that would be filled with hope and opportunity.

Knowing who I was, and from where I had come brought a nagging reminder that I had been prepared for this moment. Yet, it felt overpowering at times. Breaking through any ceiling to inspire myself would create a story to tell my children, just as it would be for the women who would look at the changing landscape in Ghana's politics and find me standing next to my husband. My voice would be theirs. My strength would have to be theirs too. It had begun to sink in that my life's work would have to mean much more than a drive to accomplish my own dreams. I had a reason to trust my instincts to believe that the next chapter of my own life would be hopeful.

This is when I realized that it is up to us, the women of Ghana, to bear the responsibility for actions needed to bring about social and economic change for ourselves. It takes a woman to understand the needs, goals and desires of other women; and to fight for the empowerment and emancipation of other women. It takes a woman to ensure that mothers and daughters and their children are not left behind in the tide of social and economic change. It takes a woman to encourage other women to band together to help end poverty—first in our homes, then in our communities and, ultimately, throughout the nation, - one woman at a time.

I could never have imagined that I would be that woman. The task had eventually fallen on me. I had to embrace it as God's purpose for my life and determine to never falter in that commitment. That was not the life I chose; it chose me.

AFTERWORD

Nana Konadu Agyeman-Rawlings writes about her life and times with passion and a fierce and insightful intellect. She demands to be taken seriously in her own right as an activist and advocate for women's rights and development. Hers is a remarkable story. She grew up at a time of hope and aspiration on the continent when everything seemed possible. We both as it happens grew up in the Gold Coast and Ghana of the 1950s and 1960s, and share childhood memories of being schooled together at that time.

My late mother Peggy Boateng, who taught Nana at the Ghana International School, always described her as one of the brightest and best of her students of whom great things were expected. She for one was not surprised by the trajectory of Nana Konadu's life.

This book is a compelling read for anyone interested in contemporary Ghanaian history, especially if seen from a much-rarified perspective. Africa's women are a source of strength, inspiration and influence. All too often this has been neglected and under-utilised in the process of nation-building. Nana Konadu Agyeman-Rawlings demonstrates in her own account of events how in the political field the women of Africa have yet to come fully into their own. She writes of her experiences with a sense of determination to see yet more recognition afforded to the role of women as leaders in every sphere of life.

The economic and political emancipation of women on the continent is a work in progress. This memoir will be an accessible and worthwhile read for men and women of every generation, but particularly, it will provide a wakeup call to the young women of Ghana and the continent. Over a hundred years ago, the great African-American jurist and activist Frederick Douglass, concerning the struggles of the peoples of Africa and its Diaspora wrote, "Power concedes nothing without a demand. It never did and it never will." This remains as true today as it ever was, even as we continue to face manifest global injustices and growing inequality within and between nations.

Nana Konadu Agyeman-Rawlings' is a powerful voice which demands to be heard. One suspects in reading this instructive and entertaining book that there may yet remain, certainly in the author's mind, at least one chapter yet to be written. I for one, as a bipartisan observer, when it comes to the internal politics of Ghana and the continent look forward to observing what may yet unfold in the life of Nana Konadu, the nation, and our beloved continent. I have certainly very much enjoyed reading this gripping account of a life to date, well and fully lived.

Rt. Hon. Lord Boateng
The House of Lords, Westminster, London-UK

ENDNOTES

Paternal Roots: Agyeman Family History

(Tracing Yesteryears – 19th Century and 20th Century)

1859–84	My great, great grandmother, Nana Afua Kobi Serwaa Ampem I, holds the title of Asantehemaa (Queen Mother of Ashanti) during the reigns of her two sons, Nana Kofi Kaakari (1867-1874) and subsequently, Nana Mensa Bonsu (1874-1883). The pair became the 10th and 11th Asantehenes (Ashanti kings), respectively.
1884	Nana Afua Kobi Serwaa Ampem I is succeeded by her daughter, Nana Yaa Akyaa (my great grandmother), as Asantehemaa.
1888	After much resistance within the Ashanti empire, my grandfather's cousin, Nana Agyeman Prempeh I (Prempeh I), ascends the Golden Stool as the 13th Asantehene while still in his teens.
1896	The British deport Prempeh I, his mother Yaa Akyaa, and all members of the immediate royal family. They are first sent to Cape Coast, then to Sierra Leone, before ending up in Seychelles, in 1901.
1901	After leading an attack on the British in 1900 to preserve Asante sovereignty, Nana Yaa Asantewaa is taken into British captivity and sent into exile in the Seychelles where she joins Prempeh I.
1902	My grandfather, Owusu Sekyere Agyeman (O S Agyeman, son of Nana Mensa Bonsu, 11th Asantehene), becomes a primary proponent for the return of the exiled king, Prempeh I, his first cousin.
1900–10	O S Agyeman enters the cocoa business—producing, buying and reselling cocoa. During this time, cocoa becomes the number one foreign exchange earner in the Gold Coast and the economy sees a cocoa export boom.
c. 1910	My grandfather, O S Agyeman, marries his first wife and my father's mother, Yaa Akyaa.

1910–19	O S Agyeman acquires ten of his own cocoa farms, making him a wealthy businessman. He sets up the business enterprise Agyeman Brothers and Company.
1912	My father, John Osei Tutu Agyeman (J O T Agyeman) is born on January 14.
1917	Prempeh I's sister, Nana Konadu Yiadom II, after whom I am named, succeeds her mother's post as Queen Mother. She serves as Regent over Asante while her family is in exile.
1918	O S Agyeman's cocoa business grows large enough to compete with the long-established European conglomerate, United Africa Company (UAC). This upsets the British.
c. 1919	To promote his cocoa business, O S Agyeman travels to the United States (Philadelphia). This makes him the first Asante to travel to America for trade, which makes him a pioneer cocoa exporter as an individual broker from the Gold Coast.
1920	Tragedy strikes my grandfather when his wife (Yaa Akyaa) is struck by jaundice in the eighth month of her pregnancy. Both Yaa Akyaa and her unborn child die during premature labour.
1924	The British pardon my grandfather's cousin, Nana Agyeman Prempeh I, who returns to Kumasi as a private citizen after almost 30 years in exile in Seychelles.
1926	Nana Agyeman Prempeh I is enstooled as Kumasihene (Chief of Kumasi). This decision follows petitions to the British monarchy from my grandfather O S Agyeman and other prominent Ashantis who request the king's formal reinstatement as Asantehene.
c. 1927	British conglomerate, UAC, plots and conspires the downfall of my grandfather.
1931	Prempeh I dies and is succeeded by Prempeh II as the next "Kumasihene."

1935	The British restore recognition of the Asante Confederacy and Prempeh II ascends the Golden Stool as the first Asantehene under the British government.
	In a disagreement about the chosen successor to the Golden Stool, my grandfather publicly protests the decision and challenges the new king's eligibility as Asantehene in court according to customary law. After lengthy litigation, the case is dismissed.
	Prempeh II files a formal grievance with the British governor requesting intervention for separation between him and his accuser, Owusu Sekyere Agyeman. The colonial governor complies and issues an order of deportation, prohibiting my grandfather, Owusu Sekyere Agyeman, from crossing a 40-kilometre radius into Asanteman (the Ashanti region).
1957	Twenty-two years later, Dr. Kwame Nkrumah, Ghana's first president, pardons Owusu Sekyere Agyeman.

Maternal Roots: Sarpong Family History

(Tracing Yesteryears – 19th Century and 20th Century)

1895–1899	My mother's father, Charles Sarpong, a pharmaceutical dispenser, marries his first wife in his hometown of Otumi (Ghana's Eastern Region).
1900-19	All ten children from my grandfather's first marriage tragically and mysteriously die at different stages during childhood. The death of each child occurs following a similar pattern of recurring symptoms - prolonged infection and chronic bodily pain. The "plague" baffles doctors.
1919	Distraught by the deaths of his children, my grandfather Sarpong leaves his wife and home in search of a new beginning. He migrates from Otumi to Kumasi. In Kumasi, my grandfather meets and marries his second wife, my grandmother, Margaret Appiah.
1921	Gold Coast government sets up a veterinary services division in the north as a means to prevent, control and cure animal diseases. The colonial government relocates my grandparents to Tamale in Ghana's Northern Region and my grandfather, Charles Sarpong, is recruited to study under Dr. Beale, an English veterinary doctor.
1921–35	My grandfather is distinguished as the first black veterinary officer in the Gold Coast. He expands his veterinary work across the country, trains students of veterinary medicine, and sets up animal care centres nationally.
1923	My mother, Felicia Sarpong, is born on October 27.
1930	My grandfather enrols my mother at Mmofra Turo Methodist School in Kumasi.
1935	December—My grandfather, Charles Sarpong, dies from a hernia complication. My mother's maternal uncle, Osei Ahenkro, becomes her legal guardian and she continues school in Kumasi.
1938	My mother enters a teacher's training program at Wesley College in Kumasi. My father's sister, Ama Serwaa, approaches my mother as a prospective wife for my father. My parents meet for the first time at my mother's college campus.
1941	After a long courtship, my parents exchange vows in a church wedding in Winneba, but live in Swedru.

| 1944 | My mother gives birth to her eldest of seven children, Yaa Achia. |
| Mid-1950's | My mother and her siblings discover they are all carriers of the sickle cell gene—a trait they inherited from my grandfather, Charles Sarpong. Through research, they realize that it was sickle cell anaemia that killed all ten of his children from his first marriage. |

INDEX

CPSIA information can be obtained
at www.ICGtesting.com
Printed in the USA
FFHW020110041118

9 781732 351912